THE RANDOM CHARACTER OF CORPORATE EARNINGS

JOSEPH E. MURPHY

EDITOR

6/6/09

Crossgar Press
2116 West Lake of the Isles Parkway
Minneapolis, Minnesota 55405

Tel. (612) 867 5837

ISBN 0-9646292-4-0

Printed in the United States of America

INTRODUCTION

You may wonder what this book is really about and how it came to be. It contains articles written over the course of three decades as part of an attempt to better understand the stock and bond markets. Many were done in collaboration with others who were interested in the same kinds of problems that I was interested in.

My first job following college and the Army was as a financial analyst. My assignment was to select and prepare reports on stocks for purchase by customers of the brokerage house where I first worked. That was in the early 1960's. Several years later, after I left the brokerage firm and joined the trust department of a bank, the task was the same. Only the selections were made for the banks trust customers rather than brokerage customers. I was assigned to write up reports on stocks that were attractive for purchase. Essentially, that meant stocks that would rise in price, stocks that would do better than average.

The question was, how do you do that? How do you pick stocks that will outperform the Dow Jones Average, or the S&P 500? What criteria do you use? There were a number of popular theories to chose from. Many of them relied on the past record. Buy the stock with high past price growth, according to one view. Select the stock with above average past earnings growth. Pick a stock that shows consistent past growth. Or, the stock with a high return on capital. Or a stock with high past growth of price and earnings and a low price/earnings ratio. There were other theories, of course. Lots of them. Every stock picker had his or her pet theory. Of the many theories, I wondered which one worked. Which was the most successful? Or, was any theory likely to work? Or work consistently?

One of the wonderful things about the stock market is that there is lots of data. Company records are public and are published. Since they are, it was quite possible to test any theory of how to select stocks. I wanted to find the best criteria. So I decided to test some of the theories. I wanted to find the best method to use in selecting stocks for purchase. I would use the extensive data on stock prices and corporate financial data to determine the most useful theory. The data I used was the *Value Line Investment Survey* data. I had it all punched up on IBM cards and arranged to use the University of Minnesota Control Data computer to do the tests. The CDC computer was one of the most powerful at the time. Yet, it had less power than a run of the mill PC of today.

A physicist at the Naval Research Laboratory by the name of M.F.M. Osborne had published a paper demonstrating that stock prices were random. Having read all of the academic articles I could find on the stock market, I had read the paper. Its conclusion was highly controversial. How could stock prices be random? Osborne's evidence was clear. Stock prices exhibited strong evidence of randomness. I knew that stock prices were affected by company earnings. So I decided to see whether corporate earnings were random. If they were, you couldn't simply use a company's past earnings growth to predict future earnings growth, and therefore its likely future price rise. If that was not the case, then past earnings growth would be a viable selection criteria. I knew that it was a popular criteria in stock selection.

The result of the study was that earnings also exhibited strong evidence of randomness. I wrote up the results, sent them into the *Financial Analysts Journal* and, following a personal interview with one of the editors (my results were at first not believed), the article was published. It is the first article in this book.

There followed a series of other studies in an attempt to ascertain what, if anything, could be used to forecast future earnings growth. The variables were those made popular in the literature of finance. Did return on equity prove a good indicator? Or dividend payout (i.e. low payout)? Of the amount of debt? Subsequent studies showed that none of these ratios was a reliable guide to future earnings growth. Earnings were simply too random. Reluctantly I discovered that corporate income and balance sheet ratios proved to be poor predictors of future earnings growth. Yet, I knew that earnings were important to stock prices. Another study proved that: it found good correlation between stock price growth and earnings growth in the same time period. That this was the case was a common view in the industry and it proved to be so. Articles 1 through 6 deal with those and related issues.

The first six articles in this book are all based on the correlation of a particular variable, like growth in earnings, to another variable, like future growth in price, or past return on equity. As one study followed another, there seemed to be a general pattern to the results. Growth variables in one historical period didn't relate to growth variables in another different historical period. And they didn't relate to ratios. Ratios seemed to be comparatively quite stable; growth variables were more random, unpredictable. The pattern led to some generalizations - rules or principles, if you will - that could be used to predict the relationship between different kinds of variables. The particular variable didn't matter; only its form - was it expressed in dollars, as a ratio, or was it a growth or percentage change variable? Articles 7 through 9 and 21 describe and demonstrate these general rules. The rules conflict with part, possibly much, of the Modern Theory of Finance. Yet, the evidence for them seems overwhelming.

Most investors, professional or otherwise, attempt to predict particular events. This stock will outperform the average, for example. Or, earnings will reach that level. Or, yields on 30-year treasuries will rise, or rise by so much. We want to know exactly what was going to happen. An alternative is to predict not a specific change, but the probability of a specific change. Or, the probabilities of several alternative changes. We could do this if we knew the distribution of changes and what factors determined their probabilities. For a random variable, the distribution tends to bell-shaped, or Gaussian. That was important. We may not know whether a company's earnings will rise or fall, or interest rates will increase or decline. But we may be able to estimate the probability of a particular rise or fall - of earnings, or interest rates, or currency prices - from their distribution. Or, so I suspected.

It was with that in mind that I contacted Maury Osborne. I said I was interested in predicting corporate loss, a subject I had worked on. I was also interested in evaluating interest rate risk. I told Osborne that I thought the approach he had used on the distribution of stock price changes could be applied to earnings, interest rates and possibly other investment variables. He agreed and we began to work together on these problems. Osborne had done something I had never seen done elsewhere. He examined how the volatility of first differences in a series (like first differences in the logarithms of stock prices) rises with the length of the difference interval. (Actually with the square root of the difference interval). Over the course of nearly two decades, we worked on a variety of problems.

The research led to six articles. All reflect to one degree or another Osborne's original paper on Brownian Motion in the Stock Market. One article deals with forecasting the probability of corporate profit or loss. A second provides a more precise description of the distribution of changes in corporate profits comparing the distribution to models in physics and engineering. A third describes how to use maturity and time to forecast the range of probable changes in interest rates for various maturities and forecast periods. A fourth applies the Brownian Motion model to changes in interest rates. The last describes departures from the normal distribution of daily changes in stock prices. The research with Osborne provided the basis for six books.

The remaining articles and unpublished papers in this book cover related topics.

In addition to Maury Osborne, I was fortunate to collaborate with four other co-authors: Richard Johnson of the University of Minnesota, Robert Larsen, formerly of Investors Diversified Services, J. Russell Nelson, past president of Arizona State University, and Harold Stevenson, former professor of finance, Arizona State University. I am also indebted to Northwestern National Bank of Minneapolis (now Norwest Bank), particularly to John Rogers, Jim Harris and Peter Heegaard who encouraged my efforts .

CONTENTS

Appendix

"The Stock Market is probably the best documented and worst described phenomena on this planet."

M.F.M. Osborne

CONTRIBUTORS

Richard S. Johnson, M.A. was Assistant Director For Applications at the National Center For Higher Education Management Systems and a Ph.D. candidate in Finance at the University of Minnesota at the time the article was published.

Robert A Larsen, C.F.A, Ph.D. in bio-chemistry, worked in bio-chemistry and subsequently managed mutual funds at Investors Diversified Services. At the time the article was written, he was Senior Analyst, Investment Department, IDS Venture Capital Management.

Joseph E. Murphy was in the investment business for over two decades. He is the author of *With Interest: How to Profit from Interest Rate Fluctuations* (Dow Jones-Irwin, 1987), *Stock Market Probability* (Probus, 1988, 1994), *The Random Character of Interest Rates* (Probus, 1990) and *Bond Tables of Probable Future Yields* (Crossgar Press, 1996).

J. Russell Nelson was Vice-Provost of the University of Colorado, Boulder at the time the article was published. He was formerly Professor of Finance, University of Minnesota, and subsequently Dean of the Business School and Chancellor of the University of Colorado, Boulder, and President of Arizona State University.

M.F.M. Osborne, Physicist with the U.S. Department of Defense (Retired). His article "Brownian Motion in the Stock Market," was the first to demonstrate randomness in stock prices. He is the author of articles in a number of fields and of *The Stock Market and Finance From a Physicist's Viewpoint,* 1977, 1995 Crossgar Press.

Harold W. Stevenson, Professor Emeritus of Finance, Arizona State University and Past President of the Western Finance Association.

1

RELATIVE GROWTH OF EARNINGS PER SHARE—PAST AND FUTURE

This article examines the correlation between relative rates of growth of earnings per share in successive periods. Based upon a study of 344 companies in 12 industries in 38 different test periods between the years 1950 and 1965, there appears to be little significant correlation between relative rates of growth of earnings per share in one period and relative growth in earnings per share in the next period. In about one-fourth of the tests companies recording below average rates of growth in earnings per share in one period tended to record above average rates of growth in the next period. In seven-tenths of the tests there was no significant correlation between relative growth in earnings per share in successive periods.

The correlation between growth and earnings per share of companies in an industry in one period and the growth of earnings per share shown by these companies in the succeeding period is examined in this study.[1] The purpose is to discover whether the correlation is positive, negative or non-existent. If it is positive, companies which record the highest rates of growth of earnings per share in one period will also, by definition, tend to record the highest rates of growth of earnings per share in the next period. That the correlation is positive is a tenet of many financial writers.

Importance of the Question

The question of correlation of relative past and future growth of earnings per share has important implications in at least four related areas: 1) theory of valuation of the firm; 2) practical appraisal of equity securities; 3) relation of growth of earnings per share to other characteristics of the firm; and 4) fluctuations in stock market prices.

Assumptions about relative growth in earning per share form an important element in theories of valuation, ranging from the early work of J. B. Williams to more recent studies. A common assumption in many of these theoretical studies is that the future growth of earnings per share is fixed at a given rate, or at a sequence of rates of growth.[2] If, for any sample of companies, the correlation between rates of change in earnings per share in two periods is positive, the assumptions have merit. On the other hand, if the correlation is negative or nil, a question is raised regarding the appropriateness of these assumptions.

In their practical valuation of the underlying value of a common stock, financial analysts and portfolio managers often make the implicit or explicit assumption that companies with high past growth of earnings per share will also exhibit high future growth of earnings per share. On the basis of this assumption, companies with high past growth of earnings per share may be assigned higher future potential growth of earnings per share, awarded higher price-earnings capitalization ratios, given better quality rankings, or on the basis of expected superior earnings trend, accorded better prospect of price appreciation.[3] Much of this reasoning is based on the premises that the correlation between rates of change in earnings per share is positive.

Relatively high growth of earnings per share is commonly described as the result of superior management, the effect of a higher return on sales or investment, or the product of inherent competitive advantages such as market share, strategic location, cost of raw materials, etc. If these factors do indeed cause persistently better rates of growth in earnings per share, the correlation between relative growth in earnings per share in two periods should be positive.

Extensive studies of stock market prices have shown that rates of change in prices for any group of companies are not cor-

14

related.[4] A lack of correlation in relative growth of earnings per share would provide a partial explanation of the non-correlation in stock prices.

Method of Analysis

To determine whether companies showing high growth in one period also showed above average growth in the next period, the following procedure was used. Three years were selected as for example 1963, 1964 and 1965. Earnings per share were recorded for each of these years for each company in the industry. Next, the growth in earnings per share between 1963 and 1964 was computed for each company in the industry. In the same way the growth in earnings per share between 1964 and 1965 was computed for each company in the industry. Then the companies showing the highest rates of growth in earnings per share between 1963 and 1964 were compared with the companies showing the highest rate of growth in earnings per share between 1964 and 1965.[5] If the companies were the same, the correlation would be positive. The degree of correlation was measured by computing the coefficient of correlation.

Adjustment of Data

Reported earnings per share are the basic data used in the analysis.[6] To insure that reported earnings per share are on a current basis, non-recurrent expenses and non-recurrent income have been excluded. Companies which shifted their fiscal year or which significantly altered their accounting practice have been excluded in order that earnings per share of each individual company be reported on a consistent basis throughout the period. Reported earnings are substantially affected by seasonal factors. To provide for seasonal comparability among companies, earnings per share for each company are for the same fiscal period, the year ending December 31.

The Companies Studied

The test was conducted on twelve industries comprising 344 companies. The industries are listed below with the number of companies in each industry given in parentheses.

Auto Parts.........(15)		Steel...........(20)
Building Materials.(29)		Petroleum........(20)
Chemical..........(25)		Natural Gas......(32)
Drug..............(22)		Electric Utility.(90)
Machinery.........(20)		Bank.............(20)
Elec. Mach, &		Railroad.........(21)
Electronics........(24)		

An additional test was performed on 207 companies consisting of all the above companies except those in the electric utility, bank and railroad industries.

The Periods Studied

The business cycle has an important effect on earnings per share. Five of the tests on successive one year periods and one of the tests on successive two year periods were made in similar phases of the business cycle. In addition, the last two tests covered periods coincident with the expansion phases of the business cycle. Tests covering similar phases of the business cycle are indicated by an asterisk (*).

For each industry thirty-eight tests were made. The tests were made for the following periods:

Successive One Year Periods

*1965/64	and	1964/63	1960/59	and	1959/58*
*1964/63	and	1963/62	1959/58	and	1958/57*
*1963/62	and	1962/61	1958/57	and	1957/56
1962/61	and	1961/60	1957/56	and	1956/55
1961/60	and	1960/59	1956/55	and	1955/54

Successive Two Year Periods

*1965/63	and	1963/61	1960/58	and	1958/56
*1964/62	and	1962/60	1959/57	and	1957/55
*1963/61	and	1961/59	1958/56	and	1956/54
1962/60	and	1960/58	1957/55	and	1955/53
1961/59	and	1959/57	1956/54	and	1954/52

Successive Five Year and One Year Periods

1965/64	and	1964/59	1960/59	and	1959/54
1964/63	and	1963/58	1959/58	and	1958/53
1963/62	and	1962/57	1958/57	and	1957/52
1962/61	and	1961/56	1957/56	and	1956/51
1961/60	and	1960/55	1956/55	and	1955/50

Successive Five Year Periods

1965/60	and	1960/55	1962/57	and	1957/52
1964/59	and	1959/54	1961/56	and	1956/51
1963/58	and	1958/53	1960/55	and	1955/50

Periods Coincident with the Business Cycle

1965/60	and	1960/57	1960/57	and	1957/53

A Summary of Results

Table I summarizes the tests by showing for each group of tests for each industry the number of tests which indicated significant positive correlation (+), the number which indicated negative correlation (-), and the number which revealed no significant correlation (0).

As may be seen, significant positive correlation was rare. It appeared in only 29 of the 492 tests. This number represents less than 6% of the tests. Since there was little evidence of positive correlation, those companies which recorded the highest rate of growth in earnings per share in one year had no more than an even chance, at best, of showing above average rate of growth in earnings per share the next year. Companies with a high rate of growth in earnings per share in one five year period had no more than an even chance of showing high rates of growth in the next five year period.

Significant negative correlation was more common than significant positive correlation. For every test which revealed significant positive correlation, more than four tests resulted in significant negative correlation. Significant negative correlation appeared in 124 tests. This number represents 25% of the total

Table I
Significant Correlation

Industry	Successive One Year Periods			Successive Two Year Periods			Successive Five and One Year Periods			Successive Five Year Periods		
	+	-	0	+	-	0	+	-	0	+	-	0
						Number of Tests						
Auto Parts	0	3	7	0	4	6	0	3	7	0	2	4
Building Materials	0	4	6	0	3	7	1	2	7	0	0	6
Chemical	0	1	9	0	4	6	1	1	8	2	0	4
Drug	2	1	7	3	0	7	1	0	9	1	0	5
Machinery	0	2	8	0	4	6	0	1	9	0	4	2
Elec. Mach.	1	3	6	1	3	6	1	3	6	0	2	4
Steel	1	3	6	0	6	4	1	3	6	1	2	3
Petroleum	2	0	8	2	3	5	0	0	10	0	0	6
Natural Gas	0	3	7	0	4	6	0	3	7	0	1	5
Elec. Utility	0	5	5	0	4	6	2	1	7	2	0	4
Bank	1	0	9	0	2	8	0	0	10	0	0	6
Railroad	0	0	10	0	3	7	1	2	7	0	2	4
Industrial Composite	1	6	3	0	8	2	1	4	5	0	3	3
Total	8	31	91	6	48	76	9	23	98	6	16	56

number of tests. Significant negative correlation appeared in 31 of the tests of successive one year period, 48 of the tests of successive two year periods, 23 of the tests of successive five year and one year periods, and 16 of the test of successive five year periods. In these tests a below average rate of growth in earnings per share in one period was likely to result in an above average rate of growth in earnings per share in the next period.

The most common results of the tests was absence of any significant correlation. In 340 of 492 tests, these was no significant correlation. This number represents 69% of the tests. No significant correlation appeared in 91 of the tests on successive one year periods, 76 of the successive two year periods, 98 of the successive five year periods. In these tests relative rates of growth of earnings per share in one period gave no significant indication of relative growth of earnings per share in the next period.

A summary table showing these results is given below:

Table II

Significant Correlation	1 Year Periods	2 Year Periods	5 & 1 Year Periods	Five Year Periods	Periods Coincident with the Business Cycle	Total
		------ Successive ------				
Positive Correlation	8	6	9	6	0	29
Negative Correlation	31	48	23	16	5	123
No Correlation	91	76	98	56	19	340
Total Tests	130	130	130	78	24	492

Conclusion

In 69% of the 493 tests covering 12 industries and 36 different test periods between 1950 and 1965, there was no significant correlation between the growth of earnings per share of companies in an industry in one period and the growth of earnings per share by these companies in the succeeding period. In another 25% of the tests the correlation was significantly negative. Significant positive correlation appeared in only 6% of the tests. The evidence of these tests points to the following conclusions: companies which record relatively high growth in earnings per share in one period have no more than an even chance of recording relatively high growth in the succeeding period. Because this conclusion is contrary to assumptions implicit in much theoretical and practical work in investment analysis, it has important implications for investment analysis. Some of the matter about which it raises questions are:

–Simple extrapolation of past rates of growth of earnings per share in projecting future growth of earnings per share and cash flow.

–Comparison of companies on the basis of past rates of growth of earnings per share.

–Use of past rates of growth of earnings per share to appraise the capability of management.

–Use of simple past growth of earnings per share in valuation of the firm, in valuation of the firm relative to other firms, or in considering the cost of capital.

–Assumption of constant growth in earnings per share in the theory of valuation of the firm.

–Relation of rates of growth of earnings per share to other variables such as return on capital, profit margins, dividend payout ratio, etc. There may be no significant relationship.

–The lack of correlation in rates of growth in earnings per share may also be significant in explaining the random walk theory of stock prices.

Footnotes

1. This article was made possible through the assistance of the Numerical Analysis Center of the University of Minnesota, which provided extensive time on its Control Data 1604 computer, and also through the assistance of the School of Business School Computer Center of the University of Minnesota. Suggestions were given by Douglas Anderson of the Numerical Analysis Center and by Harold Stevenson and Raymond Willis of the School of Business Administration, University of

Minnesota.

2. See J. B. Williams, *Theory of Investment Value*, Harvard University Press, 11938; M. J. Gordon, *The Investment, Financing and Valuation of the Firm*, Richard D. Irwin, 1962, and M. Miller and F. Modigliani, "Dividend Policy, Growth, and the Valuation of Shares," *Journal of Business,* October 1961, pp. 411-433. Also see E. F. Brigham and J. L. Pappas, "Duration of Growth, Changes in Growth rates, and Corporate Share Prices," *Financial Analysts Journal*, May-June 11966, pp. 157-161; J. Fred Weston and E. F. Brigham, *Managerial Finance*, Holt, Rinehart & Winston, 1966, pp. 300-301.

3. The literature on growth stock evaluation is extensive. Part of it, at least, contains the implicit assumption that companies with high growth in earnings per share in the past tend to experience high rates of growth in the future. Several major statistical services list companies which have recorded high rates of growth of earnings per share. Other publications provide tables which may be used, among other things, to evaluate stocks with high past growth. See Brigham and Pappas, op. cit.; Clendenin, *Theory and techniques of Growth Stock Valuation*, Bureau of Business and Economic Research, UCLA, 1957; R. M. Soldofsky and J. T. Murphy, *Growth Yields on Common Stocks. Theory and Tables*, Bureau of Business and Economic Research, State University of Iowa, 1961. Past growth in earnings per share is used as a significant variable in a large portion of the analysis done by financial analysts. It is also used as an explanatory variable in the literature on stock prices. D. Durand, "Bank Stocks and Analysis of Covariance," *Econometrica*, xxiii, 1955, pp. 30-45; M. J. Gordon, op. cit.; Scott, M. FG., "Relative Share Prices and Yields," *Oxford Economic Paper,* October 1962, pp. 218-250.

4. Studies providing this evidence are contained in P. H. Cootner, ed. *The Random Character of Stock Prices*, M. I. T. Press, 1964.

5. The measure of rate of growth in earnings per share which was used in this article is the change in the natural logarithms

of earnings per share.

6. The data is taken from *The Value Line Investment Survey*, Arnold Bernhard & Co., New York, N. Y.

2

RETURN ON EQUITY CAPITAL, DIVIDEND PAYOUT AND GROWTH OF EARNINGS PER SHARE

Growth of earnings per share determines future funds available for reinvestment in the corporation and for payment of dividends. It also influences future debt and equity financing, helps set cash income returns to shareholders and partly affects future changes of prices of equity securities. For these reasons accurate estimates of future growth of earnings per share are very important to the investor, the financial analyst, the corporate financial manager and the student of corporate finance.[1]

One method of estimating future growth of earnings per share is to extrapolate past rates of growth. In an earlier study this approach was found to have little value, at least for comparative purposes. In a study of 344 companies in 12 industries in 38 different test periods between the years 1950 and 1965, these appeared to be little significant correlation between relative growth of earnings per share in one period and relative growth of earnings per share in the next period. Only rarely did companies which recorded superior growth of earnings per share in one period show more than an even chance of recording above average growth in the next period.[2]

A second method of estimating future growth of earnings per share uses the rate of return on equity capital and the dividend payout ratio. The return on equity capital is equal to annual earnings per share divided by equity capital per share. The dividend payout ratio is equal to annual dividends per share divided by earnings per share. This method assumes that changes in the rate of return on equity capital are negligible. If the rate of return remains constant, then growth of earnings per share equals the rate of return on equity times the proportion of earnings retained.

This method of projecting growth rates of earnings per share has been widely advocated from various points of view. Gordon and Shapiro in an analysis of capital budgeting use a model which assumes that "the dividend will grow at a rate...which is the product of the fraction of income retained and the rate of return on net worth."[3] They assume that the rate will be constant and equal to the current rate. Lerner and Carleton in their recent *A Theory of Financial Analysis* use the return on investment and the payout ratio as key elements of their theory.[4] In their chapter on projecting earnings Graham, Dodd and Cottle use the return on capital and the rate of retention as a principal method. They note that "...as the payout rises, this inevitably tends to dampen down the increase in per share gains, since a smaller percentage is reinvested in the business."[5] Sauvain uses the rate of return and the payout ratio as the chief indicators of growth of per share earnings in his work on Investment Management[6] while Cummin in his article on "The Mechanics of Corporate Growth" considers "a high return on investment and a significant proportion of retained earnings" keys to superior growth of earnings per share.

Use of return on equity capital and payout ratios as indicators of future rates of growth of earnings per share is compelling both for its simple logic and for the wide range of persons who advocate the method. If the method is useful for predictive purposes, companies which have had a high return on equity capital and/or a high rate of retention of earnings in the past should tend to achieve superior rates of increase per share earnings in the future. In the study described below, eleven industries were examined to determine whether companies with high returns on equity capital and/or low payout ratios recorded superior rates of growth of earnings per share.[7]

Test Procedure

The return on equity capital was recorded for one period (e.g. 1964) for each company in the industry being studied. Next the rate of growth of earnings per share between 1964 and 1965 was computed for each company in the industry.[8] Then the companies showing the highest rates of return on common equity in 1964 were compared with the companies showing the highest rates of growth of earnings per share between 1964 and

1965. If the companies were the same, the correlation would be positive. The degree of correlation was measured computing the coefficient of correlation. The correlation payout ratios in 1964 and rates of increase in earnings per share between 1964 and 1965 was determined in a similar manner.

Reported earnings per share, dividends per share, and the rate of return on common equity are the basic data used in the analysis.[9] To insure that reported earnings are on a current basis, non-recurrent expenses and non-recurrent income have been excluded. Companies which shifted their fiscal year or which significantly altered their accounting practices have been excluded in order that earnings per share of each individual company are reported on a consistent basis throughout the period. Reported earnings are substantially affected by seasonal factors. To eliminate seasonal bias the data for each company are the same fiscal period, the year ended December 31. The data covers the years 1950-1965, inclusive. The tests were conducted on each of eleven industries comprising 244 companies. The industries are listed below with the number of companies in each industry given in parentheses:

Auto Parts	(14)	Steel	(20)
Building Materials	(28)	Petroleum	(20)
Chemical	(23)	Natural Gas	(32)
Drug	(21)	Electric Utility	(50)
Machinery	(20)	Bank	(26)
Electric Machinery & Electronics	(21)		

For each industry two groups of tests were made. In the first group of tests rates of change of earnings per share were correlated with rates of return on common equity. In the second group of tests rates of change of earnings per share were correlated with payout ratios.

The business cycle has an important effect on earnings per share. To compensate for this effect 308 tests were made in similar phases of the business cycle. For each industry two hundred and twenty tests were made so that 2,420 tests were made altogether.

Return on Equity Capital and Growth of Earnings Per Share

Table I summarizes the tests concerning the relation of the return on equity capital to growth of earnings per share. The table shows the number of tests which indicated significant positive correlation (+), the number which indicated significant negative correlation (-), and the number which revealed no significant correlation (0).

Table I

Rates of Change of Earnings Per Share and Return on Common Equity

Rate of Change of Earnings Per Share	And Return on Common Equity	Significant Correlation			Significant Correlation		
		+	-	0	+	-	0
			(Number of Tests)				
1 Year	Prior Year	1	21	88	1	14	95
2 Years	Prior Year	0	24	86	0	13	97
5 Years	Prior Year	1	20	89	2	15	93
1 Year	Prior 5 Years	3	15	92	1	14	95
2 Years	Prior 5 Years	2	11	86	3	12	84
5 Years	Prior 5 Years	1	6	59	1	8	57
		8	97	500	8	76	521

Payout ratios held constant.

As may be seen, significant positive correlation was rare. It appeared in only 8 tests. Negative correlation was more common for it appeared in 97 tests. In these tests a below average rate of return on common equity in one period was likely to result in above average growth of earnings per share in the next period. The most common result of the tests was the absence of any significant correlation. In 500 tests there was no significant correlation. This number represented 83 percent of the tests. In these tests relative rates of return on common equity in one period gave no significant indication of relative growth of earnings per share in the next period.

The absence of any significant relationship between growth of earnings per share and return on equity capital may have been due to differences in dividend payout ratios. To eliminate this effect, a second group of tests was made for which differences in payout were compensated.[10] When differences in payout were held constant, the results were the same. Relatively high or low rates of return on common equity gave no significant indication of future rates of growth of earnings per share in 521 tests, or 86 percent of the tests.

Dividend Payout and Growth of Earnings Per Share

Table II shows the results of the tests on the relationship between dividend payout ratios and rates of growth of earnings per share. As may be seen, companies with low payout ratios in one period did not tend to record above average rates of growth of earnings per share in the next period. Payout and growth were inversely correlated in only 37 tests. The most common result of the tests was absence of any significant correlation between payout ratios in one period and growth of earnings per share in the next period. In 505 tests the relationship was not significant.

Table II
Rates of Change of Earnings Per Share and Dividend Payout Ratios

Rate of Change of Earnings Per Share	And Payout Ratios	Significant Correlation			Significant Correlation		
		+	-	0	+	-	0
			(Number of Tests)				
1 Year	Prior Year	16	3	91	14	3	93
2 Years	Prior Year	21	5	84	16	6	88
5 Years	Prior Year	14	6	90	11	10	89
1 Year	Prior 5 Years	7	9	94	3	4	103
2 Years	Prior 5 Years	4	8	87	3	8	88
5 Years	Prior 5 Years	1	6	59	0	7	59
		63	37	505	47	38	52

Rates of return on common equity held constant.

To eliminate the effect of return on equity capital on the results, a final group of tests was made for which differences in the return on equity capital was compensated. When differences in the return on equity capital were held constant the results were the same. Payout bore no significant relationship to growth of earnings per share in 520 tests. This represented 86 percent of the tests.

Conclusion

In 99 percent of the tests high past rates of return on equity capital were no more indicative of above average growth of earnings per share than low rates of return. In 94 percent of the tests high rates of retention of earnings were no more a sign of above average future growth of earnings per share than low rates of retention. Neither past payout ratios nor past rates of return on equity capital proved reliable indicators of future relative rates of growth of earnings per share.

Because these results are contrary to assumptions implicit in much theoretical and practical work in financial analysis they have important implications for financial analysis. Some of the matters about which the results raise questions are:

– Assumption that changes in the rate of return on equity capital are small enough to permit use of the rate of return on equity capital and the retention ratio for predicting rate of growth of earnings per share.

– Relationship between growth of invested capital and growth of earnings per share.

– Effect of low payout ratios on growth of dividends, apart from that resulting from the capacity to raise the payout ratio.

– Justification of low payout ratios on the grounds that retention of earnings will produce significantly greater growth of earnings or dividends.

– Predictive significance of the return on equity capital, on total capital or on total assets.

– Ability to reliably predict significant differences in rates of growth of earnings per share a year or more in the future.

Footnotes

1. This article was made possible through the assistance of the Numerical Analysis Center of the University of Minnesota, which provided time on its Control Data 1604 computer, and also through the assistance of the School of Business School Computer Center of the University of Minnesota. Suggestions were given by Harold Stevenson of the School of Business Administration, University of Minnesota.

2. J. E. Murphy, "Relative Growth of Earnings Per Share— Past and Future," *Financial Analysis Journal*, November-December 1966, pp. 73-76.

3. M. J. Gordon and E. Shapiro, "Capital Equipment Analysis: The Requited Rate of Profit," E. Solomon, editor, *The Management of Corporate Capital*, Glencoe, Ill., Free Press,

1959, p. 145.

4. E. M. Lerner and W. T. Carleton, *A Theory of Financial Analysis*, New York, New York, Harcourt, Brace & World, Inc., pp.110 seq.

5. B. Graham, D. L. Dodd, & S. Cottle, *Security Analysis: Principles and Techniques*, New York, New York, McGraw-Hill, 1962, p. 457. See also chapter 33.

6. H. Sauvain, *Investment Management*, Englewood Cliffs, New Jersey, Prentice-Hall, Inc., 1959, pp. 258-64.

7. R. I. Cummin, "The Mechanics of Corporate Growth," E. M. Lerner, editor, *Readings in Financial Analysis and Investment Management*, The Institute of Chartered Financial Analysts, Inc., Homewood, Illinois, R. D. Irwin, 1963, p. 144.

8. The measure of rate of growth of earnings per share used in this study is the change in natural logarithms of earnings per share.

9. The data is taken from *The Value Line Investment Survey*, Arnold Bernhard & Co., Inc., New York, New York.

10. Differences in payout were compensated for by computing the coefficient of partial correlation.

3

PRICE/EARNING RATIOS AND FUTURE GROWTH OF EARNINGS AND DIVIDENDS

Joseph E. Murphy and Harold W. Stevenson

One of the most important market ratios used in valuation of common stocks is the price/earning ratio, or the P/E ratio. The advantage of the P/E ratio is that it permits immediate comparison of the prices of an unlimited number of stocks in terms of a common earnings base. The importance of this advantage is evident in the daily use of the P/E ratio by professional investors, its widespread publication by investment research services, its use by investment bankers in pricing new securities, its frequent presence in court in the appraisal of the value of closely held securities and its incorporation in most theoretical and empirical models of the determinants of common stock prices.

At any given time P/E ratios vary widely from one common stock to another. Besides being influenced by the level of earnings, the price of a stock, and consequently its P/E ratio, may be influenced by a number of other variables such as risk, company size, debt/equity ratio, industry, dividend yield, past growth of earnings, past growth of dividends, expected future growth of earnings and anticipated growth of dividends.

Of these other variables probably the most important is growth of earnings and dividends.

Growth is an important variable in the theoretical and empirical models of most writer, such as Benishay, Gordon, Graham, Dodd and Cottle, Holt, Lerner and Carleton, Whitbeck and Kisor and Williams, to cite a few. Different P/E ratios may be accorded to different stocks principally on the basis of expected future rates of growth of earnings and dividends. The reason for this differentiation is that a rising future earnings stream is considered to be worth more than a falling one. Graham, Dodd and Cottle, for example, assert that P/E "multipliers should advance proportionally...as the expected growth rate rises..."[1]

Holt argues that "companies with high growth rates of earnings should be valued higher than companies with low growth rates.."[2] Whitbeck and Kisor stipulate that "...we should be willing to pay more, in terms of price earnings multiples..." for stocks whose "...earnings growth will be more rapid...".[3]

The question of the actual relation between relative P/E ratios in one period and growth of earnings and dividends in a succeeding period is extremely important. Knowledge of the relationship should provide an indication of the ability of the market to judge future growth of earnings and dividends, assuming that the market tends to appraise future growth through the P/E ratio. The relation of past P/E ratios to future growth of earnings and dividends also has a bearing on the determinants of stock prices and in stock price models.

A great deal of theoretical work has been done to elucidate the relationship of future growth of earnings and dividends to present value or present price. Extensive empirical work has also been done to reveal the relationship of past growth earnings and dividends to price and to P/E multiples. Yet very little empirical work has been done on the relation of future earnings and dividend growth to past P/E ratios, the subject of this article. Only one previously published study examined this important question. In accord with traditional assumptions it found that "earnings gains are greatest in the high P/E group."[4]

Test Procedure

In examining the question of the relation between P/E ratios and future growth of earnings and dividends, two groups of tests were made. In the first group of tests, correlations were made between P/E ratios of selected companies in one period and growth of earnings and dividends of the same companies in a succeeding period. In the second group of tests, companies were grouped into quintiles on the basis of P/E ratios in one period; then average rates of growth of earnings were computed for each quintile in succeeding periods.

In order to provide consistent and comprehensive results the following was done: To provide fiscal comparability of data, all companies selected reported on the same fiscal year, the year ending December 31. Companies which shifted the fiscal year were excluded from the sample. To assure reasonable coverage the test periods covered the fifteen years 1950—1964. To reduce the possibly arbitrary effect of a single year's growth, the P/E ratio was compared with growth earnings per share not only for the next year, but also for the next two years and the next five years.[5] So that a particular year's results would not unduly influence the correlations, tests were made for each of the ten separate test periods ending 1956, 1957,...,1964. In order to avoid the effect of a particular year on the P/E ratio a second set of tests was made using the average P/E ratio over a five year period. Five year average P/E ratios were compared to growth earnings and dividends in the following year, the next two years and the following five years.

To compensate for industry effects, all tests were made by industry and separate tests were made for each of eleven industries. The industries used were auto parts (12 companies), building materials (25), chemical (20), drug (13), machinery (19), electric machinery and electronics (16), steel (15), petroleum (19), natural gas (26), electric utility (48), and bank (24). Finally, since dividend yield may affect P/E ratios, an additional set of tests was made in which the effect of dividend yield was held constant. Altogether, 2,420 separate correlations were made.

In the second group of tests the sample was smaller and one industry (bank) was excluded for ease of computation. In this group of test the P/E ratios were ranked in descending order. The companies in the industry were then divided into five groups (quintiles) on the basis of the P/E multiple. The P/E multiple was computed by dividing the stock's average annual price in one year (e.g., 1955) by earnings per share in the preceding year (1954). The rate of change of earnings per share was then computed for the following year (1956 earnings divided by 1955 earnings), and also for 1959/58, 1960/59, 1961/60. This procedure enables one to compare the forecasting ability of the P/E ratio for growth of earnings per share in successive future one year periods.

Correlation Analysis: P/E Ratios and Future Growth of Earnings Per Share

The results of the correlation tests are shown in Table I. In 488 tests, representing over eighty percent of the tests, P/E ratios bore no significant relation to future relative growth of earnings per share. Companies with relatively high P/E ratios were about as likely to record inferior future growth of earnings as superior rates of growth. Companies with relatively low P/E ratios experiences high rates of earnings growth as often as low rates of growth. In these tests, representing the bulk of the tests made, P/E ratios proved an unreliable predictor of which companies would record superior growth.

Table I
P/E Ratios and Rates of Change of Earnings Per Share

P/E Ratio	And Rates of Change of Earnings Per Share in Next	Significant Correlation A			Significant Correlation B*		
		+	-	0	+	-	0
		(Number of Tests)					
Prior Year	One Year	20	1	89	14	3	93
Prior Year	Two Years	24	0	86	20	1	89
Prior Year	Five Years	32	0	78	15	0	95
Prior 5 Years	One Year	9	3	98	10	4	96
Prior 5 Years	Two Years	12	1	86	13	3	83
Prior 5 Years	Five Years	14	1	51	9	0	57
Totals		111	6	488	81	11	513

*Dividend yield held constant.

In 111 tests, representing 18 percent of the tests, P/E ratios were directly and significantly related to future growth of earnings. In only 6 tests were P/E ratios significantly and inversely related to future growth of earnings per share.

When differences in dividend yield were held constant, similar results occurred. In 513 tests, or 85 percent of the tests, the P/E ratio was not significantly related to future growth of earnings per share.

P/E Ratios and Future Growth of Dividends Per Share

This group of tests concerned the relation between P/E ratios and future growth of dividends per share. Here again, P/E ratios were not generally related to future growth. In 544 tests, or 89 percent of the tests, relative P/E ratios gave no significant indication of future growth of dividends per share. In only a minor fraction of tests was there a significant relationship between P/E ratios and future growth of dividends per share. Similar results occurred when the dividend yield was held constant. In 501 tests, representing 83 percent of the tests, there was no significant correlation between relative P/E ratios and relative future growth of dividends per share.

P/E Quintile Ranking Ratios and Future Growth of Earnings Per Share

There is no clear evidence that the companies in the highest P/E quintile record the highest growth of earnings per share or that the companies in the lowest P/E quintile record the lowest growth. The highest P/E quintile ranked first in earnings growth one year later in only 34 of 100 tests; it ranked below average in24 tests and last in 14 tests. The lowest P/E quintile ranked first in earnings growth in 17 tests, above average in 36 tests, and lowest in only 29 tests.

The slight advantage of the highest P/E quintile seems to decline as the period lengthens. By the fourth year the highest

P/E quintile ranked first in earnings growth in only 24 tests of 100. The lowest P/E quintile ranked first in 21 tests, or nearly as many. On the basis of these tests the P/E ratios bear little systematic relation to future rates of growth of earnings per share.

It is possible that a direct correlation between P/E ratios and future growth of earnings occurs in only certain industries. It is also conceivable that a direct relation between P/E ratios and growth of earnings occurs in some years and not in others. Either alternative could produce results similar to those obtained. Close examination of results by industry and years reveals that alternative is present. The lowest P/E quintile shows higher rates of growth in earnings than the highest P/E quintile in all industries in some years. The lowest P/E quintile equaled or surpassed the highest P/E quintile in earnings growth in three of ten years in the chemical industry; in four of ten years in the auto parts, building materials and natural gas industries; in five of ten years in drugs, electric machinery and petroleum industries; and in six of ten years in the steel and electric utility industries. This evidence, which confirms the industry correlation tests, indicates that P/E ratios do not tend to be directly related to future growth of earnings in any of the industries studied.

A final test was made for a composite group of 134 companies representing all industrial companies in the sample. In three of ten years in this test the lowest P/E quintile recorded higher average growth of earnings per share than the highest P/E quintile.

Examination of the results by year reveals that there was no systematic relation between P/E ratios and growth in certain years. In no single year did the lowest P/E quintile fail to equal or exceed the growth of the highest P/E quintile in at least two industries. And in no single year did the lowest P/E quintile equal or surpass the highest in more than eight of ten industries.

Conclusion

Contrary to current assumptions the P/E ratio, according to our tests proved an unreliable judge of which companies would record superior growth of earnings per share. Both groups of tests reveal that there is little systematic relationship between relative P/E ratios in one period and relative growth of earnings per share in subsequent periods. A high P/E ratio is not a prophecy of superior earnings growth, nor is low P/E a portent of inferior earnings growth. This lack of systematic relationship characterizes all eleven industries studied and persists in all of the periods studied. The correlation tests reveled no systematic relationship between P/E ratios and future growth of dividends.

This result suggests that if the market judges future growth through the P/E ratio, it is not a good judge of growth.[6] It also calls into question the wisdom of justifying high P/E ratios in general simply on the basis of expected high future growth of earnings. The results give reason for the susceptibility of high P/E ratio stocks to sharp price decline, and they indicate that there is substantial room for picking stocks undervalued in terms of future earnings growth, provided one is able to accurately judge relative future earnings growth.

Lack of systematic relationship between P/E ratios and future growth of earnings and dividends also has a bearing on the question of appropriate stock price models and on the question of the determinants of stock prices. The wide variance in growth rates from year to year for particular P/E ratios in a given industry, and from industry to industry, suggest that price models which incorporate both growth and the P/E ratio may be unstable over time. The evidence also suggests that relative P/E ratios may be quite stable, varying little from year to year. This possibility, coupled with the unsystematic relation between past and future relative earnings growth rates shown earlier, would be a sufficient explanation of the lack of correlation between P/E ratios and future growth of earnings per share.

37

Footnotes

1. B. Graham, D. Dodd and S. Cottle, *Security Analysis: Principles and Technique*, (New York: McGraw-Hill Book Company, Inc., 1962), p. 537.

2. C.C. Holt, "The Influence of Growth Duration on Share Prices," September 1962, reprinted in E.B. Fredrickson, editor *Frontiers of Investment Analysis*, (Scranton, Pennsylvania: International Textbook Company, 1965), p. 301.

3. V. S. Whitbeck and M. Kisor, Jr., "A New Tool in Investment Decision-Making," *Financial Analysts Journal*, May-June 1963, p. 53.

4. P. F. Miller, Jr. and E. R. Widmann, "Price Performance Outlook for High & Low P/E Stocks," *The Commercial and Financial Chronicle*, September 29, 1966, p. 27.

5. The data is taken from *The Value Line Investment Survey*, (New York: Arnold Bernhard & Co., Inc.). In making the first group of tests the P/E ratio recorded for one period, for example the year 1964, for each company in the industry being studied. The P/E ratio was computed by dividing the average 1964 price (the mean of the monthly low and high prices) by 1964 earnings per share. Next the rate of growth of earnings per share between 1964 and 1965 was computed for each company in the industry. Then the companies showing the highest P/E ratios in 1964 were compared with the companies recording the highest rates of growth of earnings per share between 1964 and 1965. The degree of correlation was measured by computing coefficient of correlation.

6. Possibly because high P/E ratios may be justified by the market on the basis criteria (such as past growth of earnings, payout ratios, or return on investment) which are erroneously believed to be related to future growth of earnings. See Richard A. Brealey, "Statistical Properties of Successive Changes in Earnings," an address delivered to the Seminar in Security Prices, Chicago, March 1967; J. E. Murphy, "Relative Growth of

Earnings Per Share—Past and Future," *Financial Analysts Journal*, (November-December 1966, pp. 73-76, and "Return on Equity Capital, Dividend Payout and Growth of Earnings Per Share," *Financial Analysts Journal*, (May-June 1967), pp. 91-93.

4

EARNINGS GROWTH AND PRICE CHANGE IN THE SAME TIME PERIOD

Frequently the most important determinant of the rate of return in equity investments is the rate and direction of price change.[1] Success in investments, if it not be due to chance, is largely a function of the ability to predict price changes. The importance of predicting price changes has led to a number of studies aimed at discovering the determinants of price change. These studies may be conveniently classified into three groups: first, those studies that sought to predict future price changes from past price changes; second, those investigations that attempted to predict price changes from price ratios, such as the price/earnings ratio; and third, those studies which sought to predict price changes from past changes in other variables, such as earnings.

In the last decade a score of studies were made which attempted to discover whether future price changes could be predicted from past price changes. The results were generally disappointing. It was found that successive price changes tended to be independent; the price change of a stock in one period had little bearing on the price change in the next period. Moreover, the relative price change of a stock (relative to other stocks) in one period was not indicative of the relative price change of that stock in the next period.[2]

Although the full import of the results of these studies is not yet clear, the studies certainly have important implications for financial analysis. Some have concluded that the results call into question the very utility of fundamental financial analysis.[3] This conclusion was certainly premature and may be questioned, as will be shown below.

The results of the second and third groups of studies were only partly encouraging. The correlation between price ratios and future price changes, though promising, was frequently neither significant nor positive and price changes in one period tended to be independent of earnings changes in the preceding period.[4] None of the studies were devoted to the question of the relation between relative earnings changes and relative price changes in the same period. This question should probably have been examined first. Even though previous earnings growth was unrelated to present changes in prices, perhaps percentage changes in prices and earnings in the same period was highly correlated. Per share earnings growth could still have a substantial influence on simultaneous price changes. If there were little connection between relative changes in the same period, then the changes might be of limited value. If, on the contrary, there were high correlation between relative earnings changes and relative price changes in the same period, then the ability to predict relative earnings changes would be extremely important.[5] The purpose of this article is to report the results of a study of the influence of rates of growth of per share earnings on percentage changes in stock prices in the same period.

Test Procedure

In this study prices were defined as the average of the monthly high and low stock price during the calendar year. Earnings per share are reported earnings during the same year, adjusted to exclude the effect of non-recurrent charges or income.[6] The sample consisted of 203 companies from 10 different industries. Separate tests were made for each industry. The industries tested were auto parts (12 companies), building materials (25), chemical (20), drug (13), electric machinery and electronics (16), electric utility (44), machinery (17), natural gas (25), petroleum (19), and steel (12).

The tests were designed to determine whether the companies experiencing the highest percentage growth in earnings per share in one period also recorded the highest percentage increase in price during the same period.

To provide reasonable coverage of different time periods, tests were made for each of five different time periods: one year, two years, three years, four years, and five years. To eliminate the effect of unusual years, ten tests were made for each of the five time periods. All periods tested ended in one of the ten years 1955, 1956,...,1963, 1964. Five hundred separate tests were made altogether.

In conducting a test for one period for one industry, all companies in the industry were ranked in order of percent growth of earnings in that period. Then the companies were classified into five equal groups, or quintiles. The companies recording the highest growth in earnings per share were placed in the first quintile, next highest in growth in earnings per share were placed in the second quintile, etc. Those companies with the lowest increases in earnings per share were placed in the fifth quintile. When the above steps had been completed, the percentage change in price was computed for each company in each quintile. Then for each quintile the average percentage change in price was found.

Results of the Tests

In five year periods, and also in four year periods, the quintile with the highest rate of earnings growth tended to achieve the greatest price increase in the same period. This was true of all ten industries tested, without exception. While the tables for individual industries are not presented here, the aggregate results for all industries are shown in Table I. As that table reveals, of the 100 tests on five year periods, the first quintile in five year earnings growth ranked in the first quintile in price appreciation in 15 tests and last in price appreciation in no tests. The lowest quintile in earnings growth over a five year period ranked lowest in price appreciation in the same five year period in 82 of 100 tests. The lowest quintile in earnings growth ranked first in price appreciation in only one test. These tests indicate that price changes and earnings changes in the same five year periods were highly correlated.

A very high, but slightly lower, correspondence between relative growth of per share earnings and simultaneous price appreciation characterizes four-year periods in all industries. To

43

a lesser extent percentage changes of per share earnings and prices are highly correlated in all industries in concurrent three year periods.

In one and two year periods relative earnings growth and price appreciation still show a high degree of correlation in the aggregate. As may be seen in Table I, the top earnings growth quintile in one year periods ranked in the first price change quintile in 50 of 100 tests, in the second quintile in 25 tests and in the bottom price change quintile in only two tests. The lowest quintile in earnings growth was last in price change in 53 tests and first in only 8 tests.

In some industries the correlation between earnings growth

Table I
Earnings Growth and Price Change (Ten Industries)

EARNINGS CHANGE IN 1 YEAR AND PRICE CHANGE IN THE SAME YEAR

Earnings Growth Quintile	Number of Years in Which Price Change Ranked				
	First	Second	Third	Fourth	Fifth
First (High Growth)....	50	25	18	5	2
Second..................	18	38	21	14	9
Third...................	12	15	30	31	12
Fourth..................	12	13	23	28	24
Fifth (Low Growth)......	6	9	8	22	53

EARNINGS CHANGE IN 5 YEARS AND PRICE CHANGE IN THE SAME 5 YEARS

Earnings Growth Quintile	Number of Years in Which Price Change Ranked				
	First	Second	Third	Fourth	Fifth
First (High Growth)....	75	17	5	3	0
Second..................	16	54	25	4	1
Third...................	4	19	52	21	4
Fourth..................	4	7	14	62	13
Fifth (Low Growth)......	1	3	4	10	82

and price change in one year periods was much higher than in other industries. Earnings growth and price change in the same one year period are highly correlated in the chemical, drug, natural gas and electric utility industries. The correlation between simultaneous price appreciation is somewhat lower in building materials and the electric machinery and electronics industries. The relationship is very low in one year periods in the auto parts, machinery, petroleum and steel industries. In all industries the correlation increases between earnings growth and price appreciation in the same period as the time period is increased from one to five years.

Average annual rates of change of prices and earnings for one year and five year periods are shown in Table II. In one year periods the average rate of price change was 17.2% for companies in the highest earnings growth quintile. Companies in the lowest earnings growth quintile averaged a 3.2% increase in price. Results for the five year periods are similar. Companies in the highest earnings growth group recorded an average annual increase in price of 18.3%. Companies in the lowest earnings growth quintile recorded a mean increase in price of 3.9%.

Conclusion

Table II
Concurrent Annual Rates of Change in Price and Earnings

Earnings Growth Quintile	1 YEAR PERIOD		5 YEAR PERIOD	
	Price	Earn	Price	Earnings
First (High Growth)....	17.4%	37.3%	18.3%	14.2%
Second.................	13.5	16.5	13.4	8.2
Third.................	10.7	8.4	11.1	5.2
Fourth.................	7.5	1.0	7.8	1.7
Fifth (Low Growth)......	3.2	-13.8	3.9	-3.8

The results of above tests indicate that there is a very high correlation between relative growth of per share earnings and relative percentage changes in stock prices in the same period. Those companies recording the highest rates of growth of earnings per share show the greatest gains in market price in the same period. Companies recording the lowest earnings growth, or greatest declines of per share earnings, record the smallest price appreciation or the steepest percentage declines in price. This correspondence was true of all ten industries studied over extended periods—four to five years—and of most industries studied over shorter periods—one to two years.

These results reaffirm one of the basic premises of traditional security analysis: that fundamental variables such as earnings growth have a substantial bearing on changes in market prices. When combined with an earlier result—independence of relative past and future rates of earnings change[6]—the high correlation between rates of changes of earnings and prices in the same period provides a partial explanation of randomness in stock prices. If relative past and future rates of earnings change are independent and rates of earnings change are highly correlated with rates of price change, then successive relative percentage price change would tend to be highly stable: the companies with relatively high price/earnings ratios would always tend to have relatively high price/earnings ratios and vice versa. This suggestion stems from the mathematical fact that if price and earnings of individual stocks tend to move in the same direction at the same relative rates, their relative price/earnings ratios would tend to remain unchanged. From the viewpoint of the practicing analyst, the most important aspect of the results described above is that superior market performance will come from selecting those stocks which will record relatively superior earnings gains. Therefore, the primary effort of the analyst should be not merely to project future earnings of individual companies, but to project relative future performance so as to distinguish those companies which will show the highest percentage earnings gains from those which will record the lowest percentage gains. In this sense, the tests substantiate what is practiced by many analysts today.

Footnotes

1. All references to price changes or to earnings changes are to rates of change. This study was made possible through the assistance of the Numerical Analysis Center of the University of Minnesota, which provided time on its Control Data 1604 computer, and also through the assistance of the School of Business Center of the University of Minnesota. All of the data used refers to per share data.

2. Studies presenting this evidence are contained in P. H. Cootner, ed. *The Random Character of Stock Prices*, M. I. T. Press, 11964. Independence of successive earnings changes may be the cause of independence in stock price changes. See J. E. Murphy, "Relative Growth of Earnings Per Share—Past and Future", *Financial Analysts Journal,* November-December 1966, pp. 73-76. A. C. Rayner and I. M. D. Little, *Higgledy Piggledy Growth Again*, Basil Blackwell, Oxford, 1966. Richard A. Brealey, "Statistical Properties of Successive Changes in Earnings", an address delivered to the Seminar in Security Prices, Chicago, March, 1967.

3. E. F. Fama, "Random Walks in Stock Market Prices", *Financial Analysts Journal*, Sept.-Oct. 1965, pp. 55-58.

4. H. A. Latane, "Price Changes in Equity Securities", *Journal of Finance*, September 1951, pp. 254-264. J. D. McWilliams, "Price, Earnings and P-E Ratios", *Financial Analysts Journal*, May-June 1966, pp. 137-142. S. F. Nicholson, "Price-Earnings Ratios", *Financial Analysts Journal*, July-August 1960, pp. 43-46. H. S. Schneider, "Two Formula Methods for Choosing Common Stock", *Journal of Finance*, June 1951, pp. 221-237. M. FG. Scott, "Relative Share Prices and Yields", *Oxford Economic Papers*, October 1962, pp. 218-250. D. L. Tuttle, "An Analysis of Annual Changes in Prices of Equity Securities", unpublished Ph.D. dissertation, University of North Caroline, 1965.

5. The data is taken from The Value Line Investment Survey, Arnold Bernhard & Co., New York, N. Y.

6. See Footnote 2 above.

EFFECT OF LEVERAGE ON PROFITABILITY, GROWTH AND MARKET VALUATION OF COMMON STOCK

The replacement of equity capital by lower cost long-term debt theoretically can raise a firm's return on equity, accelerate growth of earnings and enhance the value of the common stock.[1] For this reason, leverage forms a key element in the theory of finance[2] and is an important consideration to the corporate treasurer in choice of new financing and to the financial analyst.

Leverage may be defined as the proportion of long-term capital represented by long-term debt. The higher the leverage the more a company depends on long-term creditors for its long-term capital. Long-term debt capital generally costs less than the firm is able to earn on its total capital. When two companies earn the same rate of return on total capita, the firm with the greater proportion of debt in capitalization will earn a higher return on equity capital. A higher rate of return on equity capital should produce in turn more rapid growth of earnings and dividends and higher valuation of the common stock. Thus, the return on equity capital, growth of earnings and dividends and the market's valuation of the firm's common stock are all directly tied to the leverage, at least in theory.[3]

But in appraising the significance of leverage, the financial manager needs to know more than the theoretical effect of leverage on profits and valuation. He needs to know the extent to which firms with higher leverage actually produce higher returns on common equity, record better growth of earnings and receive enhanced values in the market place.

The study described below was designed to examine the actual effect of leverage on profitability, growth and market valuation. Its purpose was to answer the questions: what bearing does the relative amount of long-term debt in a firm's capitalization have on its relative rate of return on common equity, per share, growth of stock prices, market valuation? To what extent

---

do the more highly leveraged firms actually tend to have the highest rate of return on common equity, the fastest growth of earnings, the most rapid appreciation of stock prices, the highest price/earnings ratios?

Test Procedure

Leverage is defined in this study as the ratio of long-term debt to total long-term capital. Leverage was recorded for one period (e.g., 1964) for each company in the industry being studied. Next the return on common equity was computed for each company in the industry. Then the companies with the highest proportions of leverage in 1964 were compared with the companies recording the highest rates of return on common equity in 1964. If the companies were the same a direct relationship existed between leverage and the return on common equity. The degree of relationship was measured by computing the coefficient of correlation. The relationship between leverage and growth of earnings per share was measured in a similar manner.

Reported equity and debt capital, earnings per share, prices and dividends are the basic data used in the analysis. They are taken from the Compustat annual industrial tapes published by Standard Statistics, Inc. Growth of earnings per share is computed as the rate of change of earnings per share while price/earnings ratios and dividend yields are computed from per share earnings, dividends and year-end prices. Reported earnings are substantially affected by seasonal factors. To eliminate seasonal bias and provide comparable income and price information, the data for each company are for the same fiscal period, the year ended December 31. The data covers the years 1946-1965, inclusive. The tests were conducted on each of five industries comprising 72 companies. The industries were business and electric equipment (16 companies), chemical (14), paper and container (13), petroleum (17) and steel (12). For each industry tests were made for five different length periods: one, two, three, four and five-year periods. For each length period ten tests were made, one for each of the periods ending 1956, 1957,...,1965. Thus, fifty tests were made in each industry for each question being investigated. In addition a number of tests were made on related questions. Altogether more than 2,000 separate tests were conducted.

Results of the Tests

The proportion of long-term debt in total capitalization turned out to be generally unrelated to the rate of return on common equity. Firms with heavy leverage showed no tendency to record higher rates of return on common equity capital in all time periods in four of the five industries: business and electrical equipment, chemical, petroleum and steel. In the paper and container industry leverage was less completely but still predominantly, unrelated to the return on common equity. These results are illustrated in Table I which presents the tests for one and five-year periods for the petroleum industry.

Table I
The Relation of Leverage of Rates of Return on Common Equity and Other Variables in the Petroleum Industry

	Significant Correlations					
	One Year Period			Five Year Periods		
Long-Term Debt/Total Capital	+	-	0	+	-	0
and						
Rate of Return on Common Equity	0	9	1	0	10	0
Price/Earnings...............	0	10	0	0	10	0
Price/Dividends................	0	8	2	0	10	0
% Change in Cash Flow..........	0	10	0	0	10	0
% Change in Earnings...........	0	10	0	0	10	0
% Change in Price..............	0	10	0	0	10	0

The absence of relation between leverage and return on equity raises doubt about the effect of leverage on growth and market valuation. The next group of tests revealed that the ratio of long-term debt to total capitalization bore little relation to growth of earning per share. Indeed, in two of five industries, companies with lower leverage showed a slight tendency to record higher rates of growth of earnings per share. In the chemical industry leverage was entirely unrelated to growth of earnings per share. In the chemical industry leverage was entirely unrelated to growth of earnings per share, while in steel there was a very slight direct correspondence between leverage and earnings growth in one and two-year periods, but not in longer periods.

Other tests were made to determine the effect of leverage on growth of sales per share net, income before taxes per share and cash flow per share. In nearly all tests leverage bore no significant relation on growth of per share sales, net income before taxes or cash flow. Leverage was without effect on these variables in all periods in the chemical, paper and containers and petroleum industries. In the business and electrical equipment and steel industries there was some relation between leverage and growth, particularly in a minority of tests, though in the majority of tests leverage had no effect.

Examination of the effect of leverage on price appreciation revealed similar results. The proportion of long-term debt in a company's capitalization had no bearing on its relative price growth. The lack of relation between leverage and price change characterized all time periods and all industries. Moreover, in one industry, paper and containers, the more highly leveraged companies tended to record the poorest performance.

Leverage also had no appreciable effect on market valuation. The long-term debt/total capital ratio was generally unrelated to a firm's relative price/earnings ratio and to dividend yield on its common stock in all industries and all time periods. There was even some tendency for the market to value highly leveraged companies at lower rather than higher prices in terms of price/earnings multiples and dividend yields.

Conclusions

A number of theoretical arguments have suggested that the proportion of leverage in a firm's capitalization would be directly related to its relative return on common equity, growth of earnings, price appreciation and market valuation. These arguments stated that the higher proportion of debt in a firm's capitalization the more likely it was to earn a higher return on common equity, record superior growth of earnings, achieve greater price appreciation and be valued at higher price/earnings multiples in the market place. In the tests described above, the proportion of leverage in a company's capitalization proved to be generally unrelated to its relative return on common equity, to its growth of earnings, to price appreciation or to the valuation of its shares in the market place. Companies with no or little leverage did as well in these respects as firms with high proportions of leverage.

These results raise a number of questions and have several implications. The evidence suggests that the relation between leverage and the other variables is too complex or unsystematic to permit description by a few equations, such as are normally found in theories of finance. Why should this be? A sufficient explanation for the lack of relation between leverage and relative change in earnings and prices is the following: Relative changes in prices and earnings in successive time periods tend to be independent. Companies with the highest earnings and price appreciation in one period evidenced no systematic tendency to record the best growth in the next period.[4] Relative long-term debt/total capital ratios, however, tend to be stable. The same firms tend to be highly leveraged.[5] It is not likely that any direct relationship would appear between a highly stable ratio, such as leverage and a highly volatile ratio, such as relative rates of change in earnings and prices. The evidence shows that there were none. But why should leverage bear no relation on return on equity or to market valuation? Possibly these ratios are too complex being the result of long, varied and possibly arbitrary processes. This is easily seen by reflecting on the nature of the denominator of one of these ratios, the return on common equity. Common equity capital is the historical product of a broad mixture of assets in terms of age, kind and accounting procedures. The elements of the other ratios are similarly complex. Therefore, it may be unreasonable to expect any simple relationship to be evident between them. The results of the tests also raise other questions. If leverage is unrelated to a firm's relative profitability and growth, it may also bear no relation to the volatility of firm's earnings and to the volatility of its stock.

Footnotes

1. This study was made possible through the assistance of the University Computer Center of the University of Minnesota which provided time on its Control Data 6600 computer. All of the data used in the study is based on the Compustat annual industrial tape provided by Standard Securities, Inc.

2. A. A. Robichek and S. C. Myers, *Optimal Financing Decisions,* Prentice-Hall, 1965, pp. 20-49. E. F. Brigham and M. J. Gordon, "Leverage, Dividend Policy, and the Cost of Capital," *The Journal of Finance*, March 1968, pp. 85-103. F. Modigliani and M. Miller, "Dividend Policy, Growth and the Valuation of Shares," *Journal of Business,* October 1961, pp. 411-433.

3. Illustrations of this argument may be found in the work of a number of authors. For example, Lerner and Carleton state that "...the rate of return that a corporation can earn on its equity capital...will be influences by the proportion of debt to equity in the firm's capital structure." E. M. Lerner and W. T. Carleton, *A Theory of Financial Analysis*, Harcourt, Brace & World, Inc., New York, 1966, p. 18. Graham, Dodd and Cottle maintain that "...leverage tends to increase the percentage earned on the common..." B. Graham, D. L. Dodd and S. Cottle, *Security Analysis: Principles and Technique,* McGraw-Hill, 1962, p. 637. According to Lindsay and Sametz "...when a firm

borrows funds...it increases a stockholders expected returns." J. R. Lindsay and A. W. Sametz, *Financial Management: An Analytical Approach*, R. D. Irwin, 1967, p. 289. Cummin concludes "...that if an enterprise has a leveraged capital structure...the growth potential of the enterprise will be increased..." R. J. Cummin, "The Mechanics of Corporate Growth," E. M. Lerner, editor, *Readings in Financial Analysis and Investment Management*, The Institute of Chartered Financial Analysts, Inc., R. D. Irwin, 1963, p. 143.

4. J. E. Murphy, "Relative Growth of Earnings Per Share— Past and Future," *Financial Analysts Journal*, November-December 1966, pp. 73-76. P. H. Cootner, ed., *The Random Character of Stock Prices*, M.I.T. Press, 1964.

5. In a related series of tests a very high degree of correlation was found in a firm's relative common equity/total capital in successive periods.

6

A NOTE ON THE STABILITY OF P/E RATIOS

Joseph E. Murphy and J. Russell Nelson

One of the important objectives of financial research is to explain the performance of common stock prices. Recent studies of the behavior of stock prices have strongly suggested, however, that information about past price movements is not useful in predicting either the direction or magnitude of the next move, i.e., prices of common stocks appear to take random walks.[1] It has also been shown that information about past growth in earnings per share does not lead to useful predictions about future earnings per share.[2] Finally, it has been shown that earnings per share and price tend to move together. That is, although changes in prices and earnings per share appear to behave approximately as random variables when studied individually, if examined concurrently they appear to move in the same direction.[3]

Stock price models commonly relate price to dividend expectations.[4] Expectations of improved dividends are assumed to be associated with improvements in earnings, and expectations of reduced dividends follow from earnings declines. If price is a function of dividend expectations, and if dividend expectations are strongly influenced by changes in earnings, then it follows that changes in prices and earnings should move in concert. This suggests that ratios of price to earnings per share may be relatively stable through time. It is the purpose of this article to report an investigation of the behavior of P/E ratios.

Background Considerations

The basic idea examined is that rankings of P/E ratios tend to be stable from one time period to the next. In recent years many analysts have studied P/E ratios, seeing in them a way to identify well-performing securities.[5] Molodovsky, on the other hand, has argued that much of the interest in P/E ratios is misplaced because "P/E ratios have no existence of their own. As their name implies, they are nothing but quotients reflecting any of the thirteen possible different combinations of the numerator and denominator."[6] Proponents of one point of view argue that P/E ratios are useful guides to investment decisions, while others hold them to be little more than arithmetical artifacts.

We argue from a different point of view. Neither price nor earnings information can be compared directly among firms because of differences in numbers of shares outstanding, firm size, and the like. By forming these data into ratios, useful interfirm comparisons may be possible. Thus, firms for which investor expectations about future dividends and earnings are similar may well command about the same price per dollar of future earnings.[7] If long-run earnings expectations change slowly, then investor valuations of firms, as reflected in P/E ratios, also can be expected to change slowly, so that P/E ratios should retain the same relative standing over extended time periods.

A recent study of the behavior of earnings growth and price changes presented evidence that both of these variables move in the same direction within a single time period.[8] Included in that paper were estimates of the average size of price and earnings changes arranged by quintiles. Data drawn from that paper for changes occurring within one year are shown in Table I, below, together with an additional column showing the effect of these changes on the mean P/E ratio in each quintile.

Table I
Changes in Prices, Earnings, and P/E Ratios

Quintile	Average Change in Price	Earnings	Change in P/E Ratio
1	17.4%	37.3%	-15.0
2	13.5	16.5	- 3.5
3	10.7	8.4	+ 2.0
4	7.5	1.0	+ 6.0
5	3.2	-13.8	+20.0

The data show that in the extreme quintiles changes in earnings tend to be much larger than changes in price. One can infer, and this is shown in the last column at the right, that P/E ratios should change in the opposite direction in those extreme quintiles. The hypothesis that P/E ratios tend to remain in the same rank position requires that there be differences between quintile means that are large enough to offset this moderating influence.

The Tests

In order to test the stability of their rankings, P/E ratios were computed for 203 firms in 10 different industries during the years 1951 to 1965.[9] The industries included were auto parts (12 companies), building materials, (25), chemicals (30), drugs (13), electrical machinery and electronics (16), electric utilities (44), machinery (17), natural gas (25), petroleum (19), and steel (12). The first step was to divide the firms into industry groups. This was done because it was assumed that firms in an industry face more nearly common environmental forces than do firms outside the industry so that grouping them in this way should produce more dependable results.[10] Next, the P/E ratio was computed for each firm for each year from 1951-65. The P/E

Table II
Illustration of Computations for a Hypothetical Industry

Quintile	Company	P/E Ratios 1955	Mean P/E Ratio 1955	Mean P/E Ratio 1956
	A	22		
1	B	20	21	22
	C	19		
2	D	17	18	1
	E	16		
3	F	11	15	15
	G	13		
4	H	13	13	12
	I	12		
5	J	8	10	9

ratios are approximations to the mean ratio for the year, but because of data limitations they were calculated by dividing the mean of monthly high and low prices during a calendar year by the earnings reported the same year. Firms were then ranked from highest to lowest within the industry and by year according to the size of the P/E ratio. Five equal groups of firms, or quintiles, were formed and the mean P/E for each quintile was computed.[11] Holding the firms in each quintile constant, the mean P/E for those same firms was computed for the following year, and two, three, four, and five years later. Table II illustrates these steps for a hypothetical industry using 1955 as the base year and 1956 as the subsequent year.

Results

For each of the 10 industries a summary table was prepared for each of the five lag periods, making a total of 50 tables. Each table reflects comparisons of 10 time periods so that 500 comparisons were made in all. Table III shows results for the chemical industry for one and five years after the base year. The row figures show the frequency with which the mean P/E for a particular quintile in the base period ranked in the quintile indicated by the column caption in the later year. Column figures show the frequency with which the mean P/E for a particular quintile ranged in the quintile indicated by the row caption during that base period.

Table III
P/E Ratio in One Year and P/E Ratio One Year Later

Initial P/E Quintile	Number of Times Subsequent P/E Ratio Ranked				
	First	Second	Third	Fourth	Fifth
First (Highest)	10	0	0	0	0
Second	0	9	1	0	0
Third	0	1	8	1	0
Fourth	1	0	1	9	0
Fifth	0	0	0	0	10

P/E Ratio in One Year and P/E Ratios Five Years Later

Initial P/E Quintile		Number of Times Subsequent P/E Ratio Ranked			
	First	Second	Third	Fourth	Fifth
First (Highest)	10	0	0	0	O
Second	0	9	0	1	0
Third	0	1	7	1	1
Fourth	0	0	3	5	2
Fifth	0	0	0	3	7

If all test results fell along the diagonal in Table III, it would mean that P/E ratios always kept the same rank. Although this is not true in the example, it is clear that the tendency to retain rank is strong. Rank correlation coefficients were computed on the initial and subsequent rankings of the data in all 50 tables, and the statistical significance of the results estimated.[12] All of the tabulations were highly significant, i.e., the tendency for quintile means to retain their initial rank was very strong.

Summary tables incorporating the data for all 10 industries were also prepared and are shown in Table IV. As that table reveals, of the 100 tests on successive years, the first quintile in P/E ratios ranked first in price earnings ratio the next year in 81 tests and last in no tests. The lowest quintile in P/E ratio in one year ranked last the next year in 82 tests and first in one. A very high, but slightly lower, correspondence exists between P/E ratios in one year and P/E ratios two years later. As the interval between years is lengthened, the relationship tends to weaken further. But even when the interval is lengthened to five years there remains a relationship that is statistically significant. As may be seen in the lower panel of Table IV, the top P/E quintile in one year ranked in the first P/E quintile in 60 tests, and in the last quintile in only four tests.

Table IV
P/E Ratio in One Year and P/E Ratios One Year Later

Initial P/E Quintile	Number of Tests in Which Subsequent P/E Ranked				
	First	Second	Third	Fourth	Fifth
First (Highest)	81	15	4	0	0
Second	12	62	17	9	0
Third	4	13	68	20	5
Fourth	2	8	16	61	13
Fifth	1	2	5	10	82

P/E Ratio in One Year and P/E Ratios Five Years Later

Initial P/E Quintile	Number of Tests in Which Subsequent P/E Ranked				
	First	Second	Third	Fourth	Fifth
First (Highest)	60	22	6	8	4
Second	19	45	16	18	2
Third	6	19	36	21	18
Fourth	11	7	30	31	21
Fifth	4	7	12	22	55

The lowest quintile in P/E ratios was last five years later in 55 tests and first in only four tests. As stated at the outset, earlier studies have shown that neither past earnings nor price performance predict future earnings or price performance. Coupled with the evidence presented here this leads one to suspect that there would be little connection between any given stock's P/E ratio and its future earnings or future price performance. It has also been shown that P/E ratios have little relation to future growth of earnings per share. The P/E ratio "proved an unreliable judge of which companies would record superior growth of earnings per share."[13]

Conclusions

The principal finding of this study is that rankings of P/E ratios tend to be stable over periods ranging up to five years. This result is not surprising given the evidence on prices and earnings that has been cited. But it does raise the question of the usefulness of P/E ratios. P/E ratios may be used in portfolio management to assess the relative strength of a stock or to help assess the relative dearness or cheapness of stock. The reciprocal of the P/E ratio may be used in financial research as a proxy for the equity cost of capital, and the P/E ratio may be used as an indicator of risk. Some, if not all, of these uses are called into doubt by our findings and evidence from elsewhere.

In general we would draw attention to the conceptual comparability of P/E ratios with that relatively discredited tool from the field of capital budgeting, the payback period. The payback period is the number of years' returns necessary to recover an initial investment. Similarly, the P/E ratio can be viewed as a measure of the number of years of earnings necessary to recover the purchase price of a share of stock. Many thoughtful analysts have rejected the payback period as a measure of capital investment performance because it ignores the value of earnings generated after payback has been completed and it treats all returns prior to payback as equally valuable regardless of when they are received.

If one assumes that an asset will have no salvage value or that disposal of the asset is deferred far into the future so that the present value of the disposal is small, and that yearly earnings are the same throughout the life of the project, then the reciprocal of the payback ratio is a reasonably good estimate of yield provided project life is at least twice the payback period. In stock price and earnings terms this means that for a stock with a P/E ratio of 20, the implicit yield of 5% is close to the true yield only if earnings are maintained at the present level for at least 40 years into the future—it actually reaches 5% only if earnings continue at this level forever.

Thus, we conclude that it now rests with the proponents of P/E ratio analysis to demonstrate the utility of such analysis.

Footnotes

1. See, for example, Eugene F. Fama, "Random Walks in Stock Market Prices," *Financial Analysts Journal*, Vol. 21, No. 5 (September-October 1965), pp. 55-59. Other studies presenting this evidence are contained in P. H. Cootner, ed., *The Random Character of Stock Prices*, M.I.T. Press, 1964.

2. See J. E. Murphy, "Relative Growth in Earnings Per Share—Past and Future," *Financial Analysts Journal*, November-December 1966, pp. 73-76; A. C. Rayner and I.M.D.Little, "Higgledy Piggledy Growth Again," Basil Blackwell, Oxford, 1966; and Richard A. Brealey, "Statistical Properties of Successive Changes in Earnings," an address delivered to the Seminar on Security Prices, Chicago, March 1967.

3. J. E. Murphy, "Earnings Growth and Price Changes in the Same Time Period," *Financial Analysts Journal,* January-February 1968, pp. 97-99.

4. Among those who have emphasized the importance of future dividends in stock valuation models are J. B. Williams, *The Theory of Investment Value*, (Cambridge: Harvard University Press), 1938; M.J. Gordon, "Dividends, Earnings and Stock Prices," *The Review of Economics and Statistics*, Vol. 41, No. 2 (May 1959), pp. 99-105; Benjamin Graham, et al, *Security Analysis*, (New York: McGraw-Hill Book Company), 1962, especially chapter 35; Philip Kotler, "Elements in a Theory of Growth Stock Valuation," *Financial Analysts Journal*, Vol. 18, No. 3 (May-June 1962), pp. 35-46.

5. Several of these studies are examined in the review article by Nicholas Molodovsky, *Financial Analysts Journal,* Vol. 23, No. 3 (May-June 1967), pp. 101-108; see also his latest article on this subject in the same publication, Vol. 24, No. 6 (November-December 1968), pp. 134-148.

6. Op. cit., pp. 195.

7. W.E. Bell, "The Price- Future Earnings Ratio: A Practical Aid to Stock Valuation," *Financial Analysts Journal,* Vol. 14 (Aug. 1958), pp. 25-28.

8. Joseph E. Murphy, Jr., "Earnings Growth and Price Change in the Same Time Period," *Financial Analysts Journal*, Vol. 24, No. 1 (January-February 1968), pp. 97-99.

9. The data were taken from *The Value Line Investment Survey*, Arnold Bernhard & Co.1 Inc., New York, N. Y. 10. This view has been challenged in an article that suggests that industries may be poor categories for identifying similar firms. See Ronald F. Whippern, "A Note on the Equivalent Risk Class Assumption," *Engineering Economist,* Vol. XI (Spring 1966), pp. 13-22.

11. Some may question the use of a mean of ratios on grounds that it ignores interfirm variations in the magnitude of earnings and prices, and so is not properly weighted. We believe, however, that in this instance the average of the ratios is a better indicator of the level of company P/E ratios within a quintile than the overall ratio would be.

12. Rank correlation analysis is discussed in most elementary statistical textbooks. See, for example, Wilfrid J. Dixon and Frank d. Massey, Jr., *Introduction to Statistical Analysis*, 2nd ed. (New York: McGraw Hill Book Co., Inc.) 1957, pp. 294-295.

13. Joseph E. Murphy, Jr. and Harold W. Stevenson, "Price/Earnings Ratios and Future Growth of Earnings and Dividends," *Financial Analysts Journal,* November-December 1967, p. 113.

7

FIVE PRINCIPLES OF FINANCIAL RELATIONSHIPS

Joseph E. Murphy & J. Russell Nelson

The growth of knowledge of a subject, the growth of a science, is partly the development of general, related and precise statements about reality and the verification of those statements, or principles, by tests. Statements about reality may be deduced from more general principles or they may rest on induction from experience. Until recently the development of financial theory has been primarily deductive; theories of finance have been inferred from more general principle, primarily from the definitions of accounting which mold the character of the data. Within the last decade, however, a change has occurred. Financial theory has begun to be developed on induction from experience. The most important instances of this change are the growth of the random walk theory of stock prices and, more recently, of the random walk theory of earnings changes, theories derived from analysis of the data. Each of these theories, however, concerns a single series of data; in the first case the series is the price series; in the second case it is the earnings series. Not many general statements covering more than a single series, or relating several series, have been developed inductively. It is the purpose of this paper to discuss some general statements that were developed inductively and that encompass and relate more than a single series. These general statements are called principles, though they might be termed hypotheses or even laws, mindful of the fact that general statements about reality are always hypothetical, never completely final, always subject to question and doubt.

This paper states five principles[1] which describe the relationships between pairs of financial variables. The principles furnish, in significant respects, a more accurate and useful statement of the relationship among financial variables than was previously available. The principles are very general; they cover many relationships involving one or two variables. This capacity to describe and predict general relationships is not provided to the same degree of accuracy by previous theories of finance.

The usefulness of the principles is illustrated by the following example: The influence of return on investment on growth of earnings is a very important question in finance. Traditional theory states that for a group of firms the rate of return will be directly related to growth of earnings.[2] Our third principle states that there will normally be no significant relationship between rate of return and growth of earnings. Extensive evidence showed that there is normally no significant relationship.[3] This example is but one of many that could be presented.

Traditional theory makes deductions from definitions of financial variables about the relationships that prevail between those variables. We define the statistical characteristics of two major classes of financial variables. Then we postulate the principles governing the relation between these variables. The relationships predicted by our principles differ in many important instances from the relationships predicted by the usual deductions of traditional theory.

A close examination of the behavior of financial variables over time uncovers an important distinction: Variables expressed in dollars, such as earnings per share, behave very differently than percentage changes in those same variables. Similarly, financial ratios, such as the price-earnings ratio, behave quite differently than percentage changes in financial ratios. Variables expressed as dollars or financial ratios appear comparatively stable and predictable over time. Successive values are fair approximations of one another. Percentage changes in dollar and financial ratio variables, or growth variables, on the other hand, tend to be erratic, volatile, and unpredictable over time. Successive values bear little relation to one another. Thus, financial variables may be placed into two classes or categories: (1) dollar and ratio variables and (2) percentage change variables.

Dollar And Ratio Variables

The first class or category of financial variable contains dollar and ratio variables. Dollar and ratio variables are restricted to three types: income statement, balance sheet and market price data expressed in dollars (for example, IBM's sales in 1968), per-share data expressed in dollars (for example, IBM's earnings per share in 1968), and financial ratios (for example, the price/earnings ratio). Examples are shown in Table 1.

Table 1
Illustrative Examples of Dollar and Ratio Variables

Total Dollar Variables	Per Share Dollar Variables	Ratio Variables
Sales	Sales/Share	Sales/Total Capital
Operating Income	Operating Income/Share	Sales/Equity Capital
Pretax Income	Pretax Income/Share	Pretax Income/Sale
Income Taxes	Income Taxes/Share	Net Income/Sales
Net Income	Net Income/Share	Net Income/Capital
Dividends Paid	Dividends Paid/Share	Dividends/Net Income
Inventory	Inventory/Share	CurrenAssets/Current Liabilities
Receivables	Receivables/Share	Plant/Equity Capital
Current Assets	Current Assets/Share	Net Current Assets/ Debt
Total Assets	Total Assets/Share	Equity Capital/Total Assets
Current Liabilities	Current Liabilities/Share	
Long Term Debt	Long Term Debt/Share	
Common Equity	Common Equity/Share	
Market Value	Market Price/Share	Price/Earnings

Percentage Change Variables

The second category of financial variables is the percentage change variable. The percentage change variable is found by computing the percentage change between successive observations of dollar and ratio variables. A good example is the rate of change of price per share. All growth variables are percentage change variables. Examples are shown in Table 2.

Table 2
Illustrative Examples of Percentage Change Variables

Percent Change in:	Percent Change in:	Percent Change in:
Sales	Sales/Share	Sales/Total Capital
Operating Income	Operating Income/Share	Sales/Equity Capital
Pretax Income	Pretax Income/Share	Pretax Income/Sales
Income Taxes	Income Taxes/Share	Net Income/Sales
Net Income	Net Income/Share	Net Income/Capital
Dividends Paid	Dividends Paid/Share	Dividends/Net Income
Inventory	Inventory/Share	Current Liabilities
Receivables	Receivables/Share	Plant/Equity Capital
Current Assets	Current Assets/Share	Net Current Assets/ Debt
Total Assets	Total Assets/Share	Equity Capital/Total Assets
Current Liabilities	Current Liabilities/Share	
Long Term Debt	Long Term Debt/Share	
Common Equity	Common Equity/Share	
Market Value	Market Price/Share	Price/Earnings

The Five Principles of Financial Relationships

By concentrating on general classes of variables, a simpler and more general framework for observing financial process is provided. Extensive testing of many particular variables in a variety of times periods suggests that we are able to make accurate and realistic descriptive statements about many important financial relationships. We have reduced these to five statements, or principles, describing the relationship, or correlation, between two financial variables. The five principles are presented on the following pages together with examples and justifications.

First Principle

For a group of firms, the values of a dollar or ratio variable in one period will typically be directly related to values of that same dollar or ratio variable in the next period.

Example:

Sales is a dollar variable. Sales in 1967 of nine companies in the chemical industry, for example, were directly related to the sales of the same firms in 1968. In other words, the values of dollar variables in one period were directly related to the values of that variable in the next period. The data in the next column illustrates the first principle.[4]

	Sales 1967 (Millions $)	Rank	Sales 1968 (Millions $)	Rank
DuPont	$3,100	1	$3,480	1
Union Carbide	2,540	2	2,680	2
Monsanto	1,630	3	1,790	3
Grace, W. R.	1,580	4	1,740	4
Dow Chemical	1,380	5	1,650	5
Hercules, Inc.	640	6	720	6
GAF Corp.	520	7	570	7
Stauffer Chemical	420	8	480	8
Rohm & Haas	370	9	420	9

Correlation Positive $r^2 = .99$

Justification

Dollar and ratio variables change very slowly, on average, from year to year, or from period to period. Because these values change slowly, firms change their relative positions slowly. If firms change their relative position slowly from period to period, then values in one period will be closely related to the values in the next period. This means that the coefficient of correlation will be positive and significant, on average. This will be true whatever method of correlation is used, parametric or nonparametric. This analysis assumes wide dispersion of values among firms as is generally the case. The causes of positive correlation, of statistical non-independence, stem from a variety of sources such as the tendency of management to retain assets and the effort of management to sustain and improve sales and profits.

Evidence

Very few published studies have been devoted to instances of the first principle as such, though the few that have been done uphold the validity of it. The ratio variable price/earnings, for example, has been found to be correlated in successive periods.[5] To test the first principle we made 6,100 correlations using per-share data for 150 companies from eight industries. Tests were made using both dollar and ratio variables for successive one, two, three, four and five-year periods. The data were derived from the Compustat annual tapes, were restricted to calendar year companies for all industries except retail trade, and spanned the period 1947 through 1966.

The results for 1,220 one-year period tests are given in Table 3. The results presented in the table reveal the number of correlations which recorded a direct relationship between the values of a variable in one year and the values of that variable in the next year for the firms in the industry. Although only the results for successive one-year periods are shown in the table, the results for longer periods were similar. The columns on the

Table 3
Tests of First Principle
Per Share Variables in Successive One Year Periods

Number of Significantly Positive Correlations Out of Every Ten Tests

Industry	Dollar Variables														Ratio Variables					Total			Percent of	
	Sales	Pretax Income	Cash Flow	Deprec. Chgs.	Fixed Chgs.	Income Tax	Earn	Div	Inv Cap	Cap Exp	Price High	Price Low	Price close	Debt/ Cap	Price/ Earn	Earn Eqty	Pretax Margin	Div/ Earn	Div/ Price	Actual	Predicted	Possible	Predicted	Possible
Business & Elec. Equip.	10	10	10	10	10	10	NA	10	10	10	10	10	10	10	NA	10	10	5	10	163	153	170	108	97
Chemical	10	10	10	10	10	10	NA	10	10	10	10	10	10	10	NA	10	10	9	10	164	153	170	107	96
Drug	10	10	10	10	10	10	10	10	10	NA	NA	NA	NA	10	NA	10	10	10	NA	130	117	130	111	100
Finance	10	10	NA	NA	10	10	NA	10	10	NA	10	9	10	9	NA	8	8	10	10	135	126	140	107	96
Machinery	10	10	10	10	NA	10	NA	10	10	NA	10	10	10	10	NA	10	10	10	10	150	135	150	111	100
Petroleum	10	10	10	10	10	10	10	10	10	10	10	10	10	10	9	10	10	8	10	187	171	190	109	98
Retail Trade	10	10	10	10	10	10	10	10	10	NA	10	10	10	10	7	10	10	7	10	174	162	180	107	97
Steel	NA	10	10	10	NA	10	NA	10	10	NA	NA	NA	NA	10	NA	10	NA	9	NA	89	81	90	110	90
Total																				1194	1098	1220	109	98

NA designates those tests which the sample size was less than 10 or the required data was not available.

In all other tests the sample size ranged between 10 and 30 companies. If, for example, between 65% and 75% of the tests were positive correlations, then a 7 was recorded representing approximately 7 out of 10.

right of the table give the total number of positive correlations, the predicted number of positive correlations and the total number of possible positive correlations. The possible number of positive correlations is simply the total number of tests run while the predicted number of positive correlations is the number one would expect at the five per cent level of significance, i.e., 90 per cent of the possible number. The last column on the right shows the actual number of tests which were significantly positive expressed as a per cent of the possible number. In 98 per cent of the tests the relationship was significantly positive, or direct, providing substantial evidence in support of the first principle.

Second Principle

For a group of firms, the values of a percentage change variable in one period will typically be unrelated to the values of that same percentage change variable in the next period.

Example:

Percentage change in earnings per share is a percentage change variable. The percentage change in earnings per share between 1966 and 1967 of nine companies in the chemical industry, for example, bore no relationship to the percentage change in earnings per share of the same firms between 1967 and 1968. In other words, the values of a percentage change variable in one period were not related to the values of that variable in the next period. The following data illustrate the second principle.

	Per Cent Change in Earn/Share 1966-1967	Rank	Per Cent Change in Earn/Share 1967-1968	Rank
Dow Chemical	7%	1	-2%	8
GAF Corp.	-4	2	5	6
Stauffer Chemical	-7	3	-2	7
Hercules, Inc.	-12	4	14	3
Monsanto	-13	5	11	5
Rohm & Haas	-17	6	18	2
DuPont	-20	7	19	1
Grace, W. R.	-22	8	13	4
Union Carbide	-26	9	-8	9

Correlation not significant r^2 = .08

Justification

Percentage change variables change very rapidly and erratically from year to year, or from period to period. Because they change so rapidly, a firm's rank in one period bears little or no relation to its rank in the next period. Consequently, for a group of firms, there is very little relationship between the values of a percentage change variable in one period and the values of that variable in the succeeding period; the relationship between the variables tends to be not significant. Again, wide dispersion of values among firms is generally the case and is assumed. The causes of rapid changes in rate of change variables include such factors as circumstances uncontrollable by management.

Evidence

Extensive research has demonstrated the validity of the second principle when applied to rates of change of prices per share.[6] Considerable evidence has demonstrated the applicability of this principle to percentage changes of earnings per share.[7] And some past evidence has revealed the validity of this principle when applied to percentage changes of dividends per

Table 4
Tests of Second Principle
Per Share Percentage Change Variables in Successive One-Year Periods

Number of Zero Correlations Out of Every Ten Tests

| Industry | Dollar Variables | | | | | | | | | | | | | Ratio Variables | | | | | | Total | | | Percent of | |
	Sales	Pretax Income	Cash Flow	Depr.	Fixed Chgs.	Income Tax	Earn	Div	Inv Cap	Cap Exp	Price High	Price Low	Price close	Debt/ Cap	Price/ Earn	Earn Eqty	Pretax Margin	Div/ Earn	Div/ Price	Actual	Pre-dicted	Pos-sible	Pre-dicted	Pos-sible
Business & Elec. Equip.	6	5	7	3	9	7	NA	9	3	4	8	8	8	NA	NA	6	6	6	10	101	144	160	70	63
Chemical	10	10	9	10	NA	10	NA	9	8	8	10	9	10	NA	NA	9	9	10	10	140	135	150	104	93
Drug	5	7	NA	NA	NA	10	10	NA	NA	NA	NA	NA	NA	NA	NA	NA	NA	NA	NA	32	36	40	89	80
Finance	9	10	NA	NA	9	8	NA	7	8	6	8	9	8	9	NA	9	8	9	9	126	135	150	93	84
Machinery	7	7	7	8	NA	8	NA	NA	8	NA	10	9	10	NA	NA	8	6	NA	NA	88	99	110	89	80
Petroleum	9	10	10	10	5	4	10	10	7	7	9	10	9	8	7	9	9	9	8	160	171	190	94	84
Retail Trade	6	3	7	8	NA	5	NA	NA	8	NA	9	9	10	NA	NA	2	2	NA	NA	69	99	110	70	63
Steel	NA	4	7	8	NA	NA	NA	NA	10	NA	NA	NA	NA	NA	NA	3	NA	NA	NA	32	45	50	73	64
Total																				748	864	960	85	76

NA designates those tests which the sample size was less than 10 or the required data was not available. In all other tests the sample size ranged between 10 and 30 companies. If, for example, between 65% and 75% of the tests were zero correlations, then a 7 was recorded representing approximately 7 out of 10.

share.[8]

To test the second principle we performed 4,800 correlations on percentage changes in per-share dollar variables and percentage changes in ratio variables for successive one, two, three, four and five-year periods. The results for 960 one-year period tests are given in Table 4. The table presents the number of correlations which recorded no significant relationship, positive or negative, between the values of a percentage change variable in one year and the values of that variable in the next year for the firms in the industry. Although only the results for successive one-year periods are shown in the table, the results for longer periods were similar, that the relationship was not significantly different from zero in at least 70 per cent of the predicted tests in any industry and in 87 per cent of the predicted results of all tests. These results provide substantial evidence in support of the second principle.

Third Principle

For a group of firms, the values of a percentage change variable in one period will typically be unrelated to the values of a dollar or ratio variable in the same period.

Example:

Percentage change in earnings per share is a percentage change variable; rate of return on common equity is a ratio variable. The percentage change in earnings per share between 1967 and 1968 of nine firms in the chemical industry, for example, were not related to the rates of return on common equity of the same firms in 1967. That is to say, the values of a percentage change variable in one period were not related to the values of a ratio variable in the same period. The table in the next column illustrates the third principle.

77

	Rate of Return on Common Equity in 1967	Rank	Per Cent Change in Earn/Sh. 1967-1968	Rank
Dow Chemical	14.1%	1	-2%	8
DuPont	13.3	2	19	1
Hercules, Inc.	13.1	3	14	3
Stauffer Chemical	11.7	4	-2	7
Union Carbide	10.3	5	-8	9
Rohm & Haas	10.1	6	18	2
Monsanto	9.1	7	11	5
Grace, W. R.	8.6	8	13	4
GAF Corp.	5.8	9	5	6

Correlation not significant $r^2 = .00$

Justification

If, for a group of firms, values of one variable are highly correlated from period to period, and if values of another variable are not related from period to period, then it follows that (in general) values of the first variable will not be related to values of the second variable. This fact will, on reflection, be seen to be true. It is necessarily true by deduction from the first and second laws for all periods but one.

Evidence

A number of past investigations demonstrate important instances of the third principle. The percentage change variable growth of price has been shown to be unrelated to the ratio variables, price/earnings and leverage.[9] The percentage change variable growth of earnings per share has been demonstrated to be unrelated to the ratio variables, price/earnings, leverage, dividend payout and rate of return on equity capital.[10]

To test the third principle we made 6,750 correlations on the relationship between percentage change variable and ratio

Table 5
Tests of Third Principle
Ratio and Percentage Change Variables in Coincident One-Year-Periods

Number of Zeros Correlations Out of Every Ten Tests

Industry	Debt/Cap Sales	Debt/Cap Pretax Cash Income Flow	Debt/Cap Earn	Debt/Cap Price Close	Price/Earn Sales	Price/Earn Pretax Cash Income Flow	Price/Earn Earn	Price/Earn Price Close	Earn/Eqty Sales	Earn/Eqty Pretax Cash Income Flow	Earn/Eqty Earn	Earn/Eqty Price Close	Pretax Margin Sales	Pretax Margin Pretax Cash Income Flow	Pretax Margin Earn	Pretax Margin Price Close	Div/Earn Sales	Div/Earn Pretax Cash Income Flow	Div/Earn Earn	Div/Earn Price Close	Total Actual	Total Predicted	Total Possible	Percent Predicted	Percent Possible
Business & Elec. Equip.	6	10	NA	9	NA	NA	NA	NA	0	7	NA	6	3	6	NA	8	7	3	NA	9	93	144	160	65	58
Chemical	10	8	NA	9	NA	NA	NA	NA	7	3	NA	8	9	7	NA	9	8	6	NA	8	120	144	160	83	75
Drug	10	10	8	NA	NA	NA	NA	NA	8	10	10	NA	9	8	8	NA	10	7	10	NA	146	144	160	101	91
Finance	9	NA	NA	9	9	7	NA	5	9	8	NA	9	10	NA	NA	9	10	NA	NA	9	128	135	150	95	85
Machinery	6	8	NA	9	NA	4	NA	NA	6	8	NA	7	10	7	NA	8	9	8	NA	8	120	144	160	83	75
Petroleum	10	10	10	10	6	8	NA	8	6	8	8	9	9	9	7	9	9	7	10	10	213	225	250	95	85
Retail Trade	10	10	10	NA	8	4	7	10	8	3	7	7	NA	3	NA	NA	7	3	7	8	189	225	250	84	76
Steel	NA	10	10	NA	NA	3	NA	NA	NA	NA	NA	NA	NA	NA	NA	NA	NA	6	NA	NA	38	54	60	70	63
Total																					1047	1215	1350	85	76

NA designates those tests which the sample size was less than 10 or the required data was not available.

In all other tests the sample size ranged between 10 and 30 companies. If, for example, between 65% and 75% of the tests were zero correlations, then a 7 was recorded representing approximately 7 out of 10.

variables in the same period. Tests were made for periods varying from one to five years. The results for 1,350 one-year periods are given in Table 5. The table presents the number of correlations which recorded no significant relationship, positive or
negative, between the values of a percentage change variable in
one year and the values of a ratio variable at the beginning of
that period for firms in the industry. Although only the results
for one-year periods are shown, the results for longer periods
were comparable. As may be seen in the total columns of the
table, the correlations were not significantly different from zero
in 86 per cent of the predicted tests and in 78 per cent of all
tests. The results give substantial evidence in support of the
third principle.

The first three principle, and the relationship the describe,
are illustrated in Diagram 1.

DIAGRAM 1

DIAGRAM OF FIRST, SECOND AND THIRD PRINCIPLE

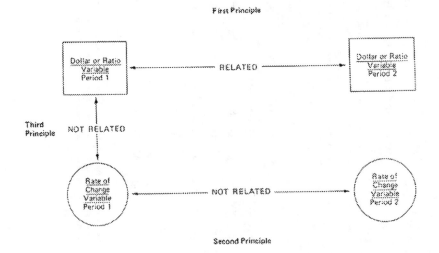

80

Fourth Principle

For a group of firms, when one variable is a component of another variable, the two variables will typically be related. The degree of relationship will depend on the extent to which the one variable includes the other.

Example:

Net income per share is a component of cash flow per share. In 1968 of nine companies in the chemical industry, for example, earnings per share was directly related to cash flow of the same firms in 1968. In other words, one variable was a component of the other and the two variables were directly related. The data illustrating the fourth principle is given below.

	Cash Flow Per Share 1968	Rank	Earnings Per Share 1968	Rank
DuPont	$14.31	1	$7.82	1
Rohm & Haas	10.41	2	5.68	2
Dow Chemical	9.70	3	4.27	3
Monsanto	8.53	4	3.30	4
Dow Chemical	6.41	5	2.60	8
Grace, W. R.	6.17	6	2.86	6
Stauffer Chemical	6.12	7	3.11	5
Hercules, Inc.	5.03	8	2.69	7
GAF Corp.	2.64	9	1.22	9

Correlation positive $r^2 = .94$

Justification

If one variable is so large a component of the other that it includes all of it, the two variables will be identical and the relationship between the values of one variable and the values of the other will be perfect; the two variables will be perfectly correlated. As one variable includes less and less of the other, the relationship diminishes gradually.

Evidence

Past evidence is not readily available on the validity of the fourth principle. To test it we made 7,800 correlations on the relationship between variables when one was a component of the other. Although tests were made on both dollar and on percentage change variables, only the results for dollar variables are presented here. In general far more correlations were significantly positive for dollar variables than for percentage change variables. Tests were made for one, two, three, four and five-year periods. The results for 780 tests on one-year data are given in Table 6. The table presents the number of correlations which recorded a direct relationship between values of a per-share dollar variable in one year and the values of a component of that variables in the same year for the firms in the industry. While the results are restricted to one-year periods, the results for longer periods were comparable. As may be seen from the table, when one variable formed a sizable component of the other, the proportion of significantly positive correlations was high. For example, in all of the instances where data was available, dividends and earnings were positively correlated; but in only 41 per cent of the tests were dividends and sales positively correlated. Earnings per share and pretax income were positively correlated in 92 per cent of the tests; earnings per share and sales per share were positively correlated in only 23 per cent of the tests. On the basis of the tests shown, which are restricted to per-share dollar variables, the fourth principle is borne out.

Table 6

Tests of Fourth Principle

Dollar Variables (Per Share) in One-Year Periods

Industry	Sales & Pretax Income	Sales & Cash Flow	Sales & Deprec.	Sales & Income Tax	Sales & Earn	Sales & Div	Pretax Income & Income Tax	Pretax Income & Earn	Pretax Income & Div	Cash Flow & Deprec	Cash Flow & Earn	Cash Flow & Div	Earn & Div	Total
						Number of Significantly Positive Correlations Out of Every Ten Tests								
Elec. Equip.	2	2	0	3	NA	6	10	NA	9	10	NA	5	NA	
Chemical	10	10	10	10	NA	8	10	NA	10	10	NA	10	NA	
Drug	9	10	10	0	0	0	10	10	10	10	10	8	10	
Finance	3	NA	NA	1	5	3	10	8	1	NA	NA	NA	10	
Machinery	4	8	10	5	NA	4	10	NA	10	9	NA	10	NA	
Petroleum	6	10	10	0	4	5	10	10	10	10	10	8	10	
Retail Trade	0	5	10	0	0	3	10	9	8	9	9	9	10	
Steel	NA	NA	NA	NA	NA	NA	10	NA	10	10	NA	10	NA	
Total	34	45	50	19	9	29	80	37	68	68	29	60	40	568
Possible	70	60	60	70	40	70	80	40	80	70	30	70	40	780
Percent of All Tests	48	75	83	27	23	41	100	92	85	97	97	86	100	73

A designates those tests which the sample size was less than 10 or the required data was not available. In all other tests the sample size ranged between 10 and 30 companies. If, for example, between 65% and 75% of the tests were zero correlations, then a 7 was recorded representing approximately 7 out of 10.

Fifth Principle

For a group of firms, by appropriate stock splits, it is possible to establish any relationship whatsoever between two per-share dollar variables.

Example:

Earnings per share in 1968 is one per-share dollar variable; price per share at the close of 1968 is another per-share dollar variable. In the following example of five hypothetical companies, earnings per share and price per share are directly related; the higher the price per share, the higher the earnings per share.

	Earnings Per Share 1968	Rank	Price Per Share 1968	Rank
Company A	$0.50	1	$7.50	1
Company B	1.00	2	10.00	2
Company C	1.50	3	12.50	3
Company D	2.00	4	15.00	4
Company E	2.50	5	17.50	5

Correlation positive $r^2 = 1.00$

Now each stock is split as follows: Company A is split 0.417 for 1; Company B is split 0.667 for 1; Company C is split 0.917 for 1; Company D is split 1.167 for 1; and Company E is split 1.414 for 1. These stock splits produce the following earnings and prices for the five companies:

84

	Earnings Per Share 1968	Rank	Price Per Share 12/31/68	Rank
Company A	$1.20	1	$18.00	5
Company B	1.50	2	13.00	4
Company C	1.63	3	13.70	3
Company D	1.72	4	12.88	2
Company E	1.76	5	12.38	1

Correlation negative $r^2 = 1.00$

After the arbitrary stock splits earning per share and price per share are inversely related—the higher the price per share,

DIAGRAM 2

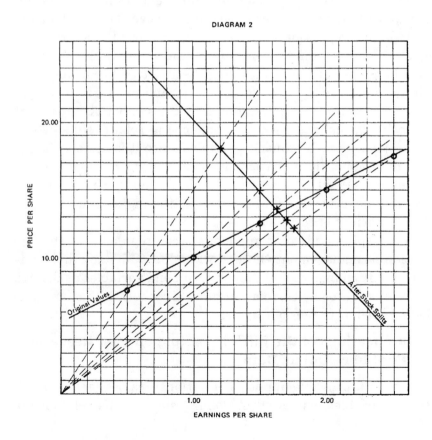

PRICE PER SHARE

EARNINGS PER SHARE

85

the lower the earnings per share. In other words, by appropriate stock splits, the relationship between two per-share dollar variables was changed from a perfect direct relationship (r=+1.0) to a perfect inverse relationship (r=-1.0).

Justification

This principle is best justified in Diagram 2. Earnings per share are represented on the horizontal axis, price per share on the vertical axis. The dots represent the original (hypothetical) values of the variables for five firms in the chemical industry in 1968. Note that the slope of the regression line is upward; the relationship (or coefficient of correlation) is positive and perfect (+1.0); the higher the price, the higher the earnings.

Next, examine the dotted lines which extend from the origin through the dots, or values, described above. The slope of the dotted line represents price/earnings ratios. By appropriate stock splits (including reverse splits) the values of the variables may be placed at any point along these dotted lines. Now split all five stocks so that the values of variables of various companies move to the points designated by the symbol "X". Note that a stock split cannot affect the underlying relationships which theoretically prevail among variables since it is merely change in a divisor, not in the basic values of the corporation. After the hypothetical splits, the relationship among the variables becomes negative; the lower the price, the higher the earnings. The coefficient of correlation is -1.0.

Stock splits and stock dividends occur regularly; at the discretion of management these stock splits and stock dividends arbitrarily change the relationships among variables as defined by regression or by correlation analysis whether that analysis be parametric or non-parametric.

Implications of the Fifth Principle on Past Research on Per-Share Dollar Data

The fifth principle applies to relationships between two per-share variables expressed in dollars, such as the relationship between earnings per share and price per share. The principle states that the relationship is arbitrary in that it can and will be significantly changed by stock splits and stock dividends which occur regularly. If the relationships revealed by regression on per-share data can be arbitrarily changed by stock splits and stock dividends, then a serious question is raised about the application of regression analysis to these kinds of per-share data. The principle is stated in terms of two variables, but the arbitrary effect of stock splits and stock dividends extends by implication to regressions involving more than two variables. And if this is so, a question is raised about the generality, if not the validity of all research which uses two or more per-share dollar variables in regression analysis. This research includes the use of valuation models and the examination of the determinants of stock prices as well as correlation involving only two variables.[11] The fifth principle, of course, does not apply to analysis restricted to ratios derived from per-share data or to percentage changes in per-share data.

Conclusions and Implications

A basic distinction may be drawn between financial variables expressed as dollars of financial ratios, and a percentage change in either of these variables. Successive values of variables expressed as dollars or financial ratios, tend to be fair approximations of one another. Given the dispersion that prevails among values of dollar or ratio variables for a group of firms, the values of a variable in one period will be positively correlated with the values in any other period. Successive values of percentage change variables on the other hand, are not good approximations of one another. Therefore, the expected correlation between values of a percentage change variable in one period and the values of that percentage change variable in another period is zero. From this, as has been shown, the values of a financial ratio, or of a variable expressed in dollars, may be expected to show a zero correlation with a growth variable.

Thus, these five principle are significant for several reasons.

They are general; they predict the relationship between the values of many pairs of financial variables. At least one of them applies to most relationships involving one or two variables for a group of firms. Among the few cases not covered is the relationship between two rate-of-change variables which are not components of one another, such as the relationship between rate of change of price and rate of change of earnings. Most other relationships involving one or two variables are covered. The principles are also more general than they appear to be in that they apply by implication to relationships involving more than two variables.[12] This capacity to predict general relationships is not provided to the same extent or accuracy by previous theories of finance.

What are the implications of these findings and the principles suggested? First, the relative stability of financial variables expressed in dollars and of financial ratios is emphasized. This relative stability in cross sectional correlation seems to have been neglected in much of financial research. Yet it seems extremely important to an understanding of financial processes. It implies, for example, that low price-earnings companies will tend to continue to retain low multiples; that firms faced with low margins will continue to have low margins; that companies beset by low rates of return on capital will continue to record low rates of return on capital. The stability principle also implies that the statement, "this company is statistically cheap," or the statement, "that company's margins are too low and will move up," are open to serious question.

Second, part of the random theory of stock prices, and the more recent random theory of earnings, are generalized by postulating that a segment of these theories applies to all growth or percentage change variables. The random theory of stock prices states that successive values of percentage change variables in prices are independent of each other. A corollary of this statement is that cross sectional correlation of percentage changes in prices will produce an expected coefficient of correlation of zero. Our second principle states that zero correlation may be expected between successive values of any growth or percentage change variable. This means that the company with the highest growth of any variable in one period, from sales on down to net income, will have only an even chance of recording above average growth of those same variables in the next period. This inconsistency of growth between different periods casts doubt on the possibility of demonstrating the superiority of one management over another on the basis of their supposed ability consistently to record superior growth of sales, earnings, market price or any other variable one cares to name. It also throws doubt on the advantages that are allegedly conferred by strategic location of plants or markets, patent protection, degree of integration, specialization, size or other frequently mentioned competitive advantages. If, indeed, such competitive advantages do exist, their influence cannot readily be detected in continued above-average growth of sales, income, dividends, or other variables of the average company.

Third, the expected average relationship, as revealed by the coefficient of correlation, between a dollar or ratio variable and a percentage change variable in the same period is zero. This is a much simpler rule than is provided by statements about particular variables. One need not recall, for example, that the expected coefficient of correlation between the price earnings ratio and the growth of price is zero or that the expected coefficient of correlation is zero between growth of earnings and return on equity, or leverage or payout. One need only remember that the expected coefficient of correlation between any financial ratio and any growth variable is zero. By concentrating in this way on general classes of variables, a simpler and more general framework is provided from which to view financial processes.

Fourth, there are implications for some of the classical questions of finance. If it is not true that the expected correlation between a financial ratio and a growth variables is zero, what is the implication for the classical questions on the relation between growth of earnings and payout, leverage or return on equity or between market growth and payout or the price-earnings ratio? Under the classical approach concepts about growth are logically derived from the definitions of finance. It is a mathematical deduction that if rates of return remain consistent, growth of earnings, for example, may be computed directly from knowledge of the rate of return and retention. From this deduction one is led almost inescapably to assume a direct relationship between rate of return, retention and subsequent growth of earnings. In making this mental transition one tends to neglect or forget the enormous effect of slight shifts in the rate of return on subsequent earnings. The effect of this neglect on growth of net income is easily seen in a shift under full payout of a rate of return from 10 per cent to 9 per cent and back to 10 per cent. This shift will produce earnings growth ranging from minus 10 per cent in the first year to plus 11 per cent in the second, a dramatic reversal. The wide prevalence and persistence of these slight shifts in return causes the classical derivation of concepts about growth to produce impressions about earnings growth that may be poor reflections of the real world. There is, in fact, no conflict between these principles and classical finance.

There are also implications about those valuation models which juxtapose a growth variable on one side of an equation and on the opposite side a financial ratio or a variable expressed in dollars. If the expected correlation between a growth variable and a financial ratio is zero, does it seem reasonable to place these variables on opposite sides of an equality sign? Our first two principles postulate the volatile character of growth variables and the stable nature of variables expressed in dollars. If this is the case, valuation models constructed on the data of one period may be expected to differ markedly from valuation models based on another period. The growth variables shift sharply from period to period, with pronounced effects upon the observed relationships. Thus, evidence from period frequently fails to predict in the next. The coefficients are not stable over time, and usually one is forced either to speculate that the market has altered its emphasis or to add some other causal explanation of the change. On the basis of our results, one is led to conclude that in most, indeed in the vast majority of cases, the volatility of growth variables would cause the growth parameters of any valuation model to shift as the data on which they were constructed were drawn from one period or another. In a true sense, then, the second principle stated here stipulates that the parameters of any valuation model, including growth variables, will change whenever the time period to which the model is applied is changed. To that extent the questions of the ability of such valuation models to predict is raised.

In summary, the principles set forth here present a view of financial processes which is from quite a different angle than those of previous theories of finance. They are in accord with strict interpretation of classical theories derived from deductions based upon the definitions of finance; yet offer a conflicting, but more realistic view of actual financial processes than some of the extensions of those deductions; they assert that nearly all valuation models that combine growth and non-growth variables will be forced to change their parameters from period to period; and extend an important part of the random theory of stock prices to include all, or most, growth variables.

Thus, the greater predictive ability of the principles suggests the usefulness of the developing laws or postulates of finance on the basis of the statistical properties of the variables rather than on the basis of deductions from the definitions by which the variables are calculated.

Footnotes

1. Our "principles" apply in the statistical sense that the relationship, as, for example, in the case of the first principle, is positive at the 5% level of significance 90% of the time. The "principles" also apply in the sense that they correctly describe the relationship in all cases that we have tested or examined. It may be that another word, such as "law" or "rule" or "postulate" would be more appropriate for the term "principle" for this discussion. In any case, the word "principle" is used in full cog-

nizance of its shortcomings.

2. See, for example, M. J. Gordon and E. Shapiro, "Capital Equipment Analysis: The Required Rate of Profit", E. Solomon, editor, *The Management of Corporate Growth,* Free Press, Glencoe, Illinois, 1959, p. 145; R. J. Cummin, "The Mechanics of Corporate Growth", E. M. Lerner, editor, *Readings in Financial Analysis and Investment Management,* The Institute of Chartered Financial Analysts, Inc., R. D. Irwin, New York, N. Y., 1968, p. 144; B. Graham, D. L. Dodd & S. Cottle, *Security Analysis: Principles and Technique,* McGraw-Hill, New York, N. Y., 1962, p. 457 and Chapter 33; E. M. Lerner and W. T. Carleton, *A Theory of Financial Analysis,* Harcourt, Brace & World, Inc., New York, N. Y., 1966; and H. Sauvain, Investment Management, Prentice-Hall, Inc., Englewood Cliffs, New Jersey, 1959, pp. 258-264.

3. J. E. Murphy, "Return on Equity Capital, Dividend Payout and Growth of Earnings Per Share", *Financial Analysts Journal,* May-June, 1967, pp. 91-93.

4. All of the data used in the examples is taken from *The Value Line Investment Survey,* Arnold Bernhard & Co., Inc., New York, N. Y.

5. J. R. Nelson and J. E. Murphy, "A Note on the Stability of P/E Ratios", *Financial Analysts Journal,* March-April, 1969, pp. 77-80.

6. The evidences is given in a number of papers contained in P. H. Cootner, editor, *The Random Character of Stock Prices,* M. I. T. Press, Cambridge, Mass., 1964.

7. A. C. Rayner and I. M. D. Little, *Higgledy Piggledy Growth Again,* Oxford: Basil Blackwell, 1966; J. E. Murphy, "Relative Growth of Earnings Per Share—Past and Future," *Financial Analysts Journal,* November-December 1966, pp. 73-76; and R. A. Brealey, "Statistical Properties of Successive Changes in Earnings", an address deliver to the Seminar on Security Prices, Chicago, March 1967, and *An Introduction to Risk and Return,* The M. I. T. Press, Cambridge, Mass., 1969, pp. 88-103.

8. M. F. Scott, "Relative Share Prices and Yields", *Oxford*

Economic Papers, October, 1962, p. 245.

9. H. A. Latane, "Price Changes in Equity Securities", *Journal of Finance*, September, 1951, p. 259; Scott, op. cit., pp. 235, 239.

10. H. W. Stevenson and J. E. Murphy, "Price/Earnings Ratios and Future Growth of Earnings and Dividends," *Financial Analysts Journal*, November-December, 1967, pp. 111-114; J. E. Murphy, "Return on Equity Capital, Dividend Payout and Growth of Earnings Per Share," *Financial Analysts Journal,* May-June 1967, pp. 91-93, and "Effect of Leverage on Profitability, Growth and Market Valuation of Common Stock," *Financial Analysts Journal*, July-August 1968, pp. 121-123.

11. M. J. Gruber, "The Determinants of Common Stock Prices,"Ph.D. Dissertation, Columbia University, 1966.

12. J. E. Murphy, "Return on Equity Capital, Dividend Payout and Growth of Earnings Per Share", *Financial Analysts Journal*, May-June 1967, pp. 91-93.

8

RANDOM AND NONRANDOM RELATIONSHIPS AMONG FINANCIAL VARIABLES: A FINANCIAL MODEL

Joseph E. Murphy, Jr. & J. Russell Nelson

I. Introduction

Careful examination of the behavior of financial variables over time uncovers an important distinction: variables expressed in dollars, such as earnings per share, behave very differently from percentage changes in those same variables. Similarly, financial ratios, such as the price/earnings ratio, behave quite differently from percentage changes in financial ratios. Variables expressed in dollars and financial ratios appear comparatively stable and predictable over time. Successive values are fair approximations of one another. Percentage changes in dollar and financial ratio variables—i.e., growth variables—on the other hand, tend to be erratic, volatile, and unpredictable over time. Successive values bear little relation to one another. This distinction between dollar and ratio, on the one hand and percentage changes in these variables—i.e., growth variables—on the other, serves as a useful basis for a financial model.[1]

Financial variables, then, may be placed in two classes or categories: (1) dollar and ratio variables, and (2) percentage change variables. Dollar and ratio variables consist of income statement, balance sheet, and market price data expressed in dollars (e.g., IBM's sales in 1968); per share data expressed in dollars (e.g., IBM's earnings per share in 1968); and financial ratios (e.g., the price/earnings ratio). A percentage change variable is found by computing the percentage change between successive observations of a dollar or ratio variable. All growth variables are percentage change variables.

The model described here postulates relationships between any two growth variables in two periods, between any dollar variables and any growth variable, and between any dollar or financial ratio variable in one period and the same variable in another period. The entire analysis is restricted to treatment of the values of the variables for many firms or, specifically, to cross-sectional linear correlation.

The model appears more general than previous financial models. It does not restrict itself to relationships between particular variables, such as between the rate of return on equity and growth of earnings. Rather, it deals with relationships between general classes of variables, such as between growth variables and financial ratios. The model also takes part of the random-walk theory of stock prices, and the more recent random-walk theory of earnings, and applies it to substantially all corporate income and balance-sheet growth variables.[2] It may pose significant implications for several classical problems of finance such as the relationship between growth of earnings and payout, leverage and return on equity, market appreciation and the price/earnings ratio.

By concentrating on general classes of variables, the model provides a simpler and more general framework for observing financial processes than is provided by those models that are restricted to combinations of particular variables. Extensive testing of many different variables in a variety of time periods suggests that the model serves as an accurate and realistic description of many financial relationships.

II. Test Procedures

The data used in testing the postulates was taken from the Compustat annual industrial tape. To insure comparability of results, only companies reporting on a calendar-year basis were included in the sample; companies that shifted their fiscal year have been excluded. To permit a large number of correlations to be run and to avoid the duplicate use of data involved in using varying length overlapping periods, all tests were run using single year periods and only companies with a full eighteen years of data (1949-1967) for all twelve variables were considered. The tests are based on six commonly used dollar variables—

sales, pretax income, cash flow, earnings, price (year-end), and dividends, all on a per share basis—and on six widely used ratios—price/earnings, dividend yield, earnings/common equity, pretax profit margins, common equity/total assets, and dividend payout. Percentage change variables were computed by finding the percent change in a particular variable in one year. The sample consisted of sixty-five companies from three different industries, with separate tests performed for each industry. The industries tested were petroleum (nineteen companies), chemical (twenty-four companies), and metals (twenty-two companies). The companies included in each industry were the firms contained in the 900-company Compustat industrial tape which met the data requirements outlined above and which were classified by Standard Statistics as belonging to the industry in question. All tests were made exactly as shown in the examples. Because of the large number of coefficients of correlation, over sixty-five thousand, only frequency distributions of the coefficients are shown and data for only one industry is given. The distributions are shown because they reveal more information than would be given by simply stating the number of coefficients that are significant at a given level; the latter information is provided in the text. While the tests are restricted to the larger firms of a few industries for selected periods, the consistency of the results suggests that the same results will be derived from tests of other samples of firms, other length periods and other years. Our other tests suggest this to be the case.[3]

III. First Postulate

The first element of the model is derived from consideration of the effect of scale on linear correlation of certain financial variables. If firms in the petroleum industry are ranked by sales in one year, these ranks are reasonable approximations of ranks in the next year. We say the same may be true of per share data and of ratios, such as the rate of return on equity. This possibility may be stated in general terms as a postulate:

The values of a dollar or ratio variable of a group of firms in one period will tend to be highly and positively correlated with the values of that same dollar or ratio variable in another period. The coefficient of correlation will tend to rise as the interval between the periods is decreased.

What are the intuitive reasons for believing that the first postulate of the model will apply to financial variables? There are several. Consider sales of major firms of the chemical industry in the last twenty years. A high degree of order characterizes annual sales of this industry. Sales of DuPont, for example, which are in billions of dollars, have been among the highest every year. Sales of Rohm & Haas, which are in the hundreds of millions have been among the smallest in all years. The same consistency of rank in sales characterized most other companies. If we correlate the sales for firms in one year with sales in another year, the coefficient of correlation will be positive and high.

To illustrate this, consider the following example, Exhibit I, of sales in two periods, 1967 and 1968, of nine companies in the chemical industry.

Exhibit I

	Sales 1967 (mil.)	Rank	Sales 1968 (mil.)	Rank
DuPont	$3,100	1	$3,480	1
Union Carbide	2,540	2	2,680	2
Monsanto	1,630	3	1,790	3
Grace, W. R.	1,580	4	1,740	4
Dow Chemical	1,380	5	1,650	5
Hercules, Inc.	640	6	720	6
GAF Corp.	520	7	570	7
Stauffer Chemical	420	8	480	8
Rohm & Haas	370	9	420	9

Note that the coefficient of correlation between sales in 1967 and sales in 1968 of the above firms is very high, approximately +1.0.

A variety of factors produce this degree of order in the sales of the chemical industry. A very large company, such as DuPont, has enormous investments in production facilities, inventory, research and development, patents, and distribution facilities. It has a tremendous heritage of experience in its employment force in the areas of production, distribution, and management. Its relations with suppliers and customers are extensive and deep. All of these factors act to produce a continuation of very high volume of sales for DuPont year after year. Rohm & Haas, on the other hand, has investments in production facilities which are but a fraction of DuPont's. Its production, distribution, and management manpower are but a small part of DuPont's. Its relations with suppliers are far less extensive. Consequently, one would expect sales of Rohm & Haas to remain consistently well below sales of DuPont. The same kind of argument may be applied to the relative sales of other firms in the chemical industry. The net effect of these factor is to establish a state which is accurately reflected by the first postulate. The same kind of arguments may be applied to other industries, to other combinations of companies, and to other financial variables.

The first postulate also applies to financial ratios that are formed by dividing one dollar variable by another. These variables include such ratios as price/earnings, earnings/sales, earnings/equity capital, debt/equity, and dividend/earnings. Why should this postulate apply to ratios? If relative sales tend to be stable, the ratio of earnings to sales will tend to be relatively stable. If cross-sectional correlation of sales and cross-sectional correlation of earnings in two periods produce high positive coefficients, the ratio formed from these two variables will produce high positive coefficients of correlation.

To test the first postulate, six dollar and six ratio variables were considered: per-share sales, pretax income, cash flow, earnings, year-end price, dividends, price/earnings, dividend yield, earnings/equity, pretax profit margins, common equity/total assets, and dividend payout. Coefficients of correlation were computed for the years between 1951 and 1967. A frequency distribution of the 192 coefficients of correlation is shown in Table 1. It is based on nineteen firms in the petroleum industry.

Table 1
Distribution of Correlation Coefficients of Dollar and Ratio Variables of Nineteen Petroleum Firms-Adjacent Years

	Coefficient of Correlation									
From:	-1.0	-.8	-.6	-.4	-.2	0	.2	.4	.6	.8
To	-.8	-.6	-.4	-.2	0	.2	.4	.6	.8	1.0

	Percent of Coefficients									
	0	0	0	0	0	0	0	1	4	95

As may be seen in Table I, all of the coefficients are positive, all are above +.4, and 95 percent of the coefficients are above +.8. Since a coefficient of 0.44 is significant at the 5 percent level, virtually all of the coefficients are significantly positive. Positive coefficients with lower average values were obtained when the interval between periods was increased. Similar results were obtained in tests of the chemical industry and is tests of the metals industry.

IV. Second Postulate

Considerable evidence has been compiled that indicates that changes in stock prices are nearly a random walk. Other evidence reveals that the rates of change of earnings perform approximately a random walk. The concept of a random walk appears to apply to other growth variables. A firm's relative growth of any variable in one year will give little clue as to its relative growth of any other variable in any succeeding or preceding year. These possibilities may be summarized as a second postulate:

The expected coefficient of correlation is zero between the values of a percentage change variable of a group of firms in one period and the values of that same, or any other, percentage change variable in another different period.

To illustrate this consider the following example, Exhibit II, of percent changes in earnings per share in two periods, 1966-1967 and 1967-1968, of nine companies in the chemical industry.

Exhibit II

	Percent Change in Earn/Share 1966-67	Rank	Percent Change in Earn/Share 1967-68	Rank
Dow Chemical	7	1	-2	8
GAF Corp.	-4	2	5	6
Stauffer Chemical	-7	3	-2	7
Hercules, Inc.	-12	4	14	3
Monsanto	-13	5	11	5
Rohm & Haas	-17	6	18	2
DuPont	-20	7	19	1
Grace, W. R.	-22	8	13	4
Union Carbide	-26	9	-8	9

Notice that the coefficient of correlation between the percent change in earnings between 1966 and 1967 and the percent changes between 1967 and 1968 is low, -0.28.

What are some of the intuitive reasons for expecting the second postulate to hold? A number of considerations do. Percentage change in most variables, such as sales, are generally small, less than plus or minus ten or fifteen percent. For companies in most industries, about half of the percentage changes, in earnings for example, may be explained by the average percentage change for the industry. This coincidence of change is caused by common influences such as changes in the economy; revival or recession; changes in the industry; the rise or fall in raw material, commodity, or final production prices; industry-wide strikes; and other common changes. Because common changes are averaged out, they do not affect the correlation between relative changes in one period and another.

It is the remaining percentage changes affecting individual companies that determine the degree of correlation. These changes are in large measure a result of erratic, uncontrollable or unpredictable changes which are outside the control of the company. These include strikes; arbitrary acts of government; the introduction of new or superior products by competitor; the death, resignation, or retirement of key personnel; arbitrary changes in consumer taste for particular styles or demand for particular products; upward or downward trends in interest rates which affect companies with dissimilar capital structure differently; and movements in population that alter demand or affect the pattern of distribution.

To test this postulate, percentage changes in the twelve variables described above were used. Coefficients of correlation were computed for the values of a percentage change variable for pairs of years, for years separated by varying intervals, and also for values of one percentage change variable in one year and another percentage variable in the other year. Based on various combinations of one-year periods, varying lags over the years 1951 to 1967, and the twelve percentage change variable, 10,608 coefficients of correlation were computed altogether. A frequency distribution of these coefficients is shown in Table 2.

Table 2

Distribution of Correlation Coefficients of Pairs of Various Percentage Change Variables in Distinct Periods and For Varying Intervals Between Periods For Nineteen Firms in the Petroleum Industry

Coefficient of Correlation

From:	-1.0	-.8	-.6	-.4	-.2	0	.2	.4	.6	.8
To	-.8	-.6	-.4	-.2	0	.2	.4	.6	.8	1.0

Percent of Coefficients

0	1	6	16	28	27	16	5	1	0

As may be seen, the average coefficient of correlation is approximately zero; 55 percent of the coefficients lie between -.2 and +.2. The proportion of coefficient that are either significantly positive (greater than +.44) or significantly negative (less than -.44) appears to be about 10 percent—or the percent one would expect from a random drawing of coefficients from an approximately normal population whose mean coefficient was zero. Similar results were obtained in the chemical and metal industries.

V. Third Postulate

By combining the two postulates presented above, we may derive a third postulate that is interesting and surprising. The first postulate stated that the coefficient of correlation between values of dollar or ratio variables in adjacent periods was high and positive. The second postulate stated that the expected coefficient of correlation between values of a percentage change variable in adjacent periods was zero. From this, one may infer that the expected coefficient of correlation between dollar or ratio variable and percentage change variable is zero. Or, more precisely:

The expected coefficient of correlation is zero between the values of a percentage change variable of a group of firms and the values of a dollar or ratio variable of the same firms.

To illustrate this postulate consider the following example, Exhibit III. Below are the rates of return on common equity, a ratio variable, for nine firms in the chemical industry in 1967, and the percent changes in earnings per share of those same firms between 1967 and 1968.

Exhibit III

	Rate of Return Common Equity in 1967	Rank	Percentage Change in Earn/Sh. 1967-1968	Rank
	%		%	
Dow Chemical14	.1	1	-2	8
DuPont	13.3	2	19	1
Hercules, Inc.	13.1	3	14	3
Stauffer Chemical	11.7	4	-2	7
Union Carbide	10.3	5	-8	9
Rohm & Haas	10.1	6	18	2
Monsanto	9.1	7	11	5
Grace, W. R.	8.6	8	13	4
GAF Corp.	5.8	9	5	6

In this example, the coefficients of correlation between rate of return on common equity in 1967 and the percentage change in earnings between 1967 and 1968 is very low, approximately zero.

What are some of the intuitive reasons for expecting the third postulate to hold? Take a specific example, the relationship between rate of return on equity and growth of earnings per share in the automobile industry. The rate of return on common equity is a comparatively stable quantity. A firm's relative rate of return in one year is a good indicator of its relative rate of return in the next year. Annual growth of earnings per share, on the other hand, is a highly volatile variable. The growth in one year for a particular company gives little indication of the growth in the next year. Since return on equity is a relatively stable variable and growth of earnings per share is a highly volatile variable, there is good reason to expect zero correlation, on average, between growth of earnings and return on equity for a group of firms. The same kind of analysis can be applied to the relationship between other financial ratios and other rate of change variables. For this reason, we may expect intuitively that the third postulate will be an appropriate description of the relationship between a ratio variable and a percentage change variable.

To investigate the third postulate, we used the six dollar variables and six ratio variables described previously and the percentage changes in them. Coefficients of correlation were computed between the values of a percentage change variable and the values of a dollar or ratio variable. Different pairs of a percentage change and a ratio or dollar ratio were considered as were different intervals of time between the test years. Through use of variables combinations, 10,608, coefficients of correlation were computed. The frequency distribution of these coefficients for the petroleum industry is given in Table 3.

Table 3

Distribution of Correlation Coefficients of Pairs of Various Percentage Dollar or Ratio and Percentage Change Variables for Varying Intervals Between Periods for Nineteen Firms in the Petroleum Industry

Coefficient of Correlation

From:	-4.0	-.8	-.6	-.4	-.2	0	.2	.4	.6	.8
To	-.8	-.6	-.4	-.2	0	.2	.4	.6	.8	1.0

Percent of Coefficients

0	1	5	14	25	28	19	6	1	0

Notice how closely Table 3 resembles Table 2. In both tables the mean coefficient of correlation is approximately zero. In Table 3, 53 percent of the coefficients fall between -.2 and +.2. The proportion of coefficients that are significantly positive (over +.44) or significantly negative (less than -.44) is roughly 10 percent or the proportion to be expected from a random selection from a population that approaches normality and has a mean coefficient of zero. Similar results were obtained in tests of the chemical and metals industries.

VI. Possible Implications

What implications does the model hold for other financial theories? First, the model emphasizes the relative stability of financial variables expressed in dollars and as ratios. This relative stability in cross-sectional correlation seems to have been a neglected past of financial research. Yet it seems extremely important to an understanding of financial processes. The model postulates, for example, that low price/earnings companies will tend to retain low multiples; that firms faced with low margins will tend to continue to have low margins; that companies beset by low rates of return on capital will continue to record low rates of return on capital.

Second, the model generalizes part of the random-walk theory of stock prices, and the more recent random-walk theory of earnings, by postulating that a segment of these theories applies to all growth or percentage changes variables. The random theory of stock prices states that successive values of percentage changes in prices are independent of each other. A corollary of this statement is that cross-sectional correlation of percentage change in prices will produce an expected coefficient of correlation of zero. The model developed here states that zero correlation may be expected between the values of one percentage change variable and the values in a different period of the same or any other percentage change variable. This means that the company with the highest growth of any variable in one period, from sales on down to net income, will have only an even chance of recording above average growth of that or any other variable in any other period. This inconsistency of growth between different periods casts doubt on the possibility of demonstrating broad general differences in managements on the basis of sustained differences in growth of sales, earnings, market prices, or other variables.

Third, the model serves as a general postulate for expressing relationships between broad classes of variables. One need not recall, for example, that the expected coefficients of correlation between the price/earnings ratio and growth of price is approximately zero or that the expected coefficient of correlation is zero between growth of earnings and return on equity, leverage, or payout. One need only remember that the expected coefficient of correlation between any financial ratio and any growth variable is zero.

Fourth, the model may have implications for some of the classical questions of finance. If it is true, as the model and the evidence here suggest, that the expected correlation between a financial ratio and a growth variable is zero, what does that imply about the classical question of the relationship between growth of earnings and payout, between leverage or return on equity, or between market growth and payout or the price/earnings ratio? What does it imply about the use of growth and dollar variables in valuation models? Will the volatility of growth variables result in models that are very time-sensitive?

In summary, the model developed here presents a view of financial processes from quite a different viewpoint than most previous theories of finance. The postulates are in accord with strict interpretation of classical theories of finance although they conflict with some deductions from those theories. They extend an important part of the random-walk theory of stock prices to include all or most growth variables. They offer a general framework for viewing financial processes. The consistency of the tests done so far suggests that the postulates of the model will hold for different times and different industries and will not become inapplicable if the test period is shifted to other times, to other industries or to samples of companies.

Footnotes

1. Acknowledgment is made to the Management Information Systems Research Center of the School of Business Administration, University of Minnesota, for use of computer facilities and to Lowell Chesborough for programming assistance.

2. The results presented here reflect the substantial background of the work on the random-theory of prices and earnings. Evidence on the random-walk theory of stock prices is given in P. H. Cootner, ed., *The Random Character of Stock Prices* (Cambridge, Mass: M.I.T. Press, 1964). Evidence on the random-walk theory of earnings changes is given in A. C. Rayner and I. M. D. Little, *Higgledy Piggledy Growth Again* (Oxford: Basil Blackwell, 1966); J. E. Murphy, "Relative Growth of Earnings Per Share-Past and Future," *Financial Analysts Journal* (November-December 1966), pp. 73-76; and R. A. Brealey, "Statistical Properties of Successive Changes in Earnings" (Chicago, Ill: March 1967), and *An Introduction to Risk and Return*, (Cambridge, Mass.: The M.I.T. Press), pp. 88-103.

3. Earlier studies were conducted on the relationships

between specific variables. All of the conclusions in the earlier studies are covered by the three general postulates developed in this paper. Some of the earlier studies include: H. W. Stevenson and J. E. Murphy, "Price/Earnings Ratios and Future Growth of Earnings and Dividends," *Financial Analysts Journal* (November-December 1967), pp. 111-114; J. E. Murphy, "Return on Equity Capital, Dividend Payout and Growth of Earnings Per Share," *Financial Analysts Journal* (May-June 1967), pp. 91-93, and "Effect of Leverage on Profitability, Growth and Market Valuation of Common Stock," *Financial Analysts Journal* (July-August 1968), pp. 121-123; and J. R. Nelson and J. E. Murphy, "A Note on the Stability of P/E Ratios," *Financial Analysts Journal* (March-April 1969), pp. 77-80.

Appendix I:

A Mathematical Statement of the Postulates

Let $x_{j,t}$ represent the value of a dollar or ratio variable for the jth firm (j=1,2,...,m) at time t (t=1,2,...,n). Furthermore, let

$$Xt=[x_{1,t},x_{2,t},...,x_{m,t}] \text{ and } X_{t+k}=[x_{1,t+k},x_{2,t+k},..., x_{m,t+k}]$$

where Xt represents the values of a dollar or ratio variable for a firm at time t and Xt+k represents the value of this same variable for the same group of firms at time t+k. To illustrate, Xt might represent earnings of firms in the chemical industry in 1968 and X_{t+k} might represent earnings of those same firms in 1969. The first postulate states

(1) $\rho(X_t,X_{t+k}) - 1$ as k $-$ 0

where "rho" stands for the expected value of coefficients of correlation between X_t and X_{t+k}. The first postulate states that the expected value of the coefficient of correlation between Xt and $X_{t,k}$ tends to 1.0 as k tends to 0.0. As the value of k departs from zero, the absolute value of the coefficients may be expect-

109

ed to decline from 1.0. Next let

$$\Delta x_{j,t} = 100 \times (x_{j,t} - x_{j,t+k} / x_{j,t+k})$$

where $\Delta x_{j,t}$ represents the percent change in a dollar or ratio variable of the jth firm between period t-k and period t.
Furthermore, let

$$\Delta X_t = [\Delta x_{1,t}, \Delta x_{2,t}, ..., \Delta x_{m,t} \text{ and } \Delta Y_{t+k} = [\Delta y_{1,t+k}, \Delta y_{2,t+k}, ..., \Delta y_{m,t+k}]$$

where ΔX_t represents the values of a percentage change variable in period t and ΔY_{t+k} represents the values of the same or a different percentage variable in period t+k. For example, ΔX_t and DYt+k might represent percentage changes in sales of firms in the chemical industry in 1968 and 1969, respectively.
Then, the second postulate states

$$(2) \; \rho \, (\Delta X_t, \Delta Y_{t+k}) = 0$$

where k is not equal to 0 or X=Y or X is not equal to Y

Equation (2) states that the expected coefficient of correlation is zero between a percentage change variable (ΔX_t) in one period and the same, or any other, percentage change variable (ΔY_{t+k}) in another different period. From postulates (1) and (2), it is possible to infer a third postulate, namely

$$(3) \; \rho(\Delta X_t, \Delta Y_{t+k}) = 0 \text{ and } X=Y \text{ or } X \text{ not equal } Y$$

where k may or may not equal zero and X_t and ΔY_{t+k} may or may not be the same variable.
Equation (3) states that the expected coefficient of correlation between a dollar or ratio variable (X_t) and a percentage change variable (ΔY_{t+k}) is zero.

9

FIVE NEW FINANCIAL PRINCIPLES: A COMMENT

Michael Hopewell

Acting Assistant Professor of Finance, University of Oregon

In an article appearing in the March-April 1971 issue of this Journal, J. E. Murphy, Jr. and J. R. Nelson (MN) develop five principles dealing with the behavior of financial data.[1] The authors argue that these principles can be used for predicting whether or not a relationship will exist between pairs of financial variables. The principles predict distinctly different behavior for two classes of variables. The first class, dollar or ratio variables, are hypothesized to exhibit quite stable temporal behavior. On the other hand, percentage change or growth variables, are alleged to be very unstable over time.

The purpose of the present comment is to examine the empirical evidence presented by MN to support the first three of their principles. The validity of the conclusions drawn by MN have been examined elsewhere.[2]

The Empirical Evidence

MN offer extensive empirical evidence concerning the behavior of financial variables. They claim that this evidence offers considerable support for the first three of their five principles.[3] However, standard statistical tests show that the empirical evidence fails to support MN's second and third principles. Before examining the evidence, the first three principles and the nature of the authors' tests will be described briefly.

The first three principles deal with the relationship between dollar or ratio variables and percentage change or growth variables and the behavior of each class of variables over time. The first principle asserts that, for a group of firms, the values of a dollar or ratio variable in one period will be positively correlated with the values of that dollar or ratio variable in the subsequent period. The second principle asserts that, for a group of firms, no relationship will exist between the values of a percentage change or growth variable in successive periods. The third principle predicts that, for a group of firms, no relationship will exist between the values of a dollar or ratio variable and the percentage changes in that variable in the same period.

Since these principles supposedly apply to a group of firms, MN do not test any individual firm time series. Rather, the authors perform numerous correlations on data for firms grouped by industry. Each individual correlation involves the values of a pair of variables for the firms in a particular industry. Furthermore, each correlation tests for a relationship in a particular annual period or a particular series of annual periods. Thus MN "test" each of the three principles by generating a large, non-random, and non-independent sample in which the individual members or the sample vary with respect to the time period, industry and specific test variables selected from the two general classes.

The authors summarize the empirical evidence on each principle by reporting both the total number of separate correlations and the actual number of correlations in which the correlation coefficient is consistent with the principle being considered. For example, in the case of the first principle MN ran 1220 separate correlations and found that 1194 or 98 per cent of the correlation coefficients were significantly different from zero and positive at the five per cent level of significance. The authors also report what they term the predicted number of positive correlations which they define in the following way:

... The predicted number of positive correlations is the number one would expect at the five per cent level of significance, i.e., 90 per cent of the possible number.[4]

Unfortunately, the expected or predicted number of significantly positive sample correlations depends not only on the level of significance but also on the assumed value of the unknown population correlation coefficient. Normally, the significance of a single sample correlation coefficient is tested against the null hypothesis of a population correlation coefficient equal to zero. In the particular case of MN's first principle, the appropriate alternative hypothesis is that the population correlation coefficient is greater than zero and the appropriate significance test of a sample correlation coefficient is a "one-tailed" test.

If a one-tailed test and the five per cent level of significance is used, there is a five per cent probability that a sample correlation coefficient will be significantly different from zero and positive even though the true population correlation coefficient is, in fact, equal to zero. This expectation is due to sampling variability alone. If a number of sample correlations were drawn from a population in which the true population correlation coefficient is equal to zero, the expected or predicted number of significantly positive correlation coefficients will be equal to five per cent of the total and not 90 per cent as stated by MN.

Either MN have failed to explain their statistical methodology sufficiently or they are in error in stating that one would expect 90 percent of the sample correlation coefficients to be positive at the five per cent level of significance. In addition, MN fail to test whether or not the actual number of significantly positive correlations is due entirely to sampling variability. In what follows, the author submits MN's empirical evidence to such a test.

Test of the First Principle

The first principle is actually supported by the empirical evidence. The null hypothesis of no relationship must be rejected in favor of accepting the alternate hypothesis of a positive population correlation coefficient. Whereas under the null hypothesis we expect five per cent of the sample correlation coefficients to be significantly positive, actually 98 per cent are significantly positive. A simple test of proportions indicates that this difference between the expected and actual proportions is too great to be due to sampling variability. Therefore, the null hypothesis is rejected and the empirical evidence supports a positive or direct relationship.

Tests of the Second and Third Principles

Both the second and third principles predict no relationship between pairs of variables. MN summarize their empirical evidence on each of these principles by reporting the proportion of sample correlation coeffcients which are not significantly different from zero at the five per cent level of significance. Again they present a predicted number, but for these two principles MN's predicted number supposedly represents the expected number of nonsignificant correlations, 90 per cent of the total.

MN's predicted number is again in error. The apparent underlying null hypothesis is that the population correlation coefficient is zero. Both principles imply an alternate hypothesis that the true population correlation coefficient is not equal to zero and a "two-tailed" test is appropriate. The authors use the five per cent level of significance to test whether or not a sample correlation coefficient is significantly different from zero. Under the null hypothesis, we expect two and one-half per cent of the sample correlations to be significantly positive and two and one-half per cent to be significantly negative due to sampling variability. We would expect that the remaining 95 per cent to be nonsignificant. This differs from MN's contention that 90 per cent of the coefficient are expected to be nonsignificant.

Now consider MN's actual results concerning the second principle. They find that 748 of the 960 or 78 per cent of the correlation coefficients are not significantly different from zero, either positive or negative. Are such sample results consistent with the null hypothesis of no relationship? Alternatively stated, is it likely that 22 per cent of the sample correlations will be significant due to sampling variability alone? Under the null hypothesis only five per cent of the correlations are expected to be significant.

A simple test of proportions can be used to test whether or not the actual proportion of significant correlations differs from the expected proportion under the null hypothesis.[5]

$Z = (p' - p)/(pq/n)^{1/2}$
where p' = observed proportion of significant correlations
p = hypothesized proportion of significant correlations
q = (1- p)
n = total number of correlations
Z = standard normal deviate

For the second principle p' = 0.22, P = 0.05, q = 0.95, and n = 960. Solving the equation, we find that Z is approximately equal to 24. This result means that the actual proportion is approximately 24 standard deviations from the proportion expected under the null hypothesis of no relationship. There is less than one chance in 10,000 that the 960 sample correlations were drawn from a population in which the true population correlation coefficient equals zero. Thus, it is extremely unlikely that the difference between the actual and expected proportions of significant correlation is due to sampling variability.[6] We must reject the null hypothesis and also must reject MN's claim that their empirical evidence supports the second principle of no relationship between percentage change variables in successive periods.

The empirical results offered by MN in support of their third principle are very similar to those analyzed above. In this case 22 per cent of the 1350 sample correlation coefficients are insignificantly different from zero when only five per cent are expected under the null hypothesis of no relationship. Using a test of proportions we find that the actual proportion is more than 29 standard deviations from the expected proportion. Again, we find it highly improbable that these sample correlations are consistent with the underlying null hypothesis, hence we must reject the authors' contention that their empirical evidence supports the third principle (no relationship between values of a dollar or ratio variable and the values of the percentage change in that dollar or ratio variable).

Some readers may find the preceding discussion to be an exercise in statistical hocus-pocus. For them we shall summarize our criticism in the following way: MN set out to create principles or laws that predict the behavior of classes of financial variables. These principles were to be based on observed empirical relationships. Two of their key principles predict no relationship between certain classes of financial variables and yet, in nearly one-quarter of the cases examined the authors find a significant non-zero relationship. MN appear too eager to ignore a significant portion of their empirical results and too eager to claim that their principles have great predictive ability.

Footnotes to Comment

1. Murphy, Joseph E., Jr. and Russell Nelson, "Five Principles of Financial Relationships," *Financial Analysts Journal*, March-April 1971, pp. 38-52.

2. Hopewell, Michael H., "Discussion," *Journal of Financial and Quantitative Analysis*, March 1971, pp. 891-93. This discussion relates to a similar paper presented by Murphy and Nelson at the 1970 Western Finance Association meetings. Their paper immediately precedes the discussion.

3. Only the first three principles are of concern here. MN's fourth and fifth principles are not subject to empirical testing. The authors offer empirical evidence on the fourth principle unnecessarily, since this principle is true by definition.

4. Murphy and Nelson "Five Principles," pp. 42-43.

5. In the case of large samples such as this, we use the normal approximation of the Binomial. Strictly speaking MN's data do not meet the random sampling and independence assumptions of this test. However, we feel justified in using this test because MN are implicitly using a similar test in drawing conclusions from a comparison of the actual and expected proportions.

6. Even if MN used a significance test with five per cent in

each tail (The ten per cent level of significance), their results fail to support the hypothesis of no relationship. With these large sample sizes, the actual proportion of 0.22 is more than 10 standard deviations away from the proportion expected to be significant under the null hypothesis. The expected proportion is equal to 0.10 if the ten per cent level is used.

Five New Financial Principles: Reply to a Comment

J. E. Murphy & J. R. Nelson

Northwestern National Bank of Minneapolis, University of Colorado.

We read with interest the comment of Dr. Hopewell on our article, "Five Principles of Financial Relationships," that appeared in the March-April 1971 issue of this Journal.[1] In his comment Dr. Hopewell states that, on the basis of standard statistical analysis, the evidence presented in the article does not support two of the five principles, and that the evidence for a third principle was unnecessary. We appreciate the comments of Dr. Hopewell, particularly his correct observation that we were using a two-tailed rather than a one-tailed test. But we disagree with his conclusions.

We remain convinced that the empirical evidence offered in support of the second and third principles was sufficient, and we find on further investigation that the evidence is far stronger than we had thought. We find that empirical evidence in support of the fourth principle is essential. We believe that the principles offer useful and broadly applicable statements for predicting relationships between general classes of financial variables.

The two principles whose evidence is questioned are:

Second Principle. For a group of firms, the values of a percentage change variable in one period will typically be unrelated to the values of that same percentage change variable in the next period.

117

Third Principle. For a group of firms, the values of a percentage change variable in one period will typically be unrelated to the values of a dollar or ratio variable in the same period.

We disagree with Dr. Hopewell for two reasons.

First, the two principles in question state that the values of one variable "will be typically unrelated" to the values of another. It is possible, of course, to quarrel about the expression "typically unrelated to," and this may be the most important of Dr. Hopewell's criticisms. In the study of financial questions one might attempt to formulate statements that are always true, i.e., in which every example is consistent with the statement. Such statements are known as tautologies and, using the methods of the propositional calculus, they can be proved to be theorems. An example of a basic financial tautology is the equation "assets = liabilities + equity".

An alternative is to develop hypotheses about the behavior of variables. An hypothesis is a provisional statement about relationships among variables to be verified, or refuted, by observation. The statement, "stable dividends lead to higher stock prices than do variable dividends," is an hypothesis. It is important to recognize that an hypothesis must be refutable in principle, else it is a tautology. The issue then is what constitutes adequate verification. At the time our article was written, 78 per cent of the cases examined were consistent with the hypothesis that values will typically be unrelated. Subsequently additional tests, reported elsewhere, showed that the hypothesis was supported in over 90 per cent of the cases examined. As additional evidence, such as that just described, is provided, it is appropriate to describe the outcome as a principle. We regard the evidence as sufficient support of the principles in question.

Second, Dr. Hopewell's statistical analysis is based upon the erroneous premise that the two principles postulate the null hypothesis about the "population of all correlation coefficients concerned." Because the principles do not assume that null hypothesis, Dr.Hopewell's tests are inapplicable and his conclusion that the "evidence fails to support" the principles is invalid.

118

However, tests performed in response to Dr. Hopewell's comment provide substantial additional evidence in support of the two principles. These tests, unlike the others, do investigate the null hypothesis that the population correlation coefficient of all correlations covered by the two principles is zero. Contrary to the fears expressed by Dr. Hopewell, approximately 95 per cent of the coefficients were nonsignificant, as is shown below. On the basis of these tests not only are the original principles confirmed, but the stronger versions of the principles suggested by Dr. Hopewell are substantiated.[3]

Second Principle

Average coefficient of correlation	0.00
Percent of coefficients nonsignificant	95%
Number of nonsignificant coefficients	1940
Total number of coefficients	2040

Third Principle

Average coefficient of correlation	-0.03
Percent of coefficients nonsignificant	94%
Number of nonsignificant coefficients	1826
Total number of coefficients	1904

In a footnote Dr. Hopewell stated that the "authors offer empirical evidence on the fourth principle unnecessarily since this principle is true by definition." Again we disagree. If the principle were true by definition, there would be no contrary cases. Since there are contrary cases, the principle is not true. by definition and empirical substantiation is essential.

In sum, the empirical evidence in support of the two principles is sufficient to support the principles as stated, and, as augmented here, is strong enough to meet the more stringent null hypothesis posed by Dr. Hopewell. The empirical evidence on the fourth principle is essential. We remain convinced, therefore, that the principles provide useful statements for predicting relations among broad classes of financial variables.

Footnotes to Reply

1. Murphy, J. E., Jr., and J. R. Nelson, "Five Principles of Financial Relationships," *Financial Analysts Journal*, March-April 1971, pp. 38-52.

2. Murphy, J. E., Jr., and J. R. Nelson, "Random and Nonrandom Relationships Among Financial Variables: A. Financial Model," *Journal of Financial and Quantitative Analysis*, March 1971, pp. 875-85, and Michael Hopewell's "Discussion" immediately following the paper.

3. The data shown represent results for 16 major companies in the petroleum industry. The tests were for the more general hypothesis suggested by Dr. Hopewell. The Z test of simple proportions, as described by Dr. Hopewell, reveals a standard normal deviate of $Z = -.20$ for the second principal and $Z = -1.81$ for the third principle. Neither proportion is unlikely. The respective Z values for the average coeffcients for the two principles are, respectively 0.01 and -0.11. Therefore we must accept the null hypothesis and also accept the view that the empirical evidence supports the second and third principles. We are indebted to Dr. Douglas H. Anderson of the University Computer Center of the University of Minnesota for reviewing our statistical procedures.

10

PREDICTING DIVIDEND CHANGES

Joseph E. Murphy, Jr. & Richard S. Johnson

Dividend income is extremely important to several classes of investors. It is important to equity common trust funds designed for income beneficiaries, to individual investors seeking dividend income, to income oriented common stock mutual funds and to corporations desiring partially tax-exempt dividend income. To these classes of investors, the current dividend yield on a common stock may not be an accurate measure of future yield since dividends are continually being increased and decreased. Despite the importance of forecasting future changes in dividend payments, relatively few empirical studies have been made on the subject.[1]

The purpose of this article is to examine past evidence on dividend changes. From a study of that evidence, the paper seeks to derive a more precise procedure than was previously available for estimating the directions and probabilities of future dividend changes.

Pattern of Dividend Changes

Dividend changes differ in important respects from changes in practically all other financial variables. Changes in dividends are normally less frequent than changes in other financial variables. For many companies dividends remain unchanged for long periods with precisely the same dividend payment being made quarter after quarter, year after year. For another, and considerably larger, group of companies, dividend changes are infrequent, less than one change every year or two. For a smaller group of companies, dividends changes are made regularly, year after year. Yet even in the last group of companies, quarterly dividend payments often remain unchanged for four quarters at a time. The net effect is that the odds of no dividend change are about four in ten, based on a sample of approximately 13,000 dividend changes among industrial companies contained in the Compustat data tape over a nineteen year period.

Compared to changes in dividends, changes in other financial variables occur almost continuously. Earnings per share vary continuously from quarter to quarter and from year to year. It is unusual, rather than the common, event that earnings per share are unchanged from period to period. Common stock prices shift continuously not only from year to year, but from day to day, from hour to hour.

Dividends differ from other financial variables in another respect. Unlike nearly all other financial variables, dividend payments can be set by company directors for most companies in most years, subject to certain restraints. While company directors, or management, cannot determine precisely other financial variables, they can, with the limitations imposed by earned income and by any existing covenants with creditors, establish the current dividend rate. It is this ability to set dividend rates which is largely responsible for the relative constancy of dividend payments.

The major uncontrollable consideration is that dividends must generally be paid from current earnings. When earnings fall below the declared dividend rate, company directors will be forced to consider reduction in the prevailing dividend rate. Otherwise directors are usually reluctant to reduce the existing dividend rate in order to prevent curtailing the income of stockholders dependent on payments.

To reveal the actual pattern of dividend changes, we show in Table 1 the number and percentage of dividend increases, dividend decreases and unchanged dividends for each of the past eighteen years for industrial companies contained on the Compustat data tape. For the total period, the frequency of dividend increases was about five in ten; the frequency of dividend decreases was about one in ten and the frequency of no change in dividend rates was just under four in ten. As also may be seen, the pattern of dividend change varies from year to year,

Table 1
Dividend Changes 1949-1967

	1967	1966	1965	1964	1963	1962	1961	1960	1959	1958	1957	1956	1955	1954	1953	1952	1951	1950	1949	Total
NUMBER OF COMPANIES																				
INCREASE:	147	608	573	508	402	372	339	428	370	277	374	450	403	299	218	184	289	380	225	6846
NO CHANGE:	206	147	196	312	317	277	203	201	257	323	325	309	367	392	395	306	228	205	95	5061
DECREASE:	27	40	54	46	60	81	117	73	97	174	108	63	82	96	124	150	142	71	150	1755
PERCENT OF TOTAL																				
INCREASE:	39	76	70	59	52	51	51	61	51	36	46	55	47	38	30	29	44	58	48	50
DECREASE:	7	5	6	5	7	11	18	10	13	22	13	8	10	12	17	23	22	11	32	13

639

partly in response to differences in changes in earnings and to changes in common stock prices. A significant rise or decline in earnings frequently leads to increases or reductions in dividend payments, while a sharp market rise generally leads to stock splits which, in turn, bring about upward adjustments, however slight, in dividend payments. The pattern of dividend changes may be seen in Table I accompanying the text.

Past Models of Dividend Safety

The income-oriented investor is generally very concerned with security, in the provision of income and in the continuance of that income. Therefore it would be very useful to have an accurate model to predict dividend changes, particularly to forecast the probability of dividend reductions.

The most commonly used model, or rule of thumb, is the coverage test. Coverage is computed by dividing earnings available for payment by the amount of dividend paid to shareholders. If earnings per share are $3.00 and the dividend payments is $1.50, coverage is computed by dividing $3.00 by $1.50 which gives a coverage ratio of 2.0 times. In this example, earnings available are 2.0 times as large as dividend payments. In using the coverage test, an appropriate ratio is arbitrarily assumed, such as a ratio of 2.0x, and ratios equal or above that ratio are deemed to provide an adequate measure of protection. The same kind of procedure is used for evaluating the safety of fixed income, including income from preferred stocks and corporate bonds.

There are a number of weaknesses in the coverage test. The coverage test implicitly assumes a linear relationship between coverage and the probability of dividend reduction even though the relationship is not, or may not be, linear. For example, a dividend covered 2.2x by earnings seems to be twice as secure as dividend covered 1.1x by earnings. In fact, however, the difference in safety is much greater than is implied by the difference in coverage ratios; the dividend covered 2.2 times by earnings is four times less likely to be reduced the next year than the dividend covered 1.1 times by earnings.

A second weakness of the coverage test is that it normally makes no distinction for differences in volatility of earnings even though these differences may, and do, have substantial implications on the safety of future dividend payments. A complete model should incorporate the effect of differences in volatility of earnings changes.

A Preliminary Model of Dividend Changes

In constructing a model to predict dividend changes it seems appropriate to begin with the fact that dividends are paid from earned income and company directors generally set the dividend payment well below the level of earnings. When earnings fall below the level of dividends, one might expect that cuts in dividend payments are more likely. Furthermore, since directors generally set the dividend rate after earnings have been reported or determined, changes in dividend rates may be expected to occur after a drop in earnings below the level of dividends. The timing of the response of dividend cuts to reductions in earnings may differ for companies whose earnings are highly seasonal, such as department stores which receive the heavy share of income in the final quarter of the year.

To determine the relative frequency of dividend cuts in response to drops in earnings below the level of dividends, we made the following test on Compustat companies over a twenty-year period. We classified stocks into two groups. The first group contained those companies with earnings greater than dividends; the second group contained those with earnings less than dividends. For each group we then asked the following questions: Were the dividends cut in the following year? Were the dividends increased in the following year? Or were the dividends unchanged?

For companies with earnings in excess of dividends, the likelihood of a reduction in dividends was relatively low. There were approximately 12,000 instances of earnings exceeding dividends. In less than 10% of these instances was the dividend cut the next year. In more than 50% of the instances the dividend was increased. In about 40% of the cases the dividend was not changed. All instances exclude stocks not paying dividends. The results are given in the total column of Table I.

The instances in which earnings fell below dividend cuts are far fewer and the frequency of dividend cuts is far higher. Altogether there were slightly over 700 cases of earnings dropping below dividends. In nearly 50% of these instances the dividend was cut. In only 10% of these instances was the dividend payment increased. In the remaining cases the dividend was unchanged.[2]

We have distinguished two major groups of cases; in one, the probability of a dividend cut is very high; in the other the probability of a dividend cut is very low. Most cuts in dividends occur in the latter category, where the probability of a dividend cut is low. Of the 1750 reductions in dividend payments in our sample, 1400 occurred among stocks with earnings in excess of dividends where the aggregate probability of a dividend cut was only one in ten. Therefore, it is important to refine the data on the frequency of dividend reductions.

Frequency of Dividend Cuts as a Function of Payout

To refine the data, we classified dividend changes by percent payout in the preceding year. Payout is computed by dividing the dividend payment by earnings per share. If dividends paid were $1.50 and earnings per share were $3.00, dividend payout would be computed by dividing $1.50 by $3.00 giving 0.50 or 50%. Dividend payout is used instead of coverage because it can be combined more easily with probable changes in earnings, as will be discussed later. The results of payout classification are show in Table 2 and are graphed in Chart 1.

The best illustration of the relation of dividend cuts to payout is given in Chart 1. Several important features of this relationship are revealed in the chart. First, between fairly wide limits, payout and the frequency of dividend cuts are directly related. Specifically, a very direct relationship exists in the range extending from a payout of 20% to a payout of 120%. The frequency of dividend reduction extends from less than 7% to a 10% payout to a frequency of dividend reduction of more than 60% at payouts of more than 120.

Note that dividend reduction is graphed on a logarithmic scale, payout on an arithmetic scale. Beyond the two extremes, the relationship becomes less direct. The frequency of dividend reductions does not rise after a payout of 120%. In fact, where earnings are negative, the frequency of dividend reduction drops from over 50% to 33%.

The evidence in Chart 1 is important in several respects. It makes it possible to predict the probability of a dividend cut the

Table 2
Annual Changes in Dividends Per Share 1949-1968

PAYOUT RATIO		NUMBER OF COMPANIES				PERCENT OF COMPANIES		
From	To	Increase	No Change	Decrease	Total	Increase	No Change	Decrease
0 - 0		192	838	0	1030	18.6	81.4	0.0
1 - 9		103	19	9	131	78.6	14.5	6.9
10 - 19		431	79	31	541	79.7	14.6	5.7
20 - 29		837	153	71	1061	78.9	14.4	6.7
30 - 39		1442	381	151	1974	73.0	19.3	7.6
40 - 49		1738	695	258	2691	64.6	25.8	9.6
50 - 59		1121	955	273	2349	47.7	40.7	11.6
60 - 69		591	747	215	1553	38.1	48.1	13.8
70 - 79		183	494	169	846	21.6	58.4	20.0
80 - 89		80	260	126	466	17.2	55.8	27.0
90 - 99		39	138	108	285	13.7	48.4	39.9
100 - 109		16	46	49	111	14.4	41.4	44.1
110 - 119		4	23	42	69	5.8	33.3	60.9
120 - 129		7	10	27	44	15.9	22.7	61.4
130 - 139		9	12	25	46	19.6	26.1	54.3
140 - or more		36	52	113	201	17.9	25.1	56.2
Negative Earnings		17	159	88	264	6.4	60.2	33.3
TOTAL		6846	5061	1755	13662	50.1	37.0	12.8

Chart 1
Payout and Incidence of Dividend Reduction

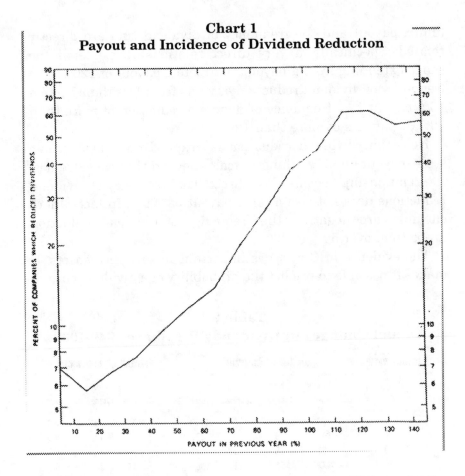

PERCENT OF COMPANIES WHICH REDUCED DIVIDENDS

PAYOUT IN PREVIOUS YEAR (%)

next year from the payout in the preceding year. The regularity of the relationship, as evidenced in Chart 1, lends credence to the possibility of prediction. Second, it is possible to combine this relationship, or function, with information on earnings changes to permit prediction of the probability of a dividend cut in any future year.

Dividend investors are primarily defensive in posture and, therefore, are mainly interested in maintenance, in non-reduction of income. Yet, the questions of dividend increases is also important since it affects the total income return. For any diversified income portfolio, increases in dividend payments may be partially, or more than, offset by reductions in dividend payments. The frequency of dividend increases in one year for various payouts in the previous year is given in the third column from right of Table 2, above.

Frequency Distribution of Earnings Changes

We have shown that the frequency distribution, or probability, of dividend reductions in one year is a function of dividend payout in the preceding year. Now, if we can predict the frequency distribution, or probability, of changes in earnings per share, then we will have a suitable basis, or model, for predicting future changes in coverage. This will enable us to forecast the probability of dividend reductions in future years. The frequency distribution of changes in earnings is bell-shaped, or approximately normally distributed. The assumption of a normal distribution of earnings changes, while subject to dispute in detail, is sufficiently precise for our purposes. The shape of the frequency distribution of earnings changes may be seen in the column of the far right of Table 3, below.

Table 3

Earnings Per Share in One Year as Percent of Earnings Per Share in Prior Year Based on Data 1956-1968

Percent		Instances	
From	To	Number	Percent
150	or more	238	6.1
140	149	113	2.8
130	139	265	6.5
120	129	449	11.0
110	119	893	21.9
100	109	949	23.3
90	99	541	13.1
80	89	258	6.3
70	79	160	3.9
Below	70	199	4.9
Total		4065	100.0

One more fact should be taken into consideration. Professional investors know from experience that sharp changes in earnings are much more likely in some industries than in others. Rates of earnings change in the electronics industry, for example, are more extreme than in electric utility or the bank industry. The dispersion of percentage change in earnings per share in the electric utility industry is far less than the dispersion in the electronics industry. Therefore, in calculating the probability of cuts in dividend payments, it is extremely important to take into account differences in volatility of earnings changes.

Summary and Conclusion

This article has been concerned with a discussion of improved techniques for analyzing and forecasting probable changes in common stock dividends. It began with a review of the coverage test and its weaknesses, it revealed the failure of coverage to provide a relative measure of probability of dividend reduction and it pointed out the absence of sufficient empirical information on the relationship between coverage and probability of dividend cuts. It stressed the need for quantitative information on the pattern of dividend changes as a prerequisite to improved methods of forecasting dividend changes and it presented the past pattern of dividend changes of 900 companies using Compustat data on industrial companies for a twenty year period. This data showed that the frequency of dividend reduction (plotted on a logarithmic scale) was a direct function of payout for payout ratios extending from 20% to 120%. The existence of this direct relationship between payout and dividend reductions makes it possible to forecast the likelihood of dividend reductions.

The existence of the direct relationship between payout and dividend reduction makes possible the development of a more precise method of forecasting dividend changes. Past work on earnings changes has shown that the frequency, or probability, of earnings changes for a group of companies tends to be normally distributed like a bell shaped curve. Past work also shows that the dispersion of changes is directly related to the length of the period over which the changed is measured. These relationships may be combined with the direct relationship between payout and the frequency of dividend reduction. The combination enables one to forecast the probability of a dividend reduction at any payout level over an extended period. Account may also be taken of differences in degree of change of different companies and industries.

This approach to analyzing and forecasting dividend changes, though it is applied here to common stock dividends, could be extended to preferred stock and corporate bond income. It represents an empirically derived model and permits a more empirically justified procedure than is provided by the traditional coverage tests in present use.

Footnotes

1. Brittan, John A., *Corporate Dividend Policy,* Washington, The Brookings Institution, 1966; Fama, Eugene F. and Babiak Harvey, Dividend Policy: An Empirical Analysis, *Journal of the American Statistical Association* (December 1968) pp. 1132-1161; Linter, John, Distribution of Incomes of Corporations among Dividends, Retained Earnings and Taxes, American *Economic Review* (May 11956) pp. 97-113; Miller, Merton H. and Modigliani, Franco, Dividend Policy, Growth and the Valuation of Shares, *Journal of Business* (October 1961), pp. 411-433; Smith, K. V., The Increasing Stream Hypothesis of Corporate Dividend Policy, *California Management Review*, (Fall 1971).

2. Acknowledgment is made to the Management Information Systems Research Center of the School of Business Administration, University of Minnesota, for the use of computer facilities and to Standard Statistics, Inc. for the use of the Compustat data tapes. The data covered the nineteen year period ended 12/31/68.

11

NEW INSIGHTS INTO CHANGES IN EARNINGS PER SHARE

Robert A. Larsen and Joseph E. Murphy, Jr.

The main purpose of the analysis of common stocks is to select those stocks that record the greatest gains in price. Price changes are positively and significantly related to earnings changes; over time, stocks recording the greatest growth in earnings tend to exhibit the highest rise in price.[1] For this reason, financial analysts seek to identify those companies that will record the highest growth in earnings and those companies whose future earnings performance will depart from the past. Unfortunately, identifying these companies is not easy.

Although coincident changes in the price and earnings series are not unrelated, each series by itself exhibits many of the characteristics of randomness. Past growth in the price of a stock reveals little about future growth in price.[2] Past increases in earnings indicate little about future increases in earnings.[3] This independence has suggested to many students that both series are random or nearly so. The randomness of the earnings series, the independence between past and future changes, complicates the task of the financial analyst. He cannot simply use past rates of change to forecast future rates of change. His problem is more complex, but is not impossible.

The difficulty faced by the financial analyst is suggested by the results. Recent studies indicate that, although analysts are able to forecast actual earnings with some accuracy, they are unable to forecast changes in earnings with the same degree of accuracy.[4] It is much easier to be within ten per cent of actual earnings than it is to be within ten per cent of the change in earnings. To distinguish correctly those companies that will record a ten per cent rise in earnings is far more exacting and difficult. Yet it is this kind of precision that is required to distinguish the stocks that will show the greatest price appreciation or price decline.

Despite the importance of predicting earnings changes, we know relatively little about the key factors that affect changes in earnings per share.[5] The purpose of this article is to report the results of an extensive investigation of a few of these factors. The variables studied are changes in equity capital per share, changes in profit margins and changes in capital turnover.

It is true by definition that:

$$\frac{\text{Earnings}}{\text{Share}} = \frac{\text{Capital}}{\text{Share}} \times \frac{\text{Earnings}}{\text{Sales}} \times \frac{\text{Sales}}{\text{Capital}}$$

It is also true by definition that:

$$\log(\text{Earnings/Share}) = \log(\text{Capital/Share})$$
$$+ \log(\text{Income/Sales})$$
$$+ \log(\text{Sales/Capital}).$$

If we compute changes as percentages, using continuous compounding, the change in earnings is exactly equivalent to the change in equity capital plus the change in profit margins plus the change in capital turnover. If we use natural logarithms and compute differences in each variable from one period to the next, the results are expressed as a compound percentage change. In our investigation, changes in each variable were expressed in terms of the first difference in the natural logarithms of the original variable.[6]

Our study was designed to determine the importance of each of these three variables—changes in capital turnover, changes in profit margins and changes in equity capital per share—to changes in earnings per share. Are changes in earnings per share primarily accompanies by corresponding changes in capital turnover? By changes in profit margins? Or by related changes in equity capital?

While we were primarily interested in the relationship of each of these components to changes in earnings, we also wanted to know whether the same pattern applied to all industries. In some industries, changes in capital turnover might be of major importance, in other industries, shifts in margins or capital per share. Finally, we wanted to know how much earnings per share changes varied around the mean change both for the composite average and for individual industries. Such information would provide an indication of the reliability of predictions.

The Compustat annual tapes supplied the data used in this study, providing per share figures of 631 companies for each of the 15 years ended December 31, 1970. Only companies for which data was available for the entire 15 year time period for all variables were included in the sample. Companies in the Compustat database not meeting this requirement were eliminated. Data for the 631 companies were classified into 102 industries on the basis of the Compustat industrial classification. Percentage changes, using continuous compounding, were computed for each of the four variables—earnings per share, capital turnover, profit margins and equity capital per share—with equity capital defined as common stock plus surplus, capital turnover defined as sales divided by equity capital, and profit margins defined as net sales divided by earnings. For each variable, annual changes were computed as well as the mean for the 15 year period.

We will first turn to the aggregate results for all years and companies. The average results for all companies in the 15 year period.

Compound Annual Change (1956 - 1970)

Change in Earnings Per Share		Change in Profit Margins	Change in Capital Turnover	Change in Capital Per Share
4.0%	=	-2.4% +	-0.7% +	7.1%

The average annual increase in earnings per share was 4.0

per cent. This change was accompanied by a 7.1 per cent increase in equity capital per share, a 2.4 per cent decline in profit margins and a 0.7 per cent fall in capital turnover. Thus, over the 15 year period ended 1970, profit margins dropped significantly, capital turnover declined very slightly and equity capital per share rose substantially. Since both capital turnover and profit margins dropped, by implication the return on equity capital also fell.

Examination of industries revealed that the pattern was similar for most industries. Earnings per share increased in all but ten industries. Equity capital per share expanded in all industries but one, the watch industry. Profit margins declined in 87 of 102 industries. Those industries with the largest increases in profit margins tended to report the largest increases in earnings per share. The pattern of capital turnover was mixed, with 54 industries reporting increases and 48 reporting declines.

To determine the precise relationship between earnings per share and each of the other variables we computed coefficients of correlation between changes in earnings and changes in each of the others. Knowledge of these relationships might permit identification of the significant variables. Coefficients of correlation (r) were determined using 15 year average values for each variable for each industry. The coefficients are shown below:

Correlation Between Changes in Earnings Per Share and Change in

	Profit Margin	Capital Turnover	Capital Per Share
r	0.725	0.014	0.500
r^2	0.526	0.002	0.250

Clearly changes in profit margins are the most important factor. Changes in profit margins are responsible for slightly over half of the variation in changes in earnings per share. The relationship is statistically significant.[7] Changes in equity capital accounted for approximately one-fourth of the variation in changes in earnings per share. This relationship is statistically significant. Shifts in capital turnover, however, bore little relation to changes in earnings, and the relationship is not significant.

To illustrate the range of changes in earnings per share, with the coincident changes in profit margins, in capital turnover and in equity capital we provide the data for the 102 industries in Table 1. The table presents the compound annual changes in these variables for the 15 year period 1956 to 1970. The industries are ranked in order of increase in earnings per share. The industry leaders in rise in earnings per share were photography, medical and hospital supply, drugs, proprietary drugs, ethical drugs, mixed manufacture gas products, motion pictures, bituminous coal, cosmetics, electric and electronic leaders and soft drinks. It is noteworthy that three of the industries are in the drug field.

In Table 2 we present the ten industries that recorded the highest rise in profit margins during the 15 year period. Two of the ten companies with the highest rise in profit margins were in the top decile of growth of earnings per share and five of the ten were in the highest quartile of earnings growth. This ranking provides further evidence on the importance of the bearing that profit margin increases have on changes in earnings.

Table 3 lists the ten industries recording the greatest increase in equity capital per share during the period 1956-1970. Half of those industries were among the top ten industries in earnings growth and six of the ten were in the top quintile of earnings growth. The strong relationship between increments in earnings and increases in equity capital per share is to be expected since it implies an improving return on equity. It is also true that firms with high returns on equity capital and low payout show relatively high increments in equity capital per share.

Table 4 presents the ten industries with the greatest

Table 1. Compound Annual Changes in Earnings Per Share with Compound Annual Changes in Profit Margins, Capital Turnover and Equity Per Share,

INDUSTRY	Change in Profit Margin %	Change in Capital Turnover %	Change in Capital Per Share %	Change in Income Per Share %
Photographic	0.6	-2.3	13.4	11.7 (15.3) [a]
Drugs-Medical, Hospital Supply	1.2	-1.7	11.5	11.0 (21.3)
Drugs-Proprietary	-0.7	-0.4	11.3	10.2 (08.1)
Drugs-Ethical	-0.2	0.0	9.9	9.7 (11.3)
Mixed Manufactured Gas Products	-2.3	2.4	9.4	9.5 (09.6)
Motion Pictures	4.9	-2.6	7.1	9.4 (59.1)
Coal-Bituminous	5.3	-3.0	6.9	9.2 (38.6)
Cosmetics	-0.4	-2.8	12.4	9.2 (38.7)
Electrical and Electrical Leaders	-2.6	0.1	11.7	9.2 (36.0)
Beverages-Soft Drinks	-2.1	2.2	8.8	8.9 (22.9)
Containers-Metal and Glass	2.6	0.0	6.2	8.8 (32.1)
Office-Business Equipment	-1.6	-2.2	12.5	8.8 (34.7)
Publishing	1.4	-5.4	12.8	8.8 (26.4)
Oil-Crude Producers	0.3	-1.7	9.8	8.4 (46.7)
Trucking	0.4	-2.9	10.9	8.4 (47.5)
Optical	-2.1	1.3	8.9	8.1 (54.4)
Business Forms—Manufacturing	-1.1	-1.0	10.1	8.0 (12.1)
Foods-Packaged	2.8	-2.0	7.1	7.9 (09.7)
Foods-Prepared Feeds for Animals	-0.3	1.7	6.2	7.6 (19.8)
Soap	0.6	0.0	6.9	7.5 (09.1)
Textile-Apparel Manufacturing	1.0	-1.0	7.2	7.2 (36.7)
Electrical-Household Appliances	-1.7	0.0	8.2	6.5 (19.3)
Food-Dairy Products	2.5	-1.5	5.5	6.5 (08.5)
Retail-Mail Order, General	-3.6	-0.3	10.4	6.5 (16.5)
Tobacco-Cigarettes	-0.7	2.4	4.8	6.5 (07.5)
Building Materials-Heat, Air Conditioning, Plumbing	-1.2	-1.4	9.0	6.4 (46.6)
Beverages-Brewers	-0.9	2.1	4.9	6.1 (54.8)
Electronics	-3.0	-3.6	12.7	6.1 (64.1)
Oil-Integrated, Domestic	-3.2	1.3	7.6	5.9 (18.0)
Auto-Trucks	-0.7	-2.0	8.4	5.7 (76.4)
Vegetable Oils	1.6	0.8	3.3	5.7 (33.7)
Machinery-Specialty	-2.4	0.5	7.3	5.4 (52.8)
Retail-Food	-2.2	0.7	6.9	5.4 (22.0)
Shoes	-1.4	1.4	5.4	5.4 (18.2)
Machinery-Steam Generating	-4.0	3.3	5.8	5.1 (39.7)
Vending Machines	-0.2	-3.7	9.0	5.1 (40.8)
Chemical and Chemical Preparations	-3.7	0.9	7.8	5.0 (39.8)
Electrical Industrial Controls	-2.6	0.3	7.3	5.0 (28.2)
Telephone Companies	-2.7	1.6	6.0	4.9 (06.6)
Watches	5.2	1.2	-1.5	4.9 (96.2)
Retail-Department Stores	-0.9	-0.3	6.0	4.8 (17.4)
Radio-TV Manufacturers	-3.9	0.0	8.5	4.6 (58.8)
Radio-TV Broadcasters	-3.2	-2.2	10.0	4.6 (53.2)
Oil-Integrated, International	-1.7	-0.5	6.7	4.5 (10.9)
Finance-Small Loans	-3.6	1.0	7.1	4.5 (09.6)
Wholesale-Not Elsewhere	-3.4	-0.3	8.1	4.4 (36.7)
Greeting Cards	-3.7	0.3	7.8	4.4 (20.3)
Automatic Temperature Controls	-2.9	-1.2	8.4	4.3 (19.7)
Metal Work-Miscellaneous	-2.7	-0.8	7.7	4.2 (78.4)
Auto Parts-Accessories	-2.2	-1.4	7.5	3.9 (62.5)

(a) Standard Deviation

Table 1. Continued

INDUSTRY	Change in Profit Margin %	Change in Capital Turnover %	Change in Capital Per Share %	Change in Income Per Share %
Beverages-Distillers	~1.5	1.6	3.8	3.9 (49.5) [a]
Confectionery	-1.0	~0.5	5.4	3.9 (17.3)
Engineering-Laboratory and Research Equipment	~3.7	-1.4	9.0	3.9 (33.9)
Sugar Cane Refiners	-1.3	~0.3	5.5	3.9 (32.3)
Food-Biscuit Bakers	-4.0	3.9	3.9	3.8 (22.7)
Foods-Canned	~0.8	1.3	3.3	3.8 (44.0)
Publishing-Books	-2.7	-1.5	8.0	3.8 (32.4)
Machinery-Industrial	-2.5	-0.9	7.0	3.6 (38.3)
Textile Products	-1.7	0.3	5.0	3.6 (54.4)
Electrical Equipment	-2.6	~1.0	7.0	3.4 (44.2)
Manufacturing Industries	-2.6	-1.0	7.0	3.4 (49.7)
Tobacco-Cigar Manufacturing	-4.4	4.9	2.9	3.4 (27.0)
Retail-Variety	-4.0	2.0	5.3	3.3 (29.5)
Machinery-Oil Well	-5.8	~0.1	9.1	3.2 (50.6)
Electronic Components	-2.4	-5.5	10.9	3.0 (36.9)
Air Transport	-4.3	-4.4	11.5	2.8 (76.7)
Shipping	2.9	-2.0	1.9	2.8 (123.0)
Aerospace	-3.7	-4.8	11.2	2.7 (58.5)
Machinery-Metal Fabricating	-2.8	~2.3	7.7	2.6 (56.9)
Aircraft-General	-3.9	-6.6	13.0	2.5 (66.6)
Retail Drug-Proprietary Store	~4.4	1.6	4.8	2.0 (37.0)
Chemicals-Specialty	-4.4	~1.0	7.3	1.9 (29.2)
Chemicals-Major	-4.0	0.6	5.2	1.8 (21.0)
Food-Meat Packers	-0.4	0.2	2.0	1.8 (76.9)
Sulfur	-4.2	~3.3	9.3	1.8 (28.9)
Machinery-Construction and Material Handling	-4.2	~0.6	6.5	1.7 (42.9)
Primary Smelting and Refining	-2.6	1.1	3.4	1.7 (55.6)
Forest Products	-4.3	-1.1	6.9	1.5 (74.0)
Retail-Apparel	-5.8	0.1	7.2	1.5 (27.1)
Sugar-Beet Refiners	-3.2	0.6	4.1	1.5 (35.6)
Tire and Rubber Goods	-3.0	-2.7	7.1	1.4 (32.7)
Machine Tools	-5.1	-0.8	6.9	1.0 (63.0)
Machinery-Agriculture	-5.0	0.9	5.0	0.9 (49.0)
Aluminum	-4.5	-0.6	5.9	0.8 (28.7)
Finance-Small Loans	-9.6	2.5	9.8	2.7 (16.2)
Paper Containers	-5.8	0.6	5.7	0.5 (41.5)
Gold Mining	-0.6	-2.8	3.8	0.4 (18.9)
Lead and Zinc	-1.9	-3.1	5.3	0.3 (38.5)
Metals-Miscellaneous	-3.1	-2.4	5.8	0.3 (66.3)
Paper	-5.2	0.2	5.2	0.2 (25.4)
Steel-Minor	-2.7	-1.8	4.7	0.2 (57.1)
Shipbuilding	-9.1	1.8	7.3	0.0 (158.4)
Railroad Equipment	-5.3	0.8	4.0	-0.5 (61.1)
Chemicals-Intermediate	-5.8	-0.9	5.7	-1.0 (61.5)
Not Elsewhere Classified	-9.1	0.0	7.3	-1.8 (77.7)
Building Materials-Roof and Wallboard	-5.7	-0.2	4.1	-1.8 (31.2)
Home Furnishing	-5.4	-0.8	3.9	-2.3 (47.8)
Motor Vehicles	-6.4	-1.7	5.3	-2.8 (98.0)
Food-Bread and Cake Bakers	-5.0	-2.3	4.2	-3.1 (52.0)
Paint	-8.0	-1.1	5.0	-4.1 (28.6)
Steel-Major	-6.4	-2.3	4.4	-4.3 (26.3)
Building Materials-Cement	-11.7	-1.7	6.2	-7.2 (37.7)

(a) Standard Deviation

Table 2. Compound Annual Changes in Profit Margins 1956-1970

Highest Ten Industries

Coal-Bituminous	5.5%
Watches	5.2
Motion Pictures	4.9
Shipping	2.9
Foods-Package	2.8
Containers-Metal and Glass	2.6
Food-Dairy Products	2.5
Vegetable Oils	1.6
Publishing	1.4

advances in capital turnover in the year 1956 to 1970. Two of the ten industries, soft drink beverages and mixed manufactured gas products, were in the top decile of earnings growth; four of the ten were in the highest quartile. On the other hand, two of the ten were in the lowest quartile of earnings growth and four were among the 50 per cent of companies with the low-

Table 3. Compound Annual Changes in Equity Capital Per Share 1956-1970

Highest Ten Industries

Photographic	13.4%
Aircraft-General	13.0
Publishing	12.8
Electronics	12.7
Office-Business Equipment	12.5
Cosmetics	12.4
Electrical and Electrical Leaders	11.7
Drugs-Medical and Hospital Supply	11.5
Air Transport	11.5
Drug-Proprietary	11.3

Table 4. Compound Annual Changes in Capital Turnover 1956-1970

Highest Ten Industries

Tobacco-Cigar Manufacturing	4.9
Food-Biscuit Bakers	3.9
Finance-Small Loans	2.5
Mixed Manufactured Gas Products	2.4
Tobacco-Cigarettes	2.4
Beverages-Soft Drinks	2.2
Beverages-Brewers	2.1
Retail-Variety	2.0
Shipbuilding	1.8
Foods-Prepared Feeds for Animals	1.7

est earnings growth. This wide range provides additional evidence that changes in capital turnover bear no direct relation to earnings growth.

Earnings Variability and Earnings Growth

We were also interested in finding out whether growth of earnings per share might be related to variability of earnings growth. It is well known that some well-known growth stocks such as American Home Products and Tampax, combined long-term growth with relatively low variability in the rate of earnings change. Annual percentage changes in earnings of those companies has been consistently positive and comparatively steady. Low variability of earnings change might provide a clue to high rates of growth over a long time period, such as the 15 year period 1956 to 1970. We chose to test this question by inquiring whether the industries exhibiting the lowest variability of earning change also portrayed the highest growth in earnings.

The results are given in the right hand column of Table 1. There we exhibit the average volatility of earnings change over

Table 5. Standard Deviation in Compound Change in Earnings Per Share 1956-1970
Ten Industries with Lowest Standard Deviation

Industry	Compound Annual Change in Earnings/Share %	Standard Deviation %
Telephone Companies	4.9	6.6
Tobacco-Cigarettes	6.5	7.5
Drugs-Proprietary	10.2	8.1
Food-Dairy Products	6.5	8.5
Soap	7.5	9.1
Mixed Manufacture Gas Products	9.5	9.6
Foods-Packaged	7.9	9.7
Finance - Small Loans	4.5	9.8
Oil-Integrated International	4.6	10.9
Drugs-Ethical	9.7	11.3

the 15 year period 1956 to 1970 of the companies in the industry. Variability or volatility is measured in terms of the standard deviation of annual percentage change in earnings. As can be seen, variability of earnings growth has no general consistent bearing on earnings growth. Industries with high growth of earnings were as likely to have high variability of earning growth as low variability. Among the industries in the top decile in earnings growth the standard deviation of earnings change ranged from a low of 8.1 per cent to a high of 59.1 per cent. The ten industries with the lowest growth all had standard deviations greater than 25 per cent. Despite the lack of significant correlation between earnings growth and variability of earning change, industries with very low variability of earnings change did tend to have generally higher rates of growth. (See Table 5 which lists the ten industries with the lowest variability of

Table 6. Standard Deviation of Growth of Earnings Per Share of the Cosmetic Industry 1956-1970

	Compound Annual Change in Earnings/Share %	Standard Deviation %
Avon Products	19.0	7.4
Faberge Corp.	14.0	75.9
Max Factor Co.	11.7	13.3
Gillette Co.	5.1	10.5
Helena Rubenstein, Inc.	5.0	24.3
Helen Curtis Industries	-2.3	119.5
Revlon, Inc.	11.7	20.0

earnings change.) Three of the industries in this table—proprietary drugs, mixed manufactured gas products and ethical drugs—were among the top ten industries in earnings growth. None of the industries in Table 5 were in the lower half of the sample with regard to earnings growth.

The higher standard deviations tend to be concentrated in those industries where earnings are cyclical—for example, the machinery, metal and motor vehicles industries. Conversely, stable industries such as the telephone industry and the drug industries have low standard deviations.

Standard deviation comparisons are most useful, however, when individual companies, rather than industrial groupings are considered. Composite industrial figures are averages and tend to be distorted by individual companies whose standard deviation is far different from the rest of the sample. The data in Table 6 for the cosmetic industry, where standard deviations ranged from 7.4 per cent to 11.95 per cent, highlights this problem. The effect of the two high figures on average for the seven in this table is appreciable.

On the other hand, the information for Faberge Corporation and Avon Products is an example of how these data are useful for individual companies. Both Faberge and Avon had good records of earnings growth but Avon's is somewhat better. The superiority of Avon's record is not fully appreciated, however, until standard deviations are considered. The standard deviation of Avon's growth was 7.4 per cent while that of Faberge was 75.9 per cent. Thus the risk of earnings disappointment has been far less for Avon than for Faberge.

Summary

This article has considered the effect on growth of earnings per share of three variables—changes in profit margins, changes in equity capital per share and changes in capital turnover—by examining these variables for 102 industries over the period 1956 to 1970. Examination revealed that the most important variable was profit margin. Changes in profit margins accounted for approximately half the observed variability in changes in earnings per share. Changes in equity capital per share accounted for approximately one-fourth. Changes in capital turnover, on the other hand, bore no significant relationship to growth of earnings.

During the time period studied, 1956 to 1970, profit margins were under pressure. The decline in profit margin was offset by a consistent rise in the equity capital per share. As a consequence, earnings per share rose, but not as much as equity capital rose.

This pattern turned out to be true, not only for the composite average of the companies in this study, but also for all the individual industries. In all cases but one, equity capital per share rose, while in 87 of 102 industries, profit margins declined.[8]

Footnotes

1. See, for example, J. E. Murphy, "Earnings Growth and Price Change in the Same Period," *Financial Analysts Journal*, January/February 1968, pp. 97-99; and Victor Niederhoffer and

Patrick J. Regan, "Earnings Changes, Analysts' Forecasts and Stock Prices," *Financial Analysts Journal*, May/June 1972, pp. 65-71.

2. Evidence is given in P. H. Cootner, editor, *The Random Character of Stock Prices,* M.I.T. Press, Cambridge, Mass., 1964.

3. A. C. Rayner, and I. M. D. Little, *Higgledy Piggledy Growth Again, Oxford,* Basil Blackwell, 1966; J. E. Murphy, "Relative Growth of Earnings Per Share - Past and Future," *Financial Analysts Journal*, November/December 1966, pp. 73-76; and R. A. Brealey, *An Introduction To Risk And Return*, M.I.T. Press, Cambridge, Mass., 1966, pp. 88-103.

4. J. G. Cragg and Burton G. Malkiel, "The Consensus and Accuracy of Some Predictions of the Growth of Corporate Earnings," *Journal of Finance*, March 1968.

5. For related theoretical and empirical work on the variables, although not in changes therein, see Sidney Cottle and Tate Whitman, *Corporate Earnings Power and Market Valuation: 1935-1955*, Duke University Press, Durham, N.C., 1959; William M. Bennett, "Capital Turnover versus Profit Margins," *Financial Analysts Journal*, March/April 1966, pp. 88-95; Myron J. Gordon, *The Investment, Financing and Valuation of the Corporation,* Homewood, Ill., R. D. Irwin, 1962; Manown Kisor, Jr., "The Financial Aspects of Growth," *Financial Analysts Journal*, March/April 1966, and Eugene M. Lerner and Willard T. Carleton, *A Theory of Financial Analysis,* Harcourt, Brace & World, Inc., New York, 1966.

6. The first difference in natural logarithms is equivalent to the percentage change if percentages are computed using continuous compounding.

7. Using the five per cent level of significance as the statistical criteria.

8. The authors wish to acknowledge with appreciation the help of Daniel F. Boehle in the compute programming work.

12

Games of Change and the Probability of Corporate Profit or Loss

Joseph E. Murphy & M.F.M. Osborne

The purpose of this paper is to describe a model for estimating the probability of future profit or loss for the individual firm. We derive the model from probability theory, show how the probability of profit or loss may be calculated for the firm, demonstrate the model's statistical reliability and use, and suggest the implications. In applying the model, we define profit as net annual income/total assets for reasons given below.

Introduction

The question of profit or loss is extremely important, both to large companies and small. Mounting losses ultimately drove the Penn Central to file for bankruptcy in 1972. Banks and investors alike lost hundreds of millions of dollars in defaulted loans and plummeting market values. But losses do not always lead to bankruptcy. More often than not, losses are temporary, particularly among large corporations.

Even these temporary losses have adverse effects. In the years and months preceding a deficit, market declines can be substantial. Credit ratings begin to be adjusted downward, thus hurting bond prices, sometimes severely. The equity base shrinks and, with it, the ability to meet coupon or principal payments. The firm's financial structure weakens, and the dividend may be placed in jeopardy. Profitable firms do not normally suffer these disadvantages. Profitable firms can usually make remittances to creditors, meet dividend and coupon payments, repay principal, and retain satisfactory credit ratings.

Despite the importance of the question of future profit or loss, to our knowledge, no systematic studies on the prediction of firm profit or loss have ever been published. This paper arose out of our earlier work in predicting deficits, begun in 1973 and

Reprinted with permission from *Financial Management*, Vol. 8, No.2. Copyright 1979, Financial Management Association, College of Business Administration, University of South Florida, Tampa, Florida. 33620. Tel. 813-974-2084. All rights reserved.

based on the analysis of profit ratios, using techniques similar to those applied to corporate bankruptcy [1,3,12]. Our earlier work on profit and loss, the inferences which may be drawn from studies on randomness in earnings, and the need for a theoretical foundation ultimately resulted in application of a form of the classical ruin problem to the estimation of the probability of future profit or loss of the individual firm.

In applying the model, we estimate the probability that a firm will report a profit, or a loss, in the year t +1 based on data available in year t. We do not assert that the firm will report a profit next year, or that it will report a loss; neither do we estimate the expected value of profit or loss. We assert the probability of profit or loss and we test the accuracy of the model in terms of relative frequencies of profit and loss among firms classified by previously estimated probabilities of profit and loss. By using probability assertions, we reflect the uncertainty of economic data.

Calculating the Probability of Profit or Loss in Games of Chance

The seventeenth century mathematician, James Bernoulli, developed a theorem for coin tossing games which has proven a significant step in the development of probability theory [7, Ch. 14]. We describe the problem and the model because we use it in estimating the probability of profit or loss of the individual firm [15].

In flipping coins, we may assign +1 to heads and -1 to tails. After a sequence of plays, our cumulative profit p, will be positive or negative. We wish to find the probability of ending up at a loss if we toss the coin an additional n times. We define zero profit as a loss; classification of zero profit as profit would modify the formula slightly.

We may calculate the probability of being at loss after n future plays by dividing the number of ways of tossing a coin n times in succession to produce an excess of p tails (call that number r) by the number of ways of tossing a coin n times (2^n).

An excess of p tails will occur if p of the future tosses are tails and at least half of the remaining tosses are also tails. A minimum of r=p+(n-p)/2 tails will produce a future loss.

For example, if after past plays we have accumulated a profit, p, of 2, the probability of remaining at profit after two future plays is 25%. Two future plays give four possible results (hh,tt,ht,th) with outcomes, 2,-2,0,0. Adding our accumulated profit of 2 to the outcomes gives four possible results (4,0,2,2). Since only one of the four possible results is zero or negative, the probability of future loss is 25%. We give additional illus-

Exhibit 1
Probability of Loss After n Future Trials From a Current Profit of 2.

Number of Future Trials n	Tails to Produce Loss r	Number of Ways to		Probability of Loss
		Obtain at least r tails	Toss a coin n times	
2	2	1	4	.25
4	3	5	16	.31
6	4	22	64	.34
8	5	93	256	.36

trations in Exhibit 1.[1]

We can calculate the probability of loss in games of chance from the binomial distributions and, if the number of future tosses is large, from the normal distribution.[2] To use the normal distribution, we must calculate the z statistic, which is formed by dividing our current profit, p, by the standard deviation of the outcomes of n future plays. In the game we have just described, the standard deviation is the square root of n which gives:

$$z = p/s$$
$$= p/\sqrt{n}$$

If our cumulative profit, p, is 2 and we toss the coin an additional 400 times, the value of z = 2/20 or 0.1. Tables of the normal distribution show that the probability of a z of 0.1 is 0.46 which means that the probability of loss is 46% after 400 more tosses. Note that as the number of future plays rises, the standard deviation increases. If the standard deviation ($\sqrt{n}$ in this example) becomes very large, z will move toward zero, and the probability of loss, or profit, will approach 50%.

Calculating the Probability of Profit or Loss for the Individual Firm

There are intuitive reasons for suspecting that the model that we have just described for coin tossing games may also be applied to estimating the probability of future profit or loss of the individual firm.

Profits of the firm represent the result of an extremely complex decision-making process involving the exchange of goods and services for money. The participants include member of the firm, suppliers, customers, investors, and lenders. Each exchange usually represents a fair trade of goods and services, or of money, between buyer and seller, and each participant has an equal opportunity to profit. The very nature of this process would lead us to expect a profit series of differences Δp_k (defined as $p_t - p_{\{t-k\}}$), very approximately characterized by a normal distribution, zero mean, and a rate of diffusion, or standard deviation, $\sigma (\Delta p_k)$, which increases with the square root of the differencing or time interval, k. This kind of distribution characterizes many random processes and may be modeled by the coin tossing game we described above [15].

Prior investigation of the profit series provides evidence that suggests application of the probability model [2, 4, 5, 6, 9, 10, 13, 16]. This evidence reveals that successive changes in profits are uncorrelated. The standard deviation of profit changes increases roughly with the square root of the differencing interval or time [8]. In most of these prior investigations, profits were measured, by definition, as the first differences in the natural logarithms of annual earnings per share. Similar tests have been performed on other firm variables, including total assets, that suggest application of the model [14].

In applying the model, we require a measure of profits that reflects net income, can assume negative values, remains unaffected by firm size, and does not exhibit severe changes when profits are close to zero. Moreover, the measure must exhibit a demonstrated capacity to distinguish future profit and loss firms.

We decided to exclude the most direct measure of profits, reported net income, since that variable does not remove differences in firm size, may exhibit unusually sharp changes after mergers and acquisitions, and cannot be conveniently scaled by converting to percentage changes, since loss firms would have to be handled separately. We can scale net income by dividing it by the firm's total assets. We chose this variable after testing a large number of profitability ratios, including pre-tax income/total assets, return on equity, return on total capital, pre-tax margins, and net profit margins. In these extensive tests, using discriminant analysis, net income/total assets proved to be the best single indicator of future profit or loss. In its ability to distinguish future profit firms from loss firms, it proved superior to any other single variable of 45 variables tested and equivalent to combinations of ratios which included itself. [12].

We define therefore as the measure of profit or loss net income available to common shareholders, excluding non-recurrent items, during the fiscal year divided by total assets of the firm at the close of the year. Whenever profit is positive, this ratio will be positive (and vice versa):

p=net annual income/total assets.

We now turn to the question of applying to the variable p the probability model that we developed earlier. We may consider the values of net income/total assets of the firm for the series of years from the beginning of the firm to the present, or by the series $p_0, p_1, ..., p_{t-1} p_t$. If we subtract each item in the above series from its successor, we obtain the first difference series of annual changes in p, or $\Delta p_1, \Delta p_2, ... \Delta p_{t-1}, \Delta p_t$. By definition, the value p in year t is the cumulative sum of the first difference series, the sum of annual changes in p since the birth of the firm. Note that the present value of net annual income/total assets, p_t, is analogous to the cumulative profit, p, in coin tossing games, described above.

In coin tossing games we estimated the probability of ending up at a future loss by dividing our present cumulative profit , p = (sum of previous Δp's), by the standard deviation, s of n future plays. This calculation gave us the z statistic where z=p/s, and s was $\sqrt{n}$.

In estimating the probability of future loss of the firm, we use the same formula. We divide our cumulative profit, p, the latest value of net annual income/total assets (sum of previous Δp's) by the standard deviation, $s = s(\Delta p_k)$, of future changes in p. This calculation for the firm gives z=p/s.

Since we do not know the value of s for future changes in p, we must estimate s from past annual changes in p, i.e., from Δp_{t-6}, Δp_{t-5}, ..., Δp_t. In the tests described below, we estimate the standard deviation, s, for one year's change, from annual changes in p over the past six years using the standard procedure for calculating an unbiased estimate of s. (The method of calculation is shown in Exhibit 2.)

Having calculated the z statistic, we may determine the probability of profit or loss from tables of the normal distribution, as illustrated in Exhibit 2.

Test of the Ability of the Model to Forecast the Probability of Future Profit or Loss of the Individual Firm

In testing the model, we wish to determine whether the estimated probabilities of future profit or loss for the individual firm are reliable and useful. Do the estimated probabilities distinguish between those firms that are more likely to experience loss and those firms that are less likely to experience loss? Do the estimated probabilities help identify those firms that are extremely likely to be profitable in the future from those that

Exhibit 2. Illustration of Computation of Probability of Profit or Loss for Year t+1 Based on Value of p for Year t.

	Fairmont Foods		Inspiration Consolidated Copper	
	$P \times 100$	$\Delta p \times 100$	$p \times 100$	$\Delta p \times 100$
1968	4.4		9.4	
1969	4.2	-0.2	20.0	10.6
1970	4.5	0.3	22.7	2.7
1971	3.2	-1.3	11.1	-11.6
1972	4.0	0.8	11.4	0.3
1973	3.5	-0.5	9.4	-2.0
1974	3.9	0.4	6.1	-3.3

$$s = \left[\frac{6}{5} \left(\overline{\Delta p^2} - (\overline{\Delta p})^2 \right) \right]^{h} = 0.76 \qquad\qquad 7.31$$

$z = p/s = \qquad\qquad 3.9/0.76 \qquad\qquad 6.1/7.31$

$z = \qquad\qquad 5.13 \qquad\qquad 0.83$

Probability
of Loss for
1975   Under 0.1%   20.6%

$$\Delta p = p_t - p_{t-1} \qquad \frac{1}{\sqrt{2\pi}} \int_{z}^{\infty} e^{-\frac{z^2}{2}} \, dz$$

Probability
of Profit for
1975   99.9%   79.4%

are not?

To test the accuracy of the estimates for individual firms, we calculated probabilities of profit and loss for a large number of firms for year t+1, using data only up to year t, classifying the firms by this estimated probability of profit or loss. Then we compared the probabilities with the actual frequency of losses in each group in year t+1. If firms for which we estimate high probability of loss for year t+1 show, in fact, a high frequency of loss in the subsequent year t + 1 (and vice versa), then we may conclude that the model is confirmed. If there is no relationship between observed frequency of future loss and predicted probability of future loss, then the model is not correct.

The date for the tests are taken from the Compustat Primary annual tape for the six test years ending 1971-1976 and from the Compustat Tertiary annual tape for the test years ending 1972-1977. The tests used all firms on the two tapes for which there were enough years of data to make the calculations for one or more test years. The total sample includes 1,343 firms, primarily large U.S. industrial corporations, but including some utility and financial firms.

In Exhibit 3, which is based on the data in Exhibit 4, we present a graph in which firms are grouped by estimated probabil-

Exhibit 3. Mean Predicted Percent Probability Based on Central Values of the Six Intervals of the Six Groups A – F.

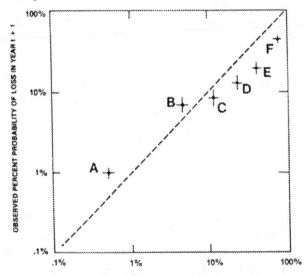

The diagonal line represents the points where theoretical percent probability = observed percent probability. The dots represent the actual relationship between observed percent probability and mean predicted percent probability. The arms of the crosses represent (very roughly) the uncertainty given by $\sigma \sim$ (expected frequency)$^{1/2}$ on each observation, i.e., $\sqrt{23}$, $\sqrt{31}$, $\sqrt{30}$, $\sqrt{85}$, $\sqrt{148}$, and $\sqrt{290}$, expressed as a percent of the number of firms in the group.

ity of loss for year t+1, from data available in year t. The vertical axis records the observed percent probability of loss in year t+1. The horizontal axis records the predicted percent probability of loss in year t+1. The predicted percent probability of loss is the central value of the six class intervals of the six groups, A-F. The class intervals, or estimated probability of loss, of the six groups are: A 0.0 - 0.9%; B 1.0 - 7.9%; C 8.0 - 14.9%; D 15.0 - 29.9%; E 30.0 - 49.9%; F 50.0 - 100.0%.

The line that runs diagonally upward from left to right on the graph of Exhibit 3 represents the theoretical relationship between observed and predicted percent probability in year t+1. The dots on the graph represent the actual relationship between observed and predicted percent probabilities. The arms of the crosses represent (very roughly) the uncertainty given by $\sigma \sim (expectedfrequency)^{1/2}$, i.e., $\pm 23^{1/2}, \pm 31^{1/2}, \pm 30^{1/2}, \pm 85^{1/2}, \pm 148^{1/2}, \pm 290^{1/2}$ (from Exhibit 4).

The first conclusion that may be drawn is that there is an increasing predicted percent probability of loss for each successive group, beginning with group A and ending with group F. Exhibit 3 shows very clearly that the observed ratios also increase in the same direction and by roughly the same amount. This correspondence is shown by the diagonally upward movement, from left to right, of the dots in exhibit 3. The correspondence is shown in the table below by the ratio of the number of

Group	A	B	C	D	E	F
Number of Loss Firms ÷ Number of Profit Firms	.011	.074	.091	.147	.242	.75
Loss Firms in Year t+1	48	47	22	4	72	165
Profit Firms in Year t+1	4585	639	242	329	297	222

loss firms in year t+1 to the number of profit firms in the year t+1 for each group.

If we consider the bottom two rows above as a contingency table, we may use the chi square test to determine whether the observed departures from independence are or are not of a magnitude ascribable to chance. Since the probability of the computed chi square of 1,279.4, with five degrees of freedom, is less than one in a billion, we reject the hypothesis of no difference between the groups.

We can also make a chi square test for independence by making 15 two by two contingency tables (one degree of freedom) of all possible pairs A-F. At a 5% level of significance, for thirteen of the fifteen possible pairs from the six groups, we reject the null hypothesis of independence, or of no difference between the groups. The exceptions are the pairs of groups B & C and C & D.

The above conclusions mean that, from a practical standpoint, we may employ the model to classify firms on the basis of predicted percent probability of loss or profit in year t+1 based on the data available in year t. We may expect that firms estimated to have low probabilities of loss in year t+1, based on data available in year t, will record a lower incidence of loss in year t+1 than firms with high estimated probabilities of loss.

The second conclusion we can draw from Exhibits 3 and 4 is that for low predicted probabilities of loss, group A, the observed frequencies are higher than predicted by the model. For high predicted probabilities of loss, groups D, E, and F, the observed frequencies are lower than predicted by the model. Except for B and C, the arms of the crosses indicate a "significant" departure of theory from observation (data not on the dashed line).

Three conditions would be sufficient to cause discrepancy between observed and theoretical frequencies: failure of the theoretical central value of the group to measure the mean probability of the group; annual departures from zero in the mean change in p for all firms; and an inverse relationship between the level of p in a particular year and the incidence of increases

156

in p in the following year. Elements of each of the three conditions appear to be present in the data. We hope to give a more detailed description of these properties in a future publication.

Although discrepancies between theoretical and observed frequencies are too large to be ascribable to chance, the evidence reveals that the model provides a useful method of classifying companies on the basis of predicted probability of loss in year t+1 from data available in year t.[3] The model is a sufficient approximation of the data to be useful in decision-making.

Summary and Implications

Exhibit 4. Summary of Results 1970-1971 to 1976-1977. Predicted Probability of Loss for Year t + 1 From Data in Year t and Observed Frequency of Loss in Year t + 1

Group		A	B	C	D	E	F	Total
z = From		∞	2.4	1.4	1.15	.55	0.0	
To		2.4	1.4	1.15	.55	0.0	– ∞	
Predicted Probability of Loss in Year t + 1 from	From	0.0	1.0	8.0	15.0	30.0	50.0	
Data in Year t	To	0.99	7.9	14.9	29.9	49.9	100.0	
Central Value of Predicted Probability of Group		.5	4.5	11.5	22.5	40.	75.	
Observed % of Firms in Group with Loss for Year t + 1		1.0	6.9	8.3	12.7	19.5	42.6	
Frequency of Loss Firms in Year t + 1 Observed		48	47	22	48	72	165	402
Predicted from Central Value by Theory		23	31	30	85	148	290	
Frequency of Profit Firms in Year t + 1 Observed		4585	639	242	329	297	222	6314
Predicted from Central Value by Theory		4610	655	234	292	221	97	
Total Number of Firms		4633	686	264	377	369	387	6716
Chi Square for Observed vs. Predicted Frequencies		8.87	3.48	1.36	12.5	37.4	83.3	
Probability ($x^2 > x^2$ obs)		.003	.062	.243	<.001	<.001	<.001	

157

We have described a model for estimating the probability of future profit or loss for the individual firm. The model, derived from probability theory, shows how to estimate the probability of future profit or loss for the firm. We have demonstrated that the model effectively groups 1,343 corporations on the basis of future frequency of loss.

The probability model and empirical evidence suggest that the standard deviation of changes in p increases with the passage of time. Since we have derived the predicted probability of future profit, or loss, from the equation $z=p/s$, a rise in s will cause z to move toward zero, at which point the probabilities of profit or loss will be equal. Consequently, as the forecast period increases, the predicted probabilities of loss and of profit will each move toward 50%. However, one should not expect this aspect of the theory to hold for indefinitely long periods.

The model implies that there will be continual adjustment of credit ratings, that the number of ratings adjusted will increase with the passage of time, and that lenders must continually monitor borrowers. The model also implies that the risk to the lender is a rough function of the square root of the maturity and that a long bond of high credit may have the same risk as a short bond of much lower credit.

The basic model provides a useful method of estimating the probability that the individual firm will be profitable or unprofitable in the future. The z statistic may be modified to reflect anticipated economic, industry, or firm changes, or other forecast periods. Such alterations will produce modified estimates of the probability of profit or loss.

Used by itself, the model provides a systematic and tested means of ranking firms on the basis of probability of future profit or loss. This ranking may be used to compare firms within the same industry, or firms drawn from different industries, regardless of firm size or the nature of the underlying business.

Footnotes

1.See Osborne for an illustration of the coin flipping model and its application to random processes, e.g., the stock market.

2. The normal distribution approximates the binomial as n tends to infinity. Use of the z statistic requires a values of n of 50 or more to reduce the error to below 1%. Below n=10, the error becomes quite large.

3. As indicated by deviations from the line in Exhibit 3 and, equivalently, the last line of Exhibit 4.

References

1. Edward I. Altman, *Corporate Bankruptcy in America*, Lexington, Mass., D. C. Heath & Company, 1971.

2. Ray Ball and Philip Brown, "Some Time Series Properties of Accounting Income," *Journal of Finance* (June 1972), p.. 663-681.

3. William H. Beaver, "Financial Ratios as Predictions of Failure," *Empirical Research in Accounting: Selected Studies*, 1966, Supplement to Vol. 4, *Journal of Accounting Research*, pp. 77-111.

4. William H. Beaver, "The Time Series Behavior of Earnings," *Empirical Research in Accounting: Selected Studies*, 1970, Supplement to Vol. 8, *Journal of Accounting Research*, pp. 62-87.

5. Richard A. Brealey, "Statistical Properties of Successive Changes in Earnings," unpublished paper, March 1967.

6. Leroy D. Brooks and Dale A. Buckmaster, "Further Evidence of the Time Series Properties of Accounting Income," *Journal of Finance* (December 1976), pp. 1359-1372.

7. William Feller, *An Introduction to Probability Theory and Its Applications,* Vol. 1, 3rd ed., New York, John Wiley & Sons, Inc., 1968.

8. Investment Strategy in Bond and Stock Portfolios, Northwestern National Bank, 1976, Chart 3.

9. John Lintner and Robert Glauber, "Higgledy Piggledy Growth in America?" paper presented to the seminar on the analysis of security prices, Graduate School of Business, University of Chicago, May 11-12, 1967.

10. I. M. D. Little and A. C. Rayner, *Higgledy Piggledy Growth Again*, Oxford, Basil Blackwell, 1966.

11. Frederick Mosteller, Robert E. K. Rourke and George B. Thomas, Jr., *Probability and Statistics*, Reading, Mass., Addison-Wesley, 1961.

12. Joseph E. Murphy, Jr. "Financial Ratios, Discriminant Analysis and the Prediction of the Odds of Corporate Deficit," 1977, unpublished.

13. Joseph E. Murphy, Jr., "Relative Growth of Earnings Per Share-Past and Future," *Financial Analysts Journal* (November/December 1966), pp. 73-76.

14. Joseph E. Murphy, Jr. and J. Russell Nelson, "Random and Nonrandom Relationships Among Financial Variables: A Financial Model," *Journal of Financial and Quantitative Analysis* (March 1971), pp. 875-885.

15. M. F. M. Osborne, "Brownian Motion in the Stock Market," *Operations Research* (March/April 1957), pp. 145-173.

16. M. F. M. Osborne, *The Stock Market and Finance From a Physicist's Viewpoint*, 1977, Crossgar Press, Minneapolis, 1995.

13

FINANCIAL ANALOGS OF PHYSICAL BROWNIAN MOTION, AS ILLUSTRATED BY EARNINGS

M.F.M. Osborne and Joseph E. Murphy

Introduction

Einstein once remarked that God does not play dice with the universe. However, in the case of corporate earnings, not only does he play dice, but the dice are loaded. How they are loaded is the subject of this paper on financial analogs of physical Brownian motion, as illustrated by earnings. The paper describes the results of an exploration of the earnings of major U.S. corporations over time from the perspective of a physicist, using mathematical concepts on Brownian motion that have been developed since Einstein's pioneering work in that field.

Brownian motion referred originally to the random movement of molecules of a liquid or gas, in all directions, apparently in chaos. Einstein first developed the theoretical law, or formula, that described important properties of that motion. We wanted to know whether the same kinds of laws could be applied to the movement of earnings of the corporation, or of a large number of corporations, over time. We also wanted to know what we might learn if we viewed earnings, or changes in earnings, from the perspective of a physicist studying Brownian motion and if we asked the same kinds of questions that he would ask.

The physicist studying molecular motion is not interested in the track of a particular molecule over a specific time interval. Rather, he is interested in the behavior of a large number of molecules over a particular slice of time. Or, he might be interested in the movements of a single molecule in many slices of time of the same length. He will then ask such questions as the following. Is there no tendency for the molecules to move more in one direction than the other? Does the particular time period have no influence? If we plot the dispersion of the changes in

Reprinted with permission from *Financial Review*, Vol. 19, No. 2, Copyright 1984. All rights reserved.

position, do they conform to a normal distribution? Does the amount of dispersion of changes increase with (the square root of) the time interval? Is the behavior of all the molecules the same?

If the answer to all of the above questions is yes, then the movement of the molecules may be described by the model of a simple random walk. That model is also called pure Brownian motion. If we substitute corporate earnings for position of the molecules, and also find that a simple random walk model will describe their change over time, the model will permit us to predict useful things. For example, we can predict the probability that a corporation might lose money next year, or ten years from now, or we can predict the proportion of firms likely to lose money, or the probability that earnings of a firm will rise by a given amount.

If the answer to the earlier questions about corporate earnings is no, then we require a more complex model, the properties of which we need to know in detail to make useful predictions. We examined the above questions for all major U.S. industrial corporations over a fifteen year span. We found that the answer to each of the above questions is no. But we also found that the departures from the simple random walk model are small, but systematic. As a result, we were able to develop a model that describes the data quite well. The model is similar to some important models of theoretical physics.

In a previous paper [16] we used a simple random walk model of constant variance per step, and zero expected advance, to describe data on the variable p=annual earnings/total assets. The data were taken from the December 1977 Compustat Primary tape for the 648 U.S. industrial firms with data for the full period 1959-1976. We estimated the probability of a deficit, $p(t + 1) < 0$, for next year, $t + 1$, given the values for this year, $p(t)$, and previous years. Previous years were used to calculate the standard deviation of one year changes in p. The probabilities

162

were sufficiently accurate for practical application by a bank [18]. There were, however, small, systematic deviations of the predicted probabilities from the observed frequencies. It is the purpose of this paper to identify a model, only slightly more complicated than a random walk, which describes these deviations.

This model has been used to describe a variety of problems in physics and has been studied by a variety of mathematical methods. The variable p = annual earnings/total assets has also been investigated in the financial and accounting literature, primarily for the purpose of forecasting earnings, not in determining the probability of a future deficit. By using a standardized variable (net income/total assets divided by the standard deviation of past changes in that ratio), we are able to apply general probability theory to the evaluation of the risk of loss [16].

Our approach to the statistical properties of the underlying data is closest to that of early work of one of the authors on common stock prices [19], and, to a degree, to early work on earnings [14, 17, 25]. The results presented here are directly concerned with a major issue raised by later work on the time series properties of earnings [1, 2, 3, 12], the nature of the underlying process. Is the earnings series generated by a simple random walk, or is the underlying process more complex? Our analysis agrees with those studies, but is expressed in a very different form, and explores some questions not taken up by them.

Data, such as earnings, are said to be stationary if their statistical properties are the same for all time periods. The data are homogeneous if the properties are the same for all firms, irrespective of industry, etc. In a controlled physics experiment, homogeneity of the population and statistical stationarity are readily achieved. Stationarity and homogeneity are less likely to characterize financial data. We are interested in departures from stationarity and homogeneity of the data, and in an evaluation of the time required to achieve a statistical steady state, or, as it is called in physics, the relaxation time to statistical equilibrium. We will find that the dice are loaded, but not so loaded that we cannot understand the game.

The Tavern in a Valley Model

Imagine a tavern on a road that crosses a bowl or saucer-shaped valley, the sides of the valley becoming higher in accordance with the formula for the elevation h from the valley bottom at $x = x_{oo}$,

$$h = 1/2k(x - x_{oo})^2$$

$x-x_{oo}$ being the horizontal distance from the tavern at the bottom of the valley. The slope of the road is then $(dh/dx) = k(x-x_{oo})$, which increases proportional to the distance from the tavern. Physicists will recognize this slope as analogous to a spring, or restoring force, proportional to the distance $x -x_{oo}$. A ball rolling freely on this road would oscillate back and forth in simple harmonic motion.

Now imagine a drunkard, staggering in a random walk in the neighborhood of the tavern. Close to the tavern, where $x - x_{oo}$ is small, or for small k, and for short intervals of time, the effect of the slope is negligible; the probability of a step (one per second, say) to the right or left is close to 1/2. We imagine that the slope of the slanting road affects the probabilities as follows. Let the step length be Δx^* taken once per time interval Δt^*.

P = probability of a step to the right $(+ \Delta x^*)$,

$$= [1/2 - k(x - x_{oo})\Delta x^*] \tag{1}$$

Q = probability of a step to the left $(- \Delta x^*)$,

$$= [1/2 + k(x - x_{oo})\Delta x^*]$$

The expected value E of one step is

$$E(\Delta x) = P(+ \Delta x^*) + Q(- \Delta x^*)$$
$$= -2k(x - x_{oo})(\Delta x^*)^2$$

Hence the drift velocity or expected displacement per unit time is

$$V(x) = - 2k(x - x_{oo})(\Delta x^*)^2/\Delta t^* \tag{2}$$

In a similar fashion the variance per unit time is

$$\sigma^2 = \{1 - 4[k(x - x_{oo})\Delta x^*]\}^2(\Delta x^{*2}/\Delta t^*) \tag{3}$$

From the above equation (2) it can be seen that there is a tendency for any drunkard to drift back toward the tavern at $x-x_{00}$, the more so the farther he happens to stagger away from it, whether to the right ($x>x_{00}$), or to the left ($x<x_{00}$). If we imagine a bus load of drunks discharged in a tight cluster in the neighborhood of the tavern, the cluster would spread out to a steady state size and its center would drift toward the tavern itself.

A measure of the time interval required for (a) the center of the cluster to reach the tavern, and b) the standard deviation of the cluster to reach a steady size, would be called in physics the relaxation time to statistical equilibrium. The two such time intervals are not quite the same [15, eq. 36].

The above situation appears in a number of different problems of physics and can be described quantitatively in a number of different ways. They were not always recognized as equivalent when first derived. References [4, 9, 13, 15, 27, 28] describe these different problems in detail. They are the Ehrenfest model of heat conduction, the Langevin equation leading to the velocity distribution of gas molecules, Brownian motion of an overdamped harmonic oscillator, and the current distribution in an electric circuit consisting of resistance and inductance agitated by a noisy random voltage. These problems can be solved by combinatorial methods with Δx^* and Δt^* finite. Alternatively, they can be considered as problems in Brownian motion [6, 7, 11, 19, 20, 21, 22, 23, 28] by taking the limit as Δx^* and Δt^* both approach zero in such a way that $(\Delta x^*)^2/\Delta t^*$ has a finite value, 2D. In this approach, the probability distribution density $\phi(x,t)$ obeys the Smoluchowski equation (see references [13, 15, and 27])

$$\partial\phi/\partial t = D(\partial^2\phi/\partial x^2) - (\partial/\partial x)[V(x)\phi]$$
$$V(x) = -\beta(x - x_{00})$$
$$\beta = 4kD$$

(4)

$V(x)$ is the drift velocity. When k=0, the drift velocity is zero, and the above is Fourier's equation for heat diffusion. The fundamental solution of Fourier's equation is just the probability distribution of position in a random walk of zero expected advance. It is a normal distribution around a starting position x_{00} with a standard deviation which increases with the square root of the time interval after the start.

Financial economists and accountants have another way of looking at the problem of barflies around a tavern, described above. The nomenclature is different, but the ultimate statistical description is practically the same. Let $X(t)$ be some financial variable of interest, evaluated once a year, t, t+1,... . For this paper $X(t)$ is annual earnings/total assets. We suppose $X(t)$ obeys a first order autoregressive scheme.

$$x(t + 1) = \alpha x(t) + f + d\,\check{\epsilon}(t). \tag{5}$$

$X(t)$ is this year's value, $X(t+1)$ next year's value, α is the regression constant and falls in the range $1 \leq \alpha \leq (t)$. $\tilde{\epsilon}(t)$ is a random variable of zero mean and unit variance. f and d are constants in the simplest case. References [1, p. 677; 2, p. 1364; 5; 8, p. 4, eq. 1; 10; 12, p. 77; 26, pp. 30, 32] give examples of sequential financial data analyzed by this equation, or slight variants of it. The equations are used to forecast X one year in the future, (t+ 1), given present (t) and past values, on which estimates of f and d may depend slightly. Ref. [24] discusses solutions of equation (5) in detail.

Let us write equation (5) in two other forms, and then interpret them, depending on the value of α.

$$X(t + 1) - X(t) = \Delta X(t + 1) = (\alpha - 1)X(t) + f + d\,\tilde{\epsilon}(t) \tag{6}$$

$$\Delta x(t + 1) = (\alpha - 1)[X(t) + f/(\alpha - 1)] + d\,\epsilon(t). \tag{7}$$

For $\alpha = 0$, equation (5) says that $X(t)$ has just the properties of the sequential control chart of some sequentially manufactured product, such as the diameter of piston rings, or calibre of an artillery shell. The expected, or intended, measure is f, with uncertainty or standard deviation d.

For $\alpha = 1$, equation (6) says that the sequential increment $\Delta X(t + 1)$ has just the properties of a step in a random walk of expected advance f (the trend per step) and standard deviation per step of d.

Intermediate values of α between zero and one are best understood in the form of equation (7). Since $\alpha - 1$ is negative, we can replace $f/(\alpha - 1)$ by $-x_{oo}$. Then equation (7) says the next expected step length $\Delta x(t+1)$ is proportional and opposite to the present distance $X(t)$ from an "equilibrium point" x_{oo} (the location of the tavern), with an uncertainty or standard deviation d. This is just the picture of our drunkard's walk near the tavern at the bottom of the valley.

In practice α can be close to the $\alpha=0$ or $\alpha=1$ cases, hence data generated by such a model would have properties close to the cases for $\alpha=0$ or $\alpha=1$. It might take a considerable span of data to distinguish between an α of zero and a small α, or between an α of one and an α close to one. In fact analyses in the literature [1], [26] of th variable p = earnings/assets have found values of $\alpha \approx 0.9$. This is quite consonant with our finding [16] that $\alpha=1$, a simple random walk, was able to represent the probabilities of a deficit one year in the future fairly well.

With this background relating the different ways in which physicists and economists have looked at different but mathematically similar problems, we turn to a description of the data. We will pay particular attention to the evidence for non-stationary and inhomogeneity in our population of 648 firms whose coordinate, measured once a year, is

p(t)=annual earnings/total assets.

We want to know whether the particular historical time period or the group of firms selected affects the statistical properties of the data and whether our model fits the data.

The Data

We can imagine our data on the variable p(t) arrayed in a table of columns, one for each year, and 648 rows, one for each firm. We want to know whether: (a) the data fits our model; (b) the ensemble is in a steady state; (c) the firms are homogeneous with respect to their statistical properties. (d) We also want to compare the sequential dispersion of earnings changes of firms across time with the dispersion across firms (Figures 4 and 3, below). The answers to these interrelated questions will strongly affect how we should best handle the data for practical purposes.

The model does fit the data. The evidence is given in Table 1 and Figure 1. The model says that when the ratio, p, is negative or low in one year, it has a higher probability of rising the next year, and vice versa. The proportion of decreases rises as you move from left to right, from 20 percent to 64 percent for all firms in the aggregate. The same pattern is true of every year, giving good evidence in support of the model.

The same results are portrayed in Figure 1. If there were no relation between the level of p and the future probability of a rise or fall in p, then the dots in the figure would form a horizontal line. The dots are not horizontal, however; they descend

Figure 1

The Deviation $k(p-p_{00})[\Delta p^*]$ In Step Probability $(1/2+k(p-p_{00})[\Delta p^*])$ From 1/2, (Equation 1, $X \rightarrow p$), vs p = Annual Earnings/Assets ($\times 100$)
$k(p-p_{00})[\Delta p^*]$

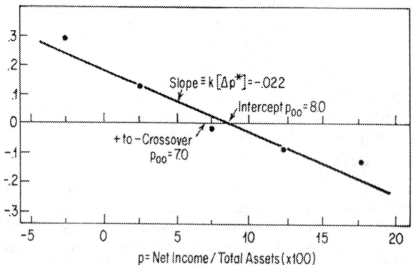

p= Net Income / Total Assets (x100)
Data Plotted At Median Of Class Intervals, From Table 1, Bottom Line

168

Table 1
Net Income/Total Assets in Year t, pt, and Probability of Decrease in Net Income/Total Assets Between Year t and Year t+1,
$$\Delta p = (p_{t+1} - p_t) < 0$$

Net Income/Total Assets in Year t (p_t x 100)

From	-5.0	0.0	5.0	10.0	15.0
To	0.0	4.9	9.9	14.9	20.0
Year					
1975	0:24	0.21	0.36	0.53	0.65
1974	0.31	0.44	0.58	0.72	0.76
1973	0:19	0.43	0.56	0.80	0.73
1972	0.14	0.22	0.39	0.58	0.38
1971	0.13	0.18	0.31	0.41	0.57
1970	0.12	0.40	0.51	0.67	0.53
1969	0.40	0.67	0.75	0.81	0.77
1968	0.20	0.51	0.68	0.72	0.74
1967	0.21	0.44	0.64	0.64	0.37
1966	0.56	0.56	0.74	0.77	0.66
1965	0.11	0.35	0.43	0.54	0.65
1964*	0.18	0.26	0.31	0.39	0.39
1963	0.09	0.17	0.27	0.25	0.50
1962	0.13	0.34	0.47	0.52	0.63
1961	0.12	0.38	0.47	0.45	0.64
1960	0.23	0.44	0.59	0.62	0.64
1959	0.31	0.60	0.67	0.77	0.71
Average	0.20	0.38	0.52	0.61	0.64
Increases:	301	2443	2360	550	150
Decreases:	76	1482	2553	824	268

Total increases: 5813   Total decreases: 5203

*A chi-square test (4 degrees of freedom) shows that for the year 1964 the increase of probability of decrease with increasing p, is not significant at the 5 percent level.

Table 2
Diffusion, s $\Delta p(k)$, Across Firms as a Function of the Differencing Interval, k

Number of Firms and Industry	1959-1976 Time Forward		1976-1959 Time Backward	
	RMS	SISR	RMS	SISR
12 Banks	.08 k$^{.32}$	.06 k$^{.38}$	.25 k$^{.13}$	.08 k$^{.37}$
14 Airlines	4.36 k$^{.28}$	4.05 k$^{.03}$	1.89 k$^{.31}$	2.27 k$^{.15}$
22 Petroleum	.97 k$^{.38}$	.74 k$^{.50}$	1.33 k$^{.28}$	1.29 k$^{.32}$
42 Retail	.97 k$^{.52}$	.90 k$^{.43}$	4.44 k$^{.12}$	1.21 k$^{.35}$
53 Chemical & Drug	2.06 k$^{.35}$	1.34 k$^{.40}$	1.53 k$^{.48}$	1.62 k$^{.41}$
113 Electric Utility	28 k$^{.45}$	.21 k$^{.50}$	.69 k$^{.15}$	.59 k$^{.16}$
648 Industrials	2.62 k$^{.25}$	1.54 k$^{.32}$	3.76 k$^{.15}$	1.89 k$^{.25}$

RMS is the root-mean-square estimate of the standard deviation. SISR is the semi-intersextile-range estimate of the standard deviation. All of the equations are significant at the 5 percent level except the SISR equations for the fourteen airlines.

to the right revealing the relationship hypothesized by the model. There are noticeable, not dramatic, but consistent departures from a straight line. From the intercept and slope of this line one can determine two relations on the three parameters of the model of equations (1) and (2): k, p_{oo} and the step length Δp^* (p replacing x). Figure 2, bottom, estimates the step length as $s_{\Delta p(k=1\ year)}$. Note that equation 5 for the autoregressive model also had just three parameters: α, f, and d.

The statistical properties of the data are not stationary. They have a tendency to change from period to period. The evidence is given in Figure 2 which records for 648 firms the mean value of p, the standard deviation of p, and the standard deviation of the annual change in p for each year 1960-1976. If these statistical measures were stationary, if the particular year had no effect, then the points would be roughly the same each year. Overall, nearly one-third of the year to year changes in the fifty-one different statistical measures were significant at the 5 percent level, or considerably more than might be expected by chance. The economy does affect all firms, as a common element, so the 648 firms are not statistically independent [3]. In much the same way the "market variable" has a common effect on the prices of common stock [19].

We can understand these results in terms of our model by imagining that if a pretty girl walks by the valley tavern, the crowd of barflies lurches to the right or left, and a systematic shift will occur in the cross-sectional mean p_f. If a fight breaks out, or conversely if the normal disorder is quelled by the arrival of a police car, the standard deviation of p or Δp will change from one year to the next.

Figures 3a, 3b, and 3 c, and the summary of those figures given in Table 2 also tell whether the data is homogeneous across firms, stationary across time, normally distributed, and characterized by a rise in dispersion characteristic of simple random walk. The underlying data used in constructing Figure 3a, 3b, and 3c is the change in p (net income/total assets) between two columns of firms for time intervals of increasing

171

Figure 2

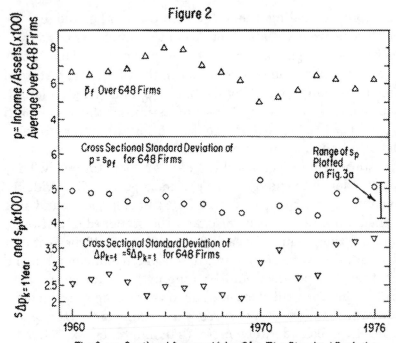

The Cross Sectional Average Value Of p, The Standard Deviation Of p, And Of $\Delta p_{k=1}$ For 648 Firms, As A Function Of Time

Figure 3a

Cross Sectional Dispersion Of $\Delta p(\tau)$ For Increasing Difference Interval τ

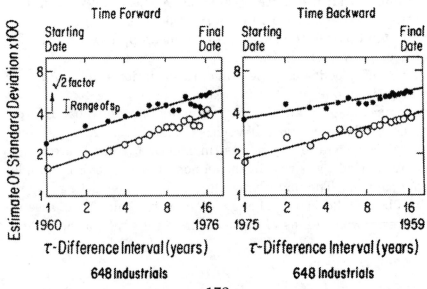

Figure 3b

Cross Sectional Dispersion Of Δp(τ) For Increasing Difference Interval τ

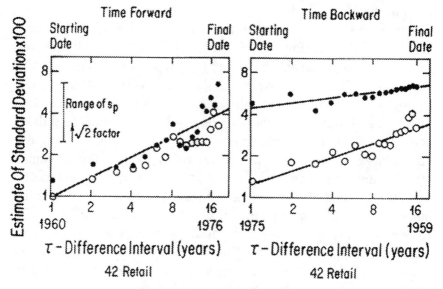

42 Retail   42 Retail

Figure 3c

Cross Sectional Dispersion Of Δp(τ) For Increasing Difference Interval τ

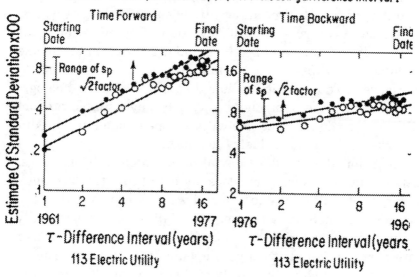

113 Electric Utility   113 Electric Utility

○ Semi-Intersextile Range
● s (Root Mean Square σ)

length, 1, 2, 3,...16 years. The standard deviation of the change in p across firms is computed from that data for each different time interval.

For a homogeneous population and a simple random walk, the standard deviation will rise with the square root of the time interval giving a straight line with a slope of one-half and the same slope for all industries. If the data were stationary, the slopes would be the same whether measured backward or forward. The slopes are generally not one-half, the standard deviation varies from one industry to the next, and the results measured forward and backward differ considerably. The evidence clearly demonstrates non-stationary and nonhomogeneity. Finally, the distributions are not normal, but have fat tails, since the standard deviation is larger than the semi-intersextile range, as may be seen by comparing the two measures in Figures 3a, 3b, 3c. Precisely the same conclusions we obtained from Figure 3 may be drawn from Table 2 where we show the parameters of straight lines fitted to each set of data.

To measure the sequential dispersion and how fast it rises as we expand the time differencing interval, we calculated the standard deviation of changes in earnings/assets for each of several different length time intervals: 1 year, 2 years,...,6 years. We give the average standard deviation of changes for firms classified by industry and by the standard deviation of the one year differencing interval and summarize the results in Table 3 and Figure 4. Those exhibits show that the data is not homogeneous and the process may not be described by a simple random walk since the dots do not rise with a slope of one-half and differ markedly from one industry to another.

In addition the standard deviation of changes in earnings/assets computed across firms does not equal the standard deviation computed across time. Overall we may conclude that the population is neither homogeneous (all drunkards equally drunk), time independent (in a steady state of drunkenness, or "stationary"), nor statistically independent (no common source of disturbance, such as the pretty girl walking by). Yet the standard deviations computed in the two ways (cross-sectional and sequential) are of the same order of magnitude, a result we have no conceptual reason to expect (see [19]).

Other Results

Table 3
The Rate of Diffusion, $s_{\Delta p(k)}$, of the Individual Firm as a Function of the Differencing Interval, k, as Shown by Industry Averages and Firms Grouped by Standard Deviation of Δp

Industry	Firms	Rate of (Sequential) Diffusion of $s_{\Delta p(k)}$	One-year (Sequential) Standard Deviation of Individual Firm Group Range	Firms	Rate of (Sequential) Diffusion of $s_{\Delta p(k)}$
Airlines	14	$2.9\ k^{.50}$	0.0-0.9	95	$.7\ k^{.48}$
Food, Beverage & Tobacco	105	$2.4\ k^{.33}$	1.0-1.9	280	$1.5\ k^{.34}$
Chemical & Drug	53	$1.6\ k^{.45}$	2.0-2.9	142	$2.4\ k^{.36}$
Retail	44	$1.8\ k^{.15}$	3.0-3.9	67	$3.4\ k^{.22}$
All Firms	648	$2.2\ k^{.28}$	4.0-4.9*	19	$4.9\ k^{.01}$
			5.0-5.9	15	$5.3\ k^{.30}$
			6.0-6.9	11	$6.0\ k^{.29}$

The nineteen firms with one-year standard deviations over 7.0 are excluded, except in the total for all firms.
*Regression equation not significant at the 5 percent level of significance.

Figure 4

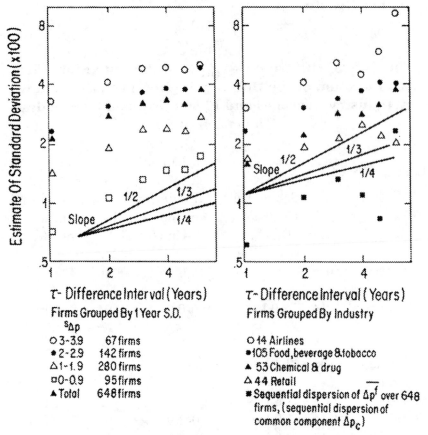

Sequential Dispersion Of Δp (τ) For Increasing Difference
Interval τ Measured By The Mean S.D. (R.M.S.σ) For Groups Of Firms

There is a property of Tables 2 and 3 which requires explanation. Practically all of the exponents are less than 0.5. The figure 0.5 is the simple random walk value, corresponding to a slope of 0.5 in Figures 3 and 4. This corresponds to a drunkard's walk on a flat surface of zero slope, or one with a constant non-zero slope (corresponding to a constant non-zero advance for the random walk). For our model of increasing slope with distance from the tavern, the standard deviation of differences approaches a constant value with increasing time interval of differencing in accordance with a formula [22, 28] of the type,

const. $(1-e^{-\beta\tau})^{1/2}$

where β is a constant. ($\beta=4kD$ in our notation). This increases like the square root of time for small intervals of time, since $1-e^{-\beta\tau}\approx\beta t$. But for large values of the time interval, it approaches a constant. Figure 5 shows this. The standard deviation increases approximately with the cube root of time for intervals of one to sixteen years. The standard deviation

Figure 5

$(1-e^{-\beta\tau})^{1/2}$ As A Function Of Time Interval
β Taken As 1/6.7 Years^{-1}

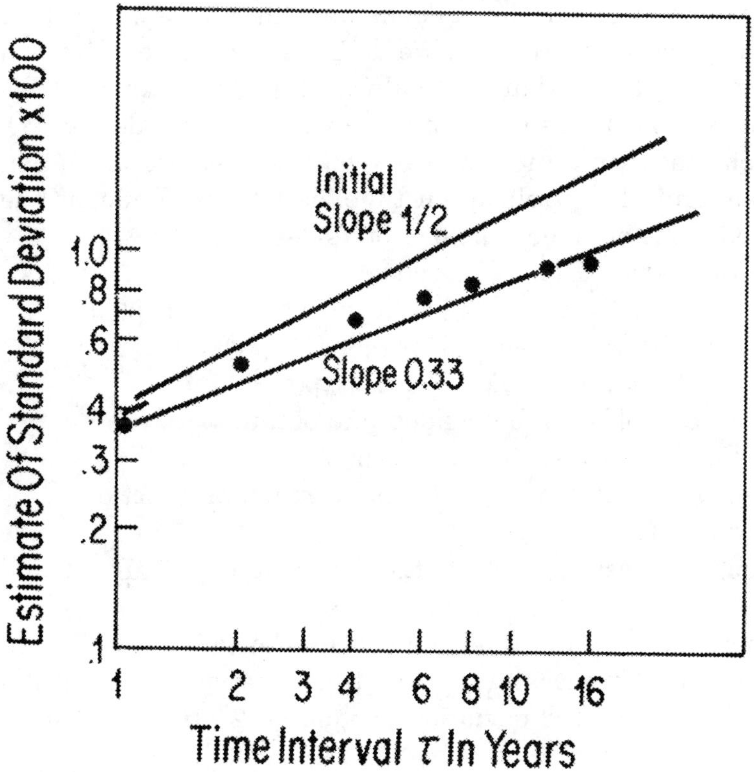

Initial Slope 1/2

Slope 0.33

Estimate Of Standard Deviation x100

Time Interval τ In Years

increases with the cube root of time because the slopes of the line of circles are approximately one-third in Figures 3 and 4 and the exponents of the regression lines, fitted to the data in Tables 2 and 3, also average 0.33.

The time interval $1/\beta=6.7$ years, taken from Figure 5, is called the relaxation time, or time interval for the variance of differences to approach to an e^{-1} approximation of its final or stationary value for very long differencing intervals. It also happens to the mean of interval for (exponential) reversion to the mean of a given initial value of the variable p = income/assets. This phenomenon has been observed in accounting studies [2] of this variable, using the autoregressive model mentioned earlier. Note the comments following equation 3.

We can evaluate this time interval in a different way, using the plots of Figure 3, but without having to make the specific assumptions of either the random walk in a valley, or a first order autoregressive scheme. We do have to assume there is a stationary state so that the values of p are bounded (this assumption is not true for a simple, unrestricted random walk).

Given that assumption, we can evaluate the autocorrelation function, and also a relaxation time, as follows. E means the expected value of an ensemble of p(t)'s.

$$E[\Delta_k p(t)]^2 = E[p(t + k) - p(t)]^2$$
$$= E[p(t + k)]^2 - 2E[p(t)p(t + k)] + E[p(t)]^2$$

By stationarity $E[p(t+ k)]^2 = E[p(t)]^2$, $E[\Delta_k p(t)] = 0$

$$E[p(t + k)p(t)] = E\ p(t)^2 - 1/2 E[\Delta_k p(t)]^2$$

Subtract $[E\ p(t)]^2$ from both sides, and obtain

$$Cov[k\ p(t)] = Var\ p - 1/2 E[\Delta_k p(t)]^2$$

Dividing by $Var[p(t)]$, we get the autocorrelation function

$$r(k) = 1 - (1/2)s^2{}_{\Delta p(k)}/s_p{}^2 \tag{8}$$

replacing E by estimates from the data given in Figures 2 and 3.

Equation (8) means that one can extrapolate the standard deviation of differences $s_{\Delta p(k)}$ to a time interval such that the extrapolated standard deviation is equal to $2^{.5}$ times the standard deviation of the variable p itself, s_p. For such intervals the autocorrelation function is zero; the random function has 'relaxed' or regressed to a steady state of independent (uncorrelated) values. The implied assumption here is that the autocorrelation function remains zero or near zero for still larger time difference values. This is true for overdamped oscillators, and in general for random series that do not have strong periodic components.

We have marked on Figure 3 the range of standard deviation for the p variable itself, and also an arrow of length the square root of two, to indicate how much the standard deviation of p should be raised before making this extrapolation. It will seem that a range from six to ten years approximates this relaxation time to equilibrium. This is also the time interval in the accounting studies for reversion of p to the mean. Since we are extrapolating on log paper, this means we are actually using a power law for this 'straight line' extrapolation. Such a determination of relaxation time is not intended to be a precise evaluation.

Summary and Conclusion

We have shown that the variable, p = annual earnings/total assets of a corporation, can be described by a statistical model (the tavern in a valley) only slightly more complicated than a simple random walk of zero expected advance, such as is used to describe stock prices. For intervals of a year, the probabilities provided by these two models are slightly, but significantly, different. The tavern in a valley model shows an appreciable, but not enormous, amount of non stationarity (i.e. different in different years) and inhomogeneity (different industries are appreciably different in their statistical properties). The principal statistic studied is the standard deviation of differences of p as dependent on the time interval of differencing. This statistic can also be used to estimate a relaxation time to statistical equilibrium for the variable p of the order of six to ten years. This corresponds approximately to the time for reversion of p to the mean of p, which has been described in other accounting studies.

The results of this paper may be applied to modify the model described earlier in [16] for evaluating the probability of future profit or loss of the individual firm. This article shows that the simple random walk model is applicable, but that it should be modified slightly by the level of the ratio p=earnings/assets (tavern in the valley model), the industry (differences in the rate of rise in the standard deviation with time), and, to a degree, the particular period.

The model can be applied by lenders, investors, or financial officers for estimating the probability that the individual firm will be profitable or unprofitable in the future [18]. It can be used to rank firms, to compare firms within the same industry, or firms from different industries, regardless of firm size or the nature of the underlying business.

References

[1] Ball, R., and R. Watts. "Some Time Series Properties of Accounting Income." *Journal of Finance* 27 June 1972):663-81.

[2] Brooks, L. D., and D. A. Buckmaster. "Further Evidence of the Time Series Properties of Accounting Income." *Journal of Finance* 31, no. 5 (December 1976):1359-73.

[3] Brown, P., and R. Ball. "Some Preliminary Findings on the Association Between the Earnings of a Firm, its Industry and the Economy." *Empirical Research in Accounting: Selected Studies*, Supplement to *Journal of Accounting Research*, 5 (1967):55-77.

[4] Chandrasekhar, S. "Stochastic Problems in Physics and Astronomy." *Reviews of Modern Physics* 15, no. 1 January 1943:1-89. (Also in [28].)

[5] Chant, P. D. "On the Predictability of Corporate Earnings Per Share Behavior."*Journal of Finance,* 35, no. 1 (March

1980):13-21.

[6] Cootner, P. H. "Stock Prices: Random vs Systematic Changes." *Industrial Management Review* 3, no. 2 (Spring 1962):24-45. In Cootner, P. H. (ed.) The Random Character of Stock Market Prices 231-53, Cambridge, Mass: MIT Press, 1964.

[7] Doob, J. L. *Stochastic Processes*. New York: Wiley, 1953.

[8] Foster, G. "Quarterly Accounting Data: Time Series Properties and Predictive-Ability Results." *The Accounting Review,* LII, no. 1 January 1977):1-21.

[9] Feller, W. *Introduction to Probability Theory and Its Applications* Vol. 1, 2nd ed., New York: Wiley, 1957.

[10] Gonedes, N. J., and H. V. Roberts. "Statistical Analysis of Random Walks and Near Random Walks." Report 7606, Center for Mathematical Studies in Business and Economics, University of Chicago, 1976.

[11] Granger, W. J., and O. Morgenstern. *Predictability of Stock Market Prices.* Lexington, MA: D. C. Heath & Co., 1970.

[12] Griffin, P. A. "The Time-Series Behavior of Quarterly Earnings, Preliminary Evidence." *Journal of Accounting Research* 15 (Spring 1977):71-83.

[13] Kac, M. "Random Walk and the Theory of Brownian Motion." *American Mathematical Monthly* 54, no. 7 (July 1947):396-89. (Also in [28].)

[14] Lintner, J., and R. Glauber. "Higgledly Piggledy Growth in America." Seminar on Analysis of Security Prices, Center for Research in Security Prices, Graduate School of Business, University of Chicago, May 11-12, 1967.

[15] Ming, Chen Wang, and G. E. Uhlenbeck. "On the Theory of the Brownian Motion II." *Reviews of Modern Physics* 17, nos. 2 & 3 (April, July 1945):323-42. (Also in [28].)

[16] Murphy, J. E., and M. F. M. Osborne. "Games of Chance and the Probability of Corporate Profit or Loss." *Financial Management* (Summer 1979):82-89.

[17] Murphy, J. E., and J. F. Nelson. "Random and Nonrandom Relationships Among Financial Variables: A Financial Model."

Journal of Financial and Quantitative Analysis 6, no. 2 (March 1971):875-85.

[18] Northwestern National Bank of Minneapolis. *P/L Forecasts*. Various editions.

[19] Osborne, M. F. M. "Brownian Motion in the Stock Market." *Operations Research* 7 (March/April 1959):145-73. (Also in Cootner, see [6].)

[20] _____ "Periodic Structure in the Brownian Motion of Stock Prices." *Operations Research* 10 (May-June 1962):345-79. (Also in Cootner, see [6].)

[21]_____ *The Stock Market and Finance From a Physicist's Viewpoint,* Vol. 1. 1977, Crossgar Press, Minneapolis, 1995.

[22]_____, and J. E. Murphy. "Brownian Motion of Corporate Earnings in a Varying Probability Field." Paper presented at the Institute For Quantitative Research in Finance, Vail, Colorado, September 1980. Available from the Institute, Columbia University, New York, NY.

[23] Perrin, J. "Brownian Movement." Encyclopedia Brittanica Volume 4, p. 270 (1950) and other editions.

[24] Quenouille, M. H. *The Analysis of Multiple Time-Series* London: Charles Griffin & Co., 1957, see esp. pp. 49, 57, 66.

[25] Rayner, A. C., and I. M. D. Little. *Higgledy, Piggledy Growth Again* Oxford: Basil Blackwell, 1966.

[26] Ruland, W. "On the Choice of Simple Extrapolative Model Forecasts of Annual Earnings." *Financial Management* 9, no. 2 (Summer 1980):30-37.

[27] Uhlenbeck, G. E., and L. S. Ornstein. "On the Theory of the Brownian Motion." *Physical Review* 36, no. 3 (September 1930):823-41. (Also in [28].)

[28] Wa, N. (ed.), *Selected Papers on Noise and Stochastic Processes*. New York, NY: Dover, 1954.

14

PREDICTING THE VOLATILITY OF INTEREST RATES

Joseph E. Murphy & M.F.M. Osborne

The purpose of this article is to examine the dispersion of changes in interest rates and to derive the law, or equation, that best describes it.

We define dispersion as the variability (standard deviation) of changes, or the degree of non-uniformity of changes. It is the most pronounced and observable characteristic of changes in interest rates. It is what makes the direction and magnitude of changes in interest rates so difficult to predict.

The equation that we will derive has important implications and uses. It demonstrates that the dispersion of changes in yields is determined by time and maturity. It reveals that changes in yields may be described by a "random walk," a major mathematical model of the physical and social sciences.

The investor can use this model to calculate the distribution of probable changes in yields between now and next year, for example, or for any future time interval. The calculation can be made for any prevailing yield level. The equation holds whether yields today are 5% or 15%, and you can use it for any maturity bond. Since yields can be converted to prices, you can estimate the distribution of changes in bond prices and then estimate the probable distribution of changes in bond returns.

Coverage, Sources, and Definitions

Past measurements of standard deviations of changes in yields have generally been restricted to a single length interval, normally a year, and to a single maturity.[1] In this article, we examine the standard deviation of a number of different length time intervals, ranging from one month to five years. We also examine dispersion for different maturity bonds.

Our measure of interest rates is the yield to maturity of a bond yield index. The yield to maturity takes account of the current price, the coupon, the value of the bond at maturity, and how long you wait until each payment in received. Yield is calculated in the same way as interest on a savings account. We use the natural logarithms of the yields instead of the yields themselves, thereby eliminating the effect of prevailing yield levels on changes in yields.

The two yield indexes we use are the Durand corporate index and the Salomon government index. The first gives annual yields from 1900 to 1965. The second provides monthly yields from 1950 to 1980. Each of these indexes had bonds ranging from one-year maturity to 20- to 30-year maturity. The two series are the most comprehensive set of data available for this kind of study.[2]

Our objective is to examine the relationship between the dispersion, or standard deviation, of changes in yields and time (the difference interval), maturity, and type of bond (government or corporate). We define the change in yield over the difference interval k as $\Delta\log_e y = \log_e y_t - \log_e y_{t-k}$.

This gives us the difference in the logarithm of yields over the difference interval k, which may be in months, quarters, years, or decades. We call this a change in yields over a particular difference interval. After we have created a times series of differences for a particular interval, such as a month, we compute the standard deviation of differences of the logs.

We will show that two factors determine the dispersion of changes in yields: 1) the maturity of the bonds and 2) the time interval, or the length of the period over which the change is measured. We will demonstrate that the equation that describes the relation has the following form:

$$\text{standard deviation } (\Delta\text{Log}_e \text{ (yield)})$$
$$= c \text{ (time interval)}^a/(\text{maturity})^b$$

The equation states that the standard deviation of changes in yields increases with time and decreases with maturity. Changes in interest rates are more variable over long periods than short periods. They are more variable for short maturity bonds than for long maturity bonds. The precise coefficients of the equation (the constant c and the exponents a and b) are important, since they tell us much about the relationship and may permit us to estimate future dispersion. The coefficients are estimated from each set of yield data.

The paper is divided into three parts. First, we describe the model, method, and data. Then we derive the general equation, demonstrating the effect on the dispersion of changes in yields of time and maturity for corporate and government bonds. Finally, we summarize the results and suggest the implications.

Model, Method, and Data

The following discussion gives the intuitive basis for our model. It is analogous to the model developed for the stock market.

We know that there is a large and competing market for bonds where bids and offers are made, where buying and selling "money" (of various maturities) occurs, and that "money's" value is measured by "yield." Yield as a "price" is the rent on a lease of money to maturity. Of course, the bond trader may deal in bond dollar prices alone.

In other markets, such as the stock market, there is good evidence and argument that equality of risk for buyers and sellers is not measured by absolute change in price $(\pm\Delta p, E\Delta p=0)$, but by equal percentage changes $(\pm\Delta\text{Log}_e p, E\Delta\text{Log}_e p=0)$, where E means the expected value of the probability distribution. Thus, a borrower or lender who faces a going rate of 10% "feels" that $\pm2\%$ in future uncertainty is the same kind of risk as 5% $\pm1\%$ in a different historical period.

There is evidence of the tendency of stock prices to change in equal percentage increments, rather than in equal dollar increments.[3] In consequence, the distribution of log price and Δlog price is more nearly normal than the distribution of price and Δprice. The same pattern appears to hold for yields.

185

Derivation of the General Equation

U.S. Corporate Bonds 1900-1965

Table I gives the standard deviations of logarithms of the Durand U.S. corporate yields for each of seven maturities (m)— 1, 5, 10, 15, 20, 25, and 30 years, and for eight differencing intervals (k)—1, 2, 3, 4, 5, 6, 7, and 8 years. Each column of the table represents a different maturity; the far left column presents a one-year maturity bond and the far right column a 30-year maturity. Each row presents a different differencing interval (k); the top row covers a one-year difference interval and the bottom row treats an eight-year difference interval.

Table I
U.S. Corporate Bonds 1900-1965 Standard Deviation of Changes of Log_e Yield

Difference Interval (years)	Maturity (years)						
	1	5	10	15	20	25	30
1.	25	.13	.09	.08	.07	.06	.06
2	.38	.19	.13	.11	.10	.09	.09
3	.45	.24	.17	.14	.13	.12	.12
4	.52	.28	.20	.17	.15	.14	.14
5	.59	.32	.23	.19	.18	.17	.17
6	.68	.38	.27	.22	.20	.19	.19
7	.77	.43	.30	.25	.23	.22	.21
8	.83	.47	.33	.27	.25	.24	.23

The matrix of standard deviation reveals the high degree of order exhibited by the dispersion of changes in yields. You see the order when you pass your eye across the matrix in different directions. From top to bottom, the standard deviation rises with increasing differencing interval, or time. Across the table, from left to right, dispersion drops as maturity rises. The standard deviation peaks in the lower left corner of the table and descends to its low point in the upper right corner. If we can derive an equation that accurately describes this dispersion change pattern shown in the matrix, we can use that equation to predict future dispersion of interest rates.

We want to examine the effects of time and maturity simultaneously to ascertain their joint effect on the standard deviation of changes in the natural logarithm of yields. On the basis of the data contained in the table of standard deviations, the form of our two-variable equations suggests a relationship such that the lines would approximate a plane if we plotted the matrix of standard deviations on a three dimensional logarithmic grid. We want the equation of this plane, so that we can estimate the standard deviation for any combination of time and maturity. The equation of such a plane has the form:

$$\log_e(\text{standard deviation}) = \log_e c$$
$$+ a(\log_e(\text{difference interval}))$$
$$- b(\log_e(\text{maturity}))$$

When we transform the logarithmic equation we obtain the equation:

$$\text{standard deviation} = c \, (\text{time interval})^a / (\text{maturity})^b$$

The standard deviation is, as before, the standard deviation in changes in the natural logarithm of yields.

Using the logarithmic form of the equation, we applied multiple regression with the standard deviation as the dependent variable, and maturity (m) and the difference interval (k) as the two independent variables. The retulting equation is:

$$\text{standard deviation} = .23 \, (\text{time interval})^{.61}$$
$$/ (\text{maturity})^{.40}$$

This single equation defines the standard deviation in terms of time, the difference interval, and maturity. The standard deviation rises with time and falls as maturity rises.

The equation provides a good explanation of the data, since the correlation is high (r=.99).[4] The estimated standard deviation for a one-year interval and a one-year maturity is s= $.23(1)^{.61}/(1)^{.40}$ or .23. The standard deviation for a five-year interval and a 10-year bond is s=$.23(5)^{.61}/(10)^{.40}$ or .24.

U.S. Government Bonds Yields 1950-1979

Table II gives the standard deviation of the Salomon U.S. Government bond yields for each of six maturities—.25, 1, 2, 5, 10, and 20 years, and for each of five difference intervals (k)— 1, 2, 4, 8, and 16 months. interval (k) as the two independent variables.

Table II
U.S. Government Bonds 1950-1979 Standard Deviation of Changes of Log_e Yield

Difference Interval (months)	Maturity (years)					
	.25	1	2	5	10	20
1	.10	.08	.07	.05	.04	.03
2	.15	.13	.11	.07	.05	.04
4	.22	.20	.16	.11	.07	.06
8	.32	.29	.24	.16	.10	.08
16	.43	.38	.31	.20	.12	.11

The standard deviation for governments are lower than those we saw in the earlier table for U.S. corporate bonds, because the difference interval here is measured in months, not years. You see the same kind of pattern, however. The numbers drop as you move your eye from left to right to longer maturities, and the numbers rise as you move your eye down the table to longer difference intervals. The standard deviation drops with increasing maturity; it rises with greater time intervals.

When we regress the standard deviation against the differencing interval and maturity, the resulting equation is:

$$\text{standard deviation} = .27 \, (\text{time interval})^{.42} / (\text{maturity})^{.35}$$

The standard deviation rises with time and falls with maturity.

The equation explains dispersion well, since the coefficient of multiple correlation is .96. Approximately 93% of the variation in the standard deviation is explained by the equation and the two variables: time and maturity.[5]

The dispersion changes in yields of government bonds resembles the dispersion of corporate bonds. The parameters of the equations that describe that dispersion are similar and the form of the equation is the same.

Two characteristics are surprising. For shorter time intervals, governments exhibit more volatility in changes in log yields than corporates, despite their lower risk. Based on the regression equations for a one-year interval the standard deviation of .27 for U.S. Government bonds is higher than the .23 standard deviation for corporate bonds.

This is not what we would expect, since governments are less risky than corporates. Part of the explanation of this unexpected result is that the government data cover the years 1950-1979, whereas the corporate data are from the period 1900-1965, two quite different eras. The rates of increase in dispersion are also different: .42 for governments and .61 for corporates. The rates of decrease in dispersion with rising maturity are similar, however, .35 vs .40. All this may be seen by comparing the equations.[6]

An Example

Using the above equation to estimate the dispersion of changes in interest rates involves four steps: 1) convert the current yield on the bond in question to natural logarithms; 2) calculate the standard deviation using the equation; 3) adjust the current yield up and down by the standard deviation; and 4) change the result back to the standard terminology of yields by taking antilogs.

Suppose the current yield to maturity on a five-year U.S. Government bond is 10%. We want to know the probable dispersion of changes in yields one year and four months in the future. The computation is as follows.

1. The natural logarithm of 10 (i.e. 10%) is 2.30.

2. The standard deviation for a 5-year maturity (maturity =5) in one year four months (i.e. differencing interval =1.33) is:

$$\text{Standard deviation} = .27 \, \frac{(\text{time interval})^{.42}}{(\text{maturity})^{.35}}$$

$$= .27 \, (1.33/(5)^{.35}$$
$$= .27 \times 1.13/1.76$$
$$= .17.$$

3. We adjust the yield in natural logarithms, or 2.30, by the standard deviation ($\pm.17$). The adjustment gives an upper figure of 2.47 (2.30 + .17) and a lower figure of 2.13 (2.30 - .17), which is the   expected range about 65% of the time. The range will be 1.96 - 2.64 about 95% of the time.

4. The antilogs of the upper and lower figures are 11.8% and 8.4% for 65% of the time and 14.0% and 7.1% for 95% of the time.

Summary and Conclusion

We have measured the dispersion of changes in interest rates by the standard deviation. For interest rates we used the natural logarithm of yields to maturity. We applied the examination to two major bond yield indexes: the Durand corporate indexes 1900-1965 and the Salomon U.S. Government indexes, 1950-1979. We found that the dispersion of changes in yields is determined by two factors: 1) the maturity of the bond and 2) the time interval, or the length of the period over which the change is measured. The equation that describes the relationship has the form:

$$\text{standard deviation } \Delta \text{ Log}_e \text{ (yield)} = c \text{ (time)}^a/\text{(maturity)}^b$$

Our model reveals that the dispersion of changes in yields, measured by the standard deviation, rises with time and declines with maturity. The model can be used to estimate the future dispersion of changes in yields.

Since we measure yields in natural logarithms, the model may be applied irrespective of the current level of yields. It may be used for any maturity within the range of data used, three months to 30 years, and it may by applied to any time period running from one month to five years.

Outside the bounds of our data, however, the model should not be used. Within the bounds of the data, the model provides a description of the dispersion (standard deviation) of changes in interest rates, measured in logs, as a function of time and bond maturity.

Footnotes

1. A partial exception is the examination of the standard deviation of the mean return from bonds over varying holding periods, as in Ibbotson, R. G. and R. A. Sinquefield, *Stocks, Bonds, Bills and Inflation: The Past and the Future*, Charlottesville: The Financial Analysts Research Foundation, 1982.

2. Salomon Brothers, *An Analytical Record of Yields and Yield Spreads*, September 1979, Part 1, U.S. Government Securities 1950-1979.

The Durand series of corporate bond yields 1900-1965 are contained in Malkiel, Burton, *The Term Structure of Interest Rates*, Princeton University Press, Princeton: 1966, Table 1, pp. 6-7.

3. See Osborne, M. F. M., "Brownian Motion in the Stock Market," *Operations Research*, Vol. 7, March-April 1959, pp.

145-173, reprinted in Cootner, P. H., ed., The *Random Character of Stock Market Prices*, MIT Press, Cambridge, Mass.: 1964, pp. 100-128.

4. The coefficient of multiple correlation (r=.99) is high and significant at the .01 level (F=3371); the standard error of estimate is low, .01, as suggested by the high value of r.

5. The coefficient of multiple correlation (r=.96) is significant at the .01 level (F=1121) and the standard error of estimate is .03.

6. Barry and Ayres derive an alternate model describing changes in yields as a function of two random variables, the consol yield, approximated by a 7-year maturity bond, and the difference between the long and short yield. Also, our results differ quantitatively from theirs, in that we find that the standard deviation of differences of yields is not independent of maturity for maturities greater than five years. Barry, J. V. and H. E. Ayres, "A Theory of the U.S. Treasury Market Equilibrium," *Management Science*, Vol. 26, No. 6, June 1980, pp. 539-569. See Osborne, M. F. M. and J. E. Murphy, "Brownian Motion in the Bond Market," presented to the Eastern Finance Association, April 27-30, 1983, New York City.

15

BROWNIAN MOTION IN THE BOND MARKET

Joseph E. Murphy and M.F.M. Osborne

One of the most important elements in the fixed-income futures market is the probability distribution of future bond prices. That distribution is determinable from the distribution of future changes in interest rates. If we can describe the dispersion of changes in future interest rates in terms of the key factors that may affect them, such as maturity and time, or holding period, then we will be in a better position to understand and evaluate fixed-income futures.

The purpose of this article is to examine the effects of holding period, bond maturity, type bond, and historical era on the dispersion of changes in interest rates and to show how the result resembles a form of "Brownian Motion".

We define dispersion as the variability or volatility (standard deviation) of changes. It is the most pronounced and observable characteristic of changes in interest rates. It is what makes changes in interest rates so difficult to predict in direction or magnitude.

I. Sources and Definitions

Past measurements of standard deviations of changes in yields have generally been restricted to a single-length interval, normally a year, and to a single maturity. In this article, we examine the standard deviation of yield changes for a number of different-length time intervals, ranging from one month to five years. We also examine the dispersion for different maturity bonds and different historical periods.

Our measure of interest rates is the yield to maturity of a bond yield index. The yield to maturity takes account of the current price, the coupon, the value of the bond at maturity, and how long one must wait until each payment is received. We use the natural logarithms of the yields instead of the yields themselves, thereby minimizing the effect of prevailing yield levels on changes in yields.

The yield indices we use are the Durand corporate index

(1900-1965), the Macaulay corporate index (1861-1937), the Salomon government index (1950-1979), the Standard & Poor's corporate index (1900-1979), and the British consol yield series (1730-1961). The first and last series are annual, and the others are monthly. The first and fourth indexes are the most comprehensive sets of data available for this kind of study. The British consol is the longest.

Our objective is to examine the relationship between the dispersion, or standard deviation, of changes in the natural logarithms of yields and time (the time interval for the changes of yield), maturity, and type of bond (government or corporate). We define the change in yield over the difference interval k as $\Delta \log_e y_t = \log_e y_t - \log_e y_{\{t-k\}}$, which defines the symbol Δ.

This gives us the difference in the logarithm of yields over the difference interval k, which may be in days, months, or years. We call this a changes in yields over a particular difference interval. After we have created a time series of a particular difference interval, such as a month, we compute the standard deviation (SD) of differences of the logs.

We also compute the semi-intersextile range (SISR) of differences of the logs. The SISR encompasses the middle two thirds of the distribution. For a normal distribution, SISR is very nearly equal to SD (see[18,20,21,22]).

We shall show that two factors determine the dispersion (i.e., SD) of changes in yields: (1) the maturity of the bond, and (2) the time interval, or length of the period over which the change is measured [16]. We shall show that two other factors that influence the dispersion of yields—the historical period and type of bond—are much less important, and that the type of bond is the least important of the four factors. We will demonstrate that the formula that describes the relation has the following form:

standard deviation ($\Delta \log_e$ [yield])

$$= c(\text{time interval})^a / (\text{maturity})^b$$

This formula states that the standard deviation of changes in $\log_e$ yields increases with time interval and decreases with maturity. Changes in $\log_e$ interest rates are more variable over

194

long time intervals than over short intervals. They are more variable for short-maturity bonds than for long-maturity bonds. The precise values of c, a, and b of the formula are important since they tell us much about the relationship and permit us to estimate future dispersion [15]. The parameters c, a, and b are estimated from the Salomon and Durand yield data, using multiple regression. The coefficient c and exponents a and b were estimated by multiple regression from the data; they are shown by the slope and intercept formed by the standard deviations on the figures.

The order of presentation is the following: First, we describe the model, methods, and data. Then, we demonstrate the effect of each of the four factors (time, interval, maturity, historical period, and type bond) on the standard deviation of each series. We evaluate the general formula for the Durand and Salomon yield data.

II. Model

The intuitive basis for our model is the following.

We know that there is a large and competing market for bonds where bids and offers are made, where buying and selling "money" (of various maturities) occurs, and where that "money's" value is measured by "yield." Yield as a "price" is the rent on the lease of money to maturity. Of course, the bond trader may, and usually does, deal in bond dollar prices alone.

In other markets, such as the stock market [17,19], there is good evidence and argument that equality of risk for buyers and sellers is not measured by absolute change in price ($\pm p$, $E \Delta p=0$), but by equal percentage changes ($\pm \Delta \log_e p$, $E \Delta \log_e p=0$), where E means the expected value of the probability distribution. Thus, a borrower or lender who faces a going rate of 10 percent "feels" that a ± 2 percent in future uncertainty is the same kind of risk as 5 percent ± 1 percent in a different historical period.

There is evidence of the tendency of common stock prices to change in equal percentage increments, rather than in equal dollar increments. In consequence, the distribution of time differences of $\log_e$ price is more nearly normal than the distribution of differences of price [17]. Similarly, the distribution of $\log_e$ yield(t+1)/yield(t) is more nearly normal than the distribution of yield(t+1) - yield(t).

In the simplest case of a random walk, the position x(t) at time t can be considered as the cumulated sum of steps x(t)= x(t) - x(t-1), taken one per unit time (second, minute, day, etc.). The probabilities are:

Prob.$((\Delta x(t)) = \nu + \sigma) = 1/2$ (1)

Prob.$((\Delta x(t)) = \nu - \sigma) = 1/2$

The expected value of one step is $E\ x(t)=\nu$ The variance of one step is

$E(\Delta(x(t))^2 - (E\Delta\ x(t))^2 = \sigma^2$. If we take a walk, which starts at time t_0 at the position $x_0 = x(t_0)$, then we imagine the change in position $x(t) - x_0$ after time $(t - t_0)$ can be expressed as,

$$x(t) - x_0 = \nu(t-t_0) \pm \sigma(t-t_0)^{0.5} \tag{2}$$

where the first term is the expected drift displacement due to "velocity" ν, or trend line, whose slope $=\nu$ may be zero, the second is the dispersion or standard deviation of position around the trend line, at position $x = x_0 + \nu(t - t_0)$. All this follows from the assumption that the steps x(t) are taken independently in the probability sense.

Departures from this simple random walk can take several forms. In the general case, one can imagine both ν and σ are nonstationary, yet both finite, both functions of time, with steps independent in a probability sense.

When the SD and SISR are unequal, the distribution is non-normal. The distribution will approach normality as the differencing interval is increased, according to the central limit theorem. When that happens, the SD and SISR will be equal.

The model can be summarized in the following way:

1. The first differences in the logs of interest rates follow a random walk whose successive steps are independent.

2. The probability distribution of expected percentage changes in interest rates themselves is lognormal and different for each maturity. The changes of $\log_e$ yields are normal.

3. The standard deviation of changes in the log of rates is

directly proportional to the square root of the time interval $t\text{-}t_0$ of the changes. This is not an exact statement. It is most nearly true for intervals $t\text{-}t_0$ of less than two years.

$\sigma = \sigma_0(t\text{-}t_0)^{0.5}$, being the value for $(t\text{-}t_0) = 1$

4. The standard deviation of changes in $\log_e$ interest rates decreases with increasing maturity.

A major purpose of the article is to demonstrate the truth of points 3 and 4. Point 3 is extremely important in determining the characteristics of changes in interest rates. But it has not been treated elsewhere insofar as we know, though it is implied in the references mentioned below. We will examine the question here by seeing how the standard deviation (the square root of the variance) changes with increases in the difference interval (time). We examine point 4 in the same way and by multiple regression.

It is useful to relate this model to others.

The model states that interest rates follow Geometric Brownian Motion. This contrasts with Bachelier in 1900 [2,7] who did not make the log transformation. Bachelier stated that the bond price (French *rente*) is a random variable, with price changes independent and identically distributed with a normal density function (Arithmetic Brownian Motion) [7, pp. 47-49]. Because Bachelier dealt with prices of short-term instruments over a short period, he may not have seen the need for the log transformation.

Since the variance of nominal changes in yields is directly related to the level of yields, it is essential to make the log transformation, just as it is with stock prices [17]. We also find evidence that volatility of changes in the logs of yields does vary between historical eras.

A number of authors have suggested or stated that changes in yields are a random walk, white noise, a stochastic process, or a variant thereof. Examples of this view appear in the work of Barry and Ayres [1], Bachelier (prices, not yields) [2], Brick and Thompson [4], Brown and Dybvig [5], Cargill and Meyer [6], Fand [8], Granger and Rees [9], Hamburger and Latta [10], Hause [11], Marsh and Rosenfeld [13], Phillips and Pippenger

[24], Pippenger [25], Roll [26], Smith [27], and others. Brick and Thompson, based on cross-correlation of two different maturities for various lags, conclude that first differences yield are random, white noise. Fand, on the basis of analysis of autoregression, stated that "knowledge of past behavior of short-term rates does not help to make better predictions of long-term rates" [8, p. 367]. Phillips and Pippenger conclude there is considerable "empirical evidence indicating that interest rates follow a random walk" [24, p. 11]. Others disagree [28, 29] and still others point out the scarcity of "empirical studies on the stochastic characteristics of interest rates" [13, p. 648].

III. Data

The examination of the dispersion of yields over time requires constant maturity yield indexes. The Durand corporate yield index covers seven maturities (m)— 1,5,10,15,20,25, and 30 years. The Salomon U.S. government yield indexes cover six maturities from 1950—1/4,1,2,5,10, and 20 years. The Macaulay and Standard & Poor's indexes are high-grade corporate yield indexes. The British consols are the actual yields of perpetuities.

IV. Method

We computed the standard deviations of changes in the natural logarithms of yields for various time intervals. In supplementary tables, not shown here, we computed the standard deviations and semi-intersextile ranges using both overlapping and nonoverlapping difference intervals.

For the figures, we used overlapping data which smooth the plots somewhat, particularly for the longer time intervals. We plotted these on the log figures shown below. The standard deviation is shown on the y-axis. The difference interval, or time, is shown on the x-axis.

This kind of chart is used so one can see whether s rises with the square root of time. If it does, the dots will lie on the straight line of slope 0.5. A solid line, included on each figure, has a slope of 0.5.

V The Evidence

One can see great similarity among the long maturities—in standard deviations and rate of increase with time. The slope is close to 0.5. This can be seen by comparing the slope of the dots with the slope of the solid line. The similarity exists, despite different types of issues (government and corporate) and different periods. The consols start in 1730, the Macaulay longs begin a century later (1857), and the Standard & Poor's longs not until 1900. Yet the dispersion of changes in long bond $\log_e$ yields is very close.

The standard deviation declines with maturity and rises with time. One can see the effect of maturity by comparing the

Figure 1.   Long maturities: standard deviation of change in Ln yield vs. differencing interval

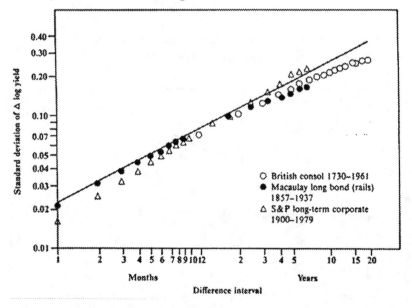

top row with the bottom row. The top is short maturities and the standard deviations are high. The bottom is long and the standard deviations are low.

One can see the effect of the holding period, or time, by looking at the rise in the line of dots. The rise is similar for short, medium, and long maturities. The slopes are roughly in accord with the exponent 0.5 hypothesized. There are departures from a straight line of slope 0.5.

The two different types of issues, corporate and government, are similar in magnitude and rate of rise for issues of similar maturity even though the time periods are different. Clearly, maturity and time intervals of differencing are the most important determinants of the dispersion of changes in interest rates.

The visual evidence of the figures is borne out by multiple-regression equations. The equation that describes the relationship between the standard deviation and time and maturity of the seven Durand corporate maturities 1900-1965 is:

standard deviation (Δ log yield)

= .23 (time interval)$^{.61}$/(maturity)$^{.48}$

Figure 2. Different maturities: standard deviation of change in Ln yield vs. differencing interval

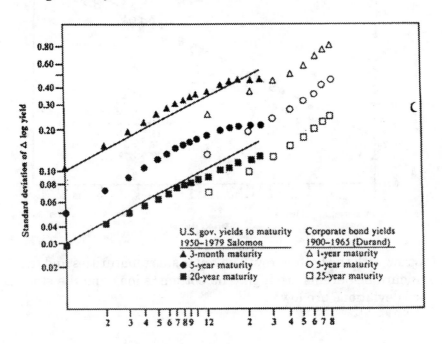

For this equation, the coefficient of multiple correlation (r=.99) is high and significant at the .01 level (F=3371); the standard error of estimate is low, .01. For one-year maturity, the standard deviation of one-year changes is .23 or approximately 26 percent.

The equation that describes the relationship between standard deviation and time and maturity of the six Salomon U.S. government maturities 1950-1979 is:

standard deviation (Δ log yield)

$$= .27 \text{ (difference interval)}^{.44}/\text{(maturity)}^{.34}$$

The coefficient of multiple correlation (r=.94) is significant at the .01 level (F=613) and the standard error of estimate is .02 or about 2 percent when for a one-year bond the standard deviation of one-year changes is .27 or approximately 31 percent. For a ten-year bond, the standard deviation of one-year changes drops to .12 or approximately 13 percent.

For individual yields series, the coefficients of correlation for the fit of SD against t were high. They were 0.9 or higher and significant at the 0.05 level for every series.

From our data, the mean change in $\log_e$ yields was not appreciably different from zero, except for perhaps 1/3 of the indices, and then only barely so.

The next three figures show separate historical periods for the same series and for different series. They present two measures of dispersion for each, the standard deviation (SD) and the semi-intersextile range (SISR).

When the two measures are the same, the distribution is probably normal. When the SISR is lower, the distribution is not normal and has fat tails. When the SISR is lower, it moves up to the values of the SD with increasing time interval, suggesting the effect of the central limit theorem. According to the central limit theorem, every distribution approaches a normal distribution as more and more independent random variables are summed, with finite variances [12], each very small compared to the sum of all of them. Lengthening the difference interval is equivalent to increasing the number of random variables summed.

Figure 3 gives comparative historical data for long bonds: the Macaulay long corporates and the British consol. One can see clearly that the historical periods differ. They differ in both volatility and normality. One can see that the historical period has more influence than the type of bond. Only the Macaulay longs have normal distributions, and then only in the earlier period. One can see the effect of the central limit theorem in the other three parts of the figure as the SISR gradually rises toward the SD. With increasing time interval, the distributions approach the normal.

Figure 4 compares the different historical periods for short bonds: the Macaulay commercial paper. Here the distributions are more normal and very similar in both periods (unlike the longs in Figure 3). There tends to be a flattening off of the rise in the dispersion.

Figure 3. Era comparison (SD vs. SISR): standard deviation of change in Ln yield vs. differencing interval

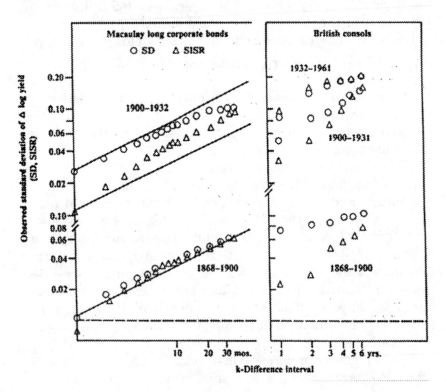

Figure 4. Era comparison (SD vs. SISR): standard deviation of change in Ln yield vs. differencing interval, Macaulay commercial paper

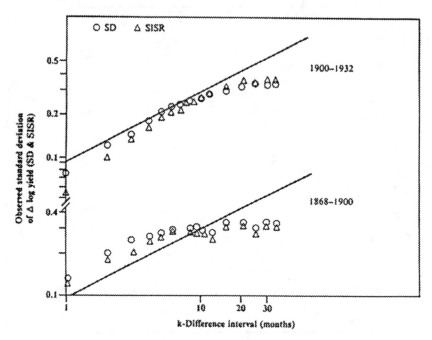

Figure 5 compares different historical periods for long bonds—this time the S&P long corporates. Again, there are slight differences between historical periods, and some difference in volatility, but the move of the SISR is toward the SD in both periods. In the earlier figures, the yields of short maturity bonds are clearly much more volatile than the yields of the longs.

Figures 6 and 7 compare bonds of different types: corporates vs. government, U.S. vs. British. Figure 6 also has different periods. We give only the standard deviation. Note the close similarity of the different types of bonds in the same period. The governments were more volatile than the corporates in the same period (Salomon vs. Durand, 1950—1965).

Figure 8 shows the effect of maturity for different historical eras for different types of securities. Here the difference inter-

Figure 5. Era comparison (SD vs. SISR): standard deviation of change in Ln yield vs. differencing interval, S&P long-term corporate

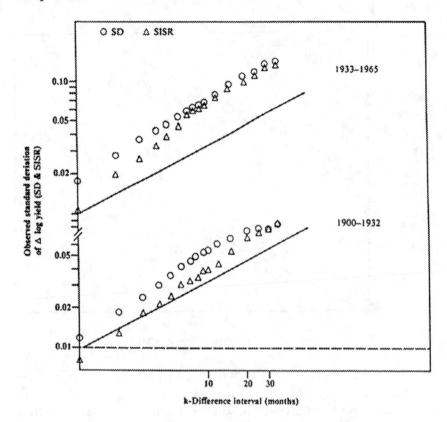

val is not varied; all plots are for a one-year difference interval. As can be seen, volatility (as measured by SD of time differences of $\log_e$ yields) declines with maturity. There are important differences between eras.

The general effect of the increasing maturity is to reduce the standard deviation, an effect already apparent in Figure 2 where we gave the data on the combined effect of time and maturity. On Figure 8, the lines are of negative slope 1/2 and 1/3.

Figure 6. Vehicle comparison: standard deviation of change in Ln yield vs. differencing interval

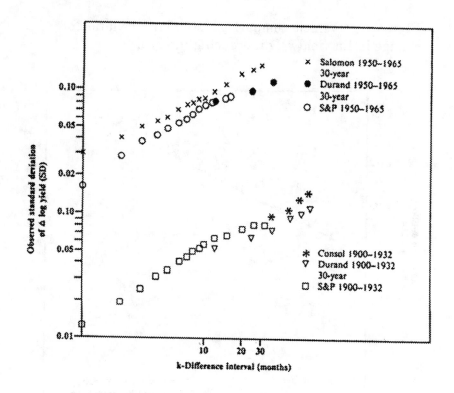

Figure 7. Vehicle comparison: standard deviation of change in Ln yield vs. differencing interval

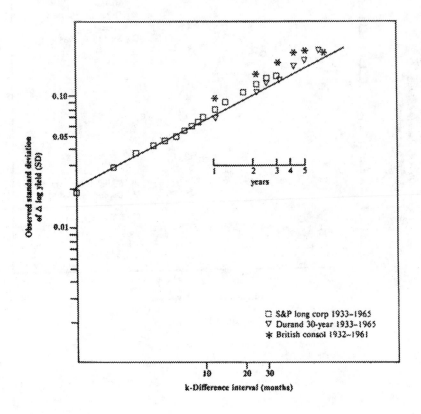

Figure 8. Era comparison (SD vs. SISR): standard deviation of change in Ln yield vs. maturity (1-year difference interval)

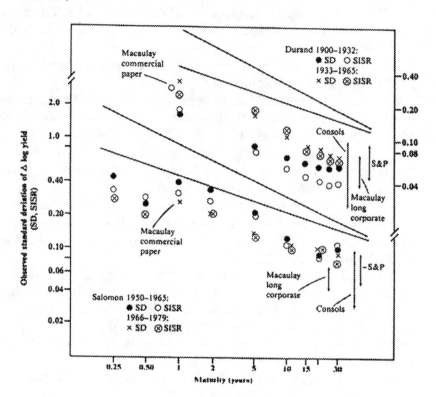

VI. Conclusion

The model developed here reveals that the dispersion of changes in $\log_e$ yields, measured by the standard deviation, rises with time and declines with maturity. The model can be used to estimate the future dispersion of changes in yields [15,16]. Since we measure yields in natural logarithms, the model may be applied irrespective of the current level of yields.

207

References

1 Barry, J.V., and H.E. Ayres. "A Theory of the U.S. Treasury Market Equilibrium." *Management Science* 26(6)(June 1980), pp. 539-69.

2 Bachelier, L., *Theory of Speculation*. Paris: Gauthier-Villers, 1900 (translated in Cootner [6]).

3 Bierwag, G.O., and M.A. Grove. "A Model of the Structure of Prices of Marketable U.S. Treasury Securities." *Journal of Money, Credit, and Banking* (August 1971), pp. 605-29.

4 Brick, John R., and Howard E. Thompson. "Time Series Analysis of Interest Rates: Some Additional Evidence." *Journal of Finance* 33(1)(March 1978), pp. 93-103.

5 Brown, Stephen J., and Philip H. Dybvig."The Empirical Implications of the Cox, Ingersoll, Ross Theory of the Term Structure of Interest Rates." *International Economic Review* 4(13)(June 1972), pp. 223-38.

6 Cargill, Thomas F., and Robert A. Meyer. "A Spectral Approach to Estimating the Distributed Lag Relationship Between Long and Short Term Interest Rates." *International Economic Review* 4(13) (June 1972), pp. 223-38.

7 Cootner, P.H. *The Random Character of Stock Market Prices.* Cambridge, MA: MIT Press, 1964.

8 Fand, Davis I. "A Time-Series Analysis of the `Bills-Only' Theory of Interest Rates." *The Review of Economics and Statistics* 48 (November 1966), pp. 361-71.

9 Granger, C.W.J. and H.J.B. Reesa. "Spectral Analysis of the Term Structure of Interest Rates," *Review of Economics and Statistics* 48 (November 1966), pp. 361-71.

10 Hamburger, Michael J., and Cynthia M. Latta. "The Term Structure of Interest Rates: Some Additional Evidence." *Journal of Money, Credit, and Banking* 1(February 1969), pp. 71-83.

11 Hause, John C. "Spectral Analysis and the Detection of Lead-lag Relations." *American Economic Review* LXI (March

1971), pp. 213-17.

12 Mandelbrot, B. "The Variance of Certain Speculative Prices." *Journal of Business* 36(1963), pp. 395-419. Also in Cootner [6].

13 Marsh, Terry A., and Eric R. Rosenfeld. "Stochastic Process for Interest Rates and Equilibrium Prices." *Journal of Finance* 38(2)(May 1983), pp. 635-50.

14 Modigliani, Franco, and Richard Sutch. "The Term Structure of Interest Rates: A Reexamination of the Evidence." *Journal of Money, Credit, and Banking* 1(February 1969), pp. 112-20.

15 Murphy, J.E. *With Interest: How to Profit from Fluctuations in Interest Rates.* Chicago: Dow Jones-Irwin, 1986.

16 Murphy, J.E., and M.F.M. Osborne. "Predicting the Volatility of Interest Rates." *Journal of Portfolio Management* (Winter 1985), pp. 66-69.

17 Osborne, M.F.M. "Brownian Motion in the Stock Market." *Operations Research* 7(1959), pp. 145-73. Also in Cootner [6].

18 Osborne, M.F.M. "Random Walks in Earnings and Fixed Income Securities." Seminar, Institute for Quantitative Research in Finance, April 1968. Available from the Institute, Columbia University, New York, NY.

19 Osborne, M.F.M. *The Stock Market and Finance from a Physicist's Viewpoint.* 1977, Crossgar Press, Minneapolis, MN 1995.

20 Osborne, M.F.M. & Murphy, J.E. "Brownian Motion of Corporate Earnings in a Varying Probability Field." Seminar, Institute for Quantitative Research in Finance, Fall 1980. Available from the Institute, Columbia University, New York, NY.

21 Osborne, M.F.M. & Murphy, J.E.. "Financial Analogs of Physical Brownian Motion, as Illustrated by Earnings." *The Financial Review* 19(2)(1984), pp. 153-72.

22 Osborne, M.F.M. & Murphy, J.E. "Brownian Motion in the Interest Rate Considered as the Price of Money." Annual Meeting, Eastern Finance Association, April 20-23, 1983, New York, NY.

23 Perrin, J. "Brownian Movement." *Encyclopedia Britannica* Vol. 4(1950), p. 270.

24 Phillips, Llad, and John Pippenger. "Preferred Habitat vs. Efficient Market: A Test of Alternative Hypotheses." *Federal Reserve Bank of St. Louis Review* 58(May 1976), pp. 11-19.

25 Pippenger, John. "A Time-Series Analysis of Post-Accord Interest Rates: A Comment." *Journal of Finance* 29(September 1974), pp. 1320-25.

26 Roll, Richard. *The Behavior of Interest Rates* New York: Basic Books, 1970.

27 Smith, V. Kerry, and Richard G. Marcis. "A Time-Series Analysis of Post-Accord Interest Rates." *Journal of Finance* 27(June 1972), pp. 589-605.

28 Smith, V. Kerry, and Richard G. Marcis. "Post-Accord Interest Rates: A Reply." *Journal of Finance* 29(September 1974), pp. 1326-27.

29 Wood, John A. "The Expectations Hypothesis, the Yield Curve, and Monetary Policy." *Quarterly Journal of Economics* 78(August 1964), pp. 457-70.

Data Sources

1 Durand, David. *Basic Yields of Corporate Bonds, 1900-1942.* National Bureau of Economic Research, Technical Paper 3, New York, NY: 1947.

2 Homer, Sidney. *A History of Interest Rates.* New Brunswick, NJ: Rutgers University Press, 1983.

3 Macaulay, Frederick R. *The Movements of Interest Rates, Bond Yields and Stock Prices in the United States since 1856.* National Bureau of Economic Research, New York, NY: 1938.

4 Malkiel, Burton G. *The Term Structure of Interest Rates.* Princeton, NJ: Princeton University Press, 1966.

5 Salomon Brothers. *An Analytical Record of Yields and Yield Spreads.* New York" 1979, 1986.

6 Standard & Poor's. *Security Price Index Record.* New York.

Commentary

Juan Ketterer Northwestern University

Given my field of research, I will direct my comments to stress the relevancy of the Murphy-Osborne paper from the point of view of theoretical analysis.

The line of research we are engaged in tries to construct theoretical models capable of assessing the relationship between macroeconomic observables and assets' returns. From a general point of view, this class of models should help us understand the determination of the spectrum of returns for the stock market and the yield curve for the bond market. Among their practical applications are capital budgeting, portfolio insurance, performance evaluation, and detection of "micro" arbitrage opportunities. Their impact on market performance can be seen in an increase of market efficiency and market liquidity.

When evaluating a particular theoretical model, we look, among other things, for two types of properties: determinacy and solvability. Determinacy is the characteristic of a model that allows us to go beyond the "general equilibrium" statement that "everything depends on everything"—that is, to establish sharper relationships among exogenous and endogenous variables. On the other hand, solvability is the ability of the model to produce empirically testable implications.

An interesting case of models that is very useful for analyzing the dynamic behavior of capital markets is the continuous-time/continuous-trading type. This class of models is based on the assumption that continuous trading can occur and that agents can instantaneously react to the information flow.

One of the key assumptions in those models refers to the properties of the stochastic process followed by asset prices. Even though the problems can be formulated in a very general fashion, to obtain a certain degree of solvability and determinacy, some restrictions have to be imposed on the price processes. At this point, the Murphy-Osborne study acquires special relevancy. One of the restrictions most commonly imposed on securities prices is that they follow a form of Brownian motion. With this assumption, the modeler can obtain a high degree of solvability in most instances. This is because of the nice mathematical properties of Brownian motion.

The Brownian motion property has been studied with great detail for the stock market. But, as far as I know, the paper presented by Mr. Murphy and Dr. Osborne is one of the first attempts to discern empirically whether the Brownian motion property is found in the bond market as well. In this sense, theorists can learn a great deal from this type of exercise.

Asserting that asset prices follow a Brownian movement implies, in a sense, a form of continuity in the underlying uncertainty. This "smoothness" in the information flow is inherited by the securities prices, giving rise to the Wiener property. However, it is an undeniable fact that sometimes "shock" occur that disrupt the continuous nature of the flow of information. It is not clear from the methodology used in the Murphy-Osborne study how those shocks have been filtered out. I will leave this question open for further consideration.

Thomas M. Kelly, Jr. Barnes & Co.

In these seminars, the academic discussant usually talks about the qualities of the model—whether it's a specific or nonspecific model—or else he criticizes the data source. Then, the industry discussant gets up and says it's all irrelevant anyway because, first, he doesn't understand it and, secondly, it doesn't apply to what industry people do in the real world. So, by and large, the industry discussant is treated with some humorous laughter by the audience but little else than that.

Be that as it may, I think the Murphy-Osborne work is a very interesting study and, as Professor Ketterer said, it's one of the first studies to apply to bond price data the kinds of statistical methods that were applied to stock price data in the late 1950s and early 1960s. You'll notice that there's no Cootner in this area. Some years ago, Professor Cootner did a study of stock prices that basically brought together all of the literature on the randomness of stock prices going back to studies of the Paris

Bourse. We don't have anything like that on bonds.

The other nice thing about the study is that it concerns the three series of numbers that everyone who has worked in this field looks at: the Macaulay studies of corporate bond yields going back to the 1860s, the Macaulay studies of municipal bond yields, and the Salomon Brothers prices. Everyone has access to these numbers and they have been worked and reworked.

A third comment I would like to make is that the logging of price changes makes a great deal of intuitive sense. Take as an example the price movement of a bond at 14 percent versus the price movement of a bond at 7 percent. The 14 percent bond, relatively speaking, will obviously move more.

There are several intuitive points that the paper addresses and seems to improve. First, when we have a period of very high rates, we should have high absolute volatility; but relative volatility during a period of low rates seems to be about the same. Also—and this is something that everyone believes—long rate ought to be less volatile than short rates although long prices, obviously, will be more volatile than short prices. The paper treats this and seems to prove it.

Another point—that corporate bond yields, municipal bond yields, and government bond yields all basically move together—again is very true, although most of the studies about divergences in yields have not been logged. For example, a government bond going from 7 to 14 is like a corporate bond going from 8 to 16. Now, most of the studies have looked at the price change between the governments and corporates and have concluded that the volatility of the corporates has increased when, really, it hasn't at all.

The interesting aspect of all this for a use of futures, bonds, and options is the forecasting ability as implied by Brownian movement given a forward rate or some sort of random process once the spot rate is determined. I'd very much like to see somebody actually take spot rate in 1945 and apply it against something, going out 10 or 20 years. All one has to do is just take any observable rate and see how well it would perform; in other words, from my viewpoint, see if one could make any money off of it.

Again, in an intuitive way of looking at this, when we're pricing options, the option pricing model assumes some sort of distribution of returns. Now, since the paper indicates a normal distribution, this would have some significant impact for the pricing of options, both options on actual securities and, to a slightly lesser extent, options on future. (See, for example, the article by Bookstaber and McDonald{1} and some of the modifications to Black-Scholes.)

To summarize, I think this is a very interesting paper and, perhaps in years ahead, will be regarded like the original paper on Brownian movement in the stock market.

1. Richard M. Bookstaber and James B. McDonald, "A Generalized Options Valuation Model for the Pricing of Bond Options," *Review of Research in Futures Markets* 4(1)(1985), pp. 60-73.

Discussion

Robert Kolb: I have two unresolved questions about the paper. First, it seems the principal measure you looked at it is equivalent to the natural log of yield relative, meaning the natural log of y_t divided by y_{t-1}. In your stock market paper, I know what the economic significance of that is because it is the natural log of the return. My first concern, then, it that I don't see what economic measure is being used. My second concern is that, if the measure that you are using follows Brownian motion, it would seem to imply that bond prices cannot follow Brownian motion. Now, if that supposition is correct, why would stock prices follow Brownian motion but not bond prices?

M. F. M. Osborne: Let's put it this way. You buy stock with dollars and you buy money by paying "rent". The interest is really the price on the money that you rented. Instead of buying stock and getting dividends, you buy bonds and get interest. That's a simplified approach to it—the interest is the price.

Now, concerning the other point—that if the yields follows Brownian motion, the price should not—that statement is strictly correct. But, in practice, it is not correct for short intervals. The reason is the relationship between yield and price. For short intervals of time, you can make a Taylor expansion and then the yield is a linear function of the price, or the price is a linear function of the yield. In that case, if one variable is going to be normal, so also will the other. So, price will also follow Brownian motion up to intervals of about a year or two, which they do. In fact, this was discovered by Bachelier, but he only went up to 45 days. He actually examined the Brownian motion of French bonds, and the same would be true in this country, too, but only up to about a year. So, if the log yields follow Brownian motion, then the yields themselves will, too, for a short interval around the starting yield. And the same will also be true for prices, again, up to about a year or two. All three will be normal, approximately. That's why I hammered on that word in the beginning.

Robert Savit: I don't quite understand something about the philosophical approach. You showed evidence that over some time interval these quantities appear to exhibit Brownian motion in the sense that certain tests are consistent with what you would get from Brownian motion. On the other hand, you also stated that for very short time intervals, the dynamics are apparently not random. Would you be content to say that your conclusions are that this randomness or Brownian motion is descriptive over some intermediate time intervals but that one should not necessarily deduce from that that the underlying dynamics are completely random?

M. F. M. Osborne: I would accept that. Certainly it is true in the stock market that, because people are trading trade-to-trade, the price bounces between the bid and the ask. So, if it bounces up to the bid, the next nonzero price will be three-to-one down. So that's certainly not random. We have not examined between-trade data in the bond market, but I would suspect the same kind of thing will be true. So that's the lower limit of time interval—between trades, maybe even between three or four trades. And there is another nonrandom effect in the stock market, which I suspect is true in the bonds, and that is the "stickiness" of the whole numbers. Prices tend to stick at $2, $3, $4, $5, $6, or $51, $52, $53, and they also bounce a little bit. I suspect that happens with bond prices, but I don't know. So, that is one lower limit and one departure from randomness.

The other one I mentioned is that at 10 years stocks change their identity. It's like Brownian motion in a chemically reacting system where particles are created and annihilated and changing. So, there is an upper limit in years. For New York Stock Exchange stocks, it was about 20 or 30 years, about 5 or 6 years for OTC stocks, and about 8 to 10 years for Amex stocks. After that amount of time, the identity of the particle—the stock—becomes fuzzy. It's no longer the same beast.

Dan Pieptea: I see that you find a linear relationship between the time intervals that you have used and the standard deviation of the variation of the log of the yields, and it also appears that, as you consider longer time intervals, you obtain some deviations from this linear relationship. I would like to suggest an explanation for this. It could be that there is a drift to this diffusion process and it probably is a mean reverting diffusion process as Cox, Ingersoll, and Ross suggest. As you look at longer time periods, the interest rates will have to fluctuate within a boundary, and they will not move like the stocks—up and up and up. Rather, they will have to drift backward. In the long run, this could possibly explain the deviation from the linear relationship that you observed for the short time periods.

M. F. M. Osborne: I think that is quite reasonable. For the infinite maturity of the bonds or the British consols, you could observe the square root of time diffusion with just a little bit of falling off after several years. But for a commercial paper, it leveled off in about a year. So, it makes sense that there really is an upper limit and a lower limit. We did not look for it, but I would not be at all surprised if it is there.

John Marshall: In the paper, you look explicitly at the relationship between yields and maturity. You don't seem to address the question of the coupon or the coupon frequency. I was somewhat surprised that you didn't also consider duration and the relationship between yield changes and duration, given that duration is a more precise explanation than maturity alone for yield at any given point in time.

M. F. M. Osborne: Well, I paint with a broad brush and hew with a dull axe. There is a formula that will give you the yield to maturity if you are given the coupon, and the indices that we worked with were derived using the formula. The coupon doesn't cut too much ice, and, sometimes, as I think Macaulay pointed out in his work, the same issuer is issuing the same bond with the same coupon, but one was payable in New York and the other was payable in London in gold, and the process would be different on those bonds because of where they were paid and despite the fact that the coupons and the maturities were exactly the same. Well, this is simply smoothed out in the statistical effect. As for your inquiry about duration, frankly, we simply didn't look at it.

Joseph Murphy: We didn't have any good data for duration. That's very hard to get.

Paul Fackler: In your last slide, it seemed that you had price volatility at long forecast horizons decreasing. I found that somewhat curious. Also, you seemed to indicate that at different periods there were different volatility regimes. I think you tried to address this by reestimating using different periods. But the implications of that forecasting is quite serious. If we use the whole 20th century as we know it so far to estimate the linear relationships that you were estimating, we are not necessarily going to obtain good forecasts for today.

M. F. M. Osborne: I think the question is, how good is good enough? We admit that one era is statistically different from another era, and this really upsets a basic concept of statistics—that you are sampling something uniform. We used different eras show that statistically they are different. If it's serious, well, I agree.

Joseph Murphy: On the first question, the bond matures; so, at that point, the volatility of the price returns to zero. That's why, as was shown in my presentation, the volatility decreases. There are several effects. One is that, as the bond gets shorter, it moves in toward the value at maturity.

Paul Farris: Going back to the academic reviewer's comments about shocks, can you say if these short-term movements that are incorporated in the data? Would you care to comment on the effects of rather substantial shocks or structural changes that might occur?

M. F. M. Osborne: I admit there are shocks. There was a dreadful one October 19 in the stock market and it hit the bond market too. Again, this is an imperfection of the basic assumptions that one can do statistics. If there are going to be these sudden jerks, we just have to admit that the fundamental basis of statistics is good most of the time but not all of the time. That's what it amounts to. I can't insist that I'm doing perfect statistics when I can clearly see that the environment has changed. The fact is that shocks do mess up statistically. In a more minor sense, different eras are different too. We can't jump from one era to the next in one day like we did a month ago, but we can jump quite a bit in a year. In other words, the shock is somewhat softened. It is not a hammer blow but a hammer blow with a pillow to cushion it for a period of time.

Joseph Murphy: We also looked at the standard deviation of the British consol series over separate 10-year periods. During most of that time, the standard deviation is within certain bounds. There are one or two decades, however, where it jumps, and that is where it corresponds to the shock effect.

16

COMPUTER GENERATED NARRATIVE DESCRIPTION

An important part of human discourse is the use of language to describe phenomena, the noninteractive construction of sentences to convey to others meaningful statements about the external world. Those sentences are conditioned partly by language itself, partly by the phenomena which is being described.

It is fully possible that part of these descriptive activities, the construction of sentences to picture observable phenomena, could be performed by machine. It is quite conceivable that these descriptions could be as accurate, varied, grammatical and elegant as those composed by individuals. It is possible that machine generated descriptions might provide social utility at economically justifiable costs, either by replacing at less effort activities now done by individuals or by providing new services not presently practicable or available. The provision of machine generated descriptions might also, as a corollary, provide insight into the nature of our language, thought and minds.

Computers are now used for descriptive activities, providing unique descriptions to unique phenomena. Label addressing is such an activity, one previously restricted to humans who alone could write and relate the document to be mailed to the address in hand. Form letters, composed of standard sentences with words inserted or form paragraphs or even sentences are also descriptive composition activities performed by computers. Experimental conversational and interrogatory programs also produce descriptive sentences, replicating in effect the human generation of descriptive statements. Yet, in the main, computers remain numerical machines devoted overwhelmingly to the processing and production of quantitative data. Most of human communication in non-numeric. Therefore, the potentially most promising and undeveloped field for computers is in the processing of language. In this field noninteractive verbal description and/or narrative probably holds the greatest and easiest potential since it is probably most amenable to solution.

Reprinted from ACM '75 *Proceedings of the Annual Conference.* Ed. J.D. White. 1975. The Association for Computing Machinery, New York, N.Y. 29-31.

The most useful machines which man has developed to replace his own effort have been those which have achieved superiority in specific functions by relinquishing general capabilities, as in the wheel, the axe, the steam turbine. By restriction they surpassed man in their functions. It seems reasonable then that computer programs designed to generate sentences will be successful if they are restricted to descriptions of limited types of phenomena. By this restriction computer capabilities in limited areas may exceed those of man, not only in economy but also in descriptive capability.

It is not easy to discern what particular subjects would be most suitable for computer generated descriptions. It occurred to me that my own field, financial analysis, was unusually appropriate for type of application. It was appropriate for several reasons. First, a great deal of human effort is expended on the verbal description of financial statements by a variety of financial institutions, from banks to brokerage house, to lawyers, by government agencies and by the news media. Second, there are a large number of firms which produce and report financial data, over 5,000 publicly owned corporations and a much large number of private corporation. Third, most of the reporting firms record and report the data in relatively uniform format. Fourth, the data of all major firms is available on magnetic tape. Consequently a program which could describe in verbal form the financial data of a single firm could be used without change on thousands of firms using commercially available financial data tapes.

The process of verbal description may be defined as the selection of strings of words in which the words match phenomena and the arrangement of words is in accord with conventional rules of grammar and style. Although we are not sure how complex this process is, or exactly how we do it, it may be a fairly simple process.

The description of corporate income and balance sheet data is restricted to a limited domain of external data and to a formal and restricted vocabulary. The vocabulary has precisely defined names, or subjects, and a limited number of verbs, adjectives and adverbs. These characteristics make it relatively easy to design a program which encompasses most or all possible variations of descriptive statements and which meets the normal conventions of communication on the subject. Because financial description is quite limited in form and content, the process of replicating this activity may make it easier to understand how we as individuals construct sentences.

In most investment reports prepared by banks, brokerage house, etc. financial descriptions form part of a longer report, occasionally interwoven with other descriptive material but often contained in separate paragraphs or standing alone. The form of description is conventional. Normally, sales or revenues are described first, then operating income, pretax income, possibly pretax margins, finally net income and per share earnings. Each of these items has a unique name. For each of these variables the number of possible predicates is limited and the same set of predicates is used for every variable. Sales, for example, may be described as at or reaching a given value for a given time, as rising or falling to a given value from a former value, or as rising or falling a given percentage or dollar amount between two periods. If the periods are quite separate the rise or fall may have been consistent, or interrupted. Precisely the same predicates and predicate modifiers, and those alone, which are used for sales are also balance sheet items. The actual values which appear as adverbs or as participle modifiers are unique to each firm and period. Thus the domain of verbal descriptions which are used in word strings with specific financial names, such as "sales" is common to and may be used with all income and balance sheet names and all firms and periods. The value of any item, the amount of sales of IBM in 1975, is unique to each firm and each period. The verbs are most general, the specific financial names are more specific and the actual values are unique.

The activity of composing descriptive statements is simply a matter of placing in a string in conventional order the financial name, one of several alternative but equally appropriate verbs plus the unique value of the items for the time and firm in question. For example, we can say sales rose (advanced, climbed, increased, moved up, etc.) from $600 million in 1973 to $620 in 1974. The verb rose may be replaced by any of several alternative verbs, such as advanced. The financial name "sales" in this case may be net income in another case, but the balance of the sentence, apart from the dollar figures and the dates, must be in this or a very similar form.

In composing descriptions the writer generally uses the above format, or some variations of it, examines the data, decides whether sales have risen or fallen, adds the appropriate verb to sales, inserts other modifiers, the amounts and the dates. He uses a similar procedure for the descriptive statements he applies to the remaining income statement or balance sheet items be chooses to include in the description. Normally he will vary the verbs, the modifiers, and generally the sentence structure so as to provide a total description which has reasonable variety and style. Frequently, particularly if new at the task, the writer will compose an original draft in which some verbs or adjectives or sentence structures may be repeated. He then simply alters, the original, switching one word for another of similar meaning, or altering sentence structure. Having prepared many of these descriptions and read many more, I believe I am accurately describing the process, or at least one example of its practice.

The program which was developed to prepare narrative descriptions of corporate income and balance sheet data was designed to accomplish several things. It should describe them accurately. It should use appropriate sentences for each variable and it should characterize changes correctly. It should use varied sentence structure and wording so as not to be repetitive either in form or vocabulary. It should be complete, providing a descriptive statement for every important change. And, finally it should furnish descriptive reasons or causal statements on important changes in significant variables such as net income. the last capability, if possessed by a writer, takes considerable training to acquire and requires careful examination of the data and a number of computations. It could be built into the program without difficulty. The only requirement of the program was that the data be in standard format and that the date and identity of each item be available.

The program operates with and on six files, a company data file, a vocabulary file, a sentence structure file, a duplicate sentence structure file, a duplicate word file, and a sentence selector file.

Each word in the vocabulary has an assigned identification number. Each data element in the company file, such as sales, is converted to a alphanumeric number (A Format) from the original decimal or integer form and each computed number, such as the percent change in sales, is converted to an alphanumeric. Each of these is often assigned an unused unique identification number and added up to the vocabulary file. The last activity occurs while the program is in execution.

The program is controlled by the sentence selector file which determines what financial items will be described, what years of data will be used, and what sentences will be selected. The sentences are simply strings of number representing words and codes for operations. The operation codes determine whether a number is to be converted into alphanumeric representation, a computation made or one of several words of different meaning to be chosen. When a sentence has been processed, the stored output is simply a string of numbers. After all sentences have been processed, the complete stored output is a much larger string of numbers. The entire operation so far, is very similar to that used by a writer except that instead of a draft containing strings of words, the draft contains strings of numbers. The numbers are then examined and alternate numbers are inserted to vary words of similar meaning.

The variation uses each equivalent only once and then randomizes the alternate words before repeating the variation. The variation in sentence structure was done earlier during the program. The result, at this point is a string of numbers each of which corresponds with a single word in the program vocabulary. The next step is to replace the numbers with the corresponding words and print the results.

To enlarge the program it is only necessary to add additional sentence generators to the sentence file and/or new words to the vocabulary. To alter the general format of the composition, one need only change the sentence selection file. These files stand as independent entities and may be changed without changing the program.

Every description is unique insofar as the data is unique. Several descriptions of the same data for the same firm ran in succession will also differ from each other since the program varies both wording and sentence structure. The following is an example of the report for General Mills for the year that ended May 31, 1974.

Exhibit I

Between 1972 and 1973 net sales increased sharply to $11774.0 million from $9759.0 million. During the same period pretax margins declined from 4.1 to 3.7. Reflecting a 20.6 percent increase in net sales and a - 9.5 percent decline in pretax margins pretax income advanced to $449.0 million compared with $407.0 million in the earlier interval. Net income rose 15.9 percent to $255.0 million from $220.0 million. On the basis of higher sales/shares, lower pretax margins and slightly increased tax retention earnings/share increased to $4.68 from $4.20.

Between 1968 and 1973 net sales increased to $11774.0 million against $7444.0 million in the prior period. In the corresponding interval pretax margins fell substantially from 8.1 to 3.7. In response to a 58.1 percent advance in net sales and a -53.6 percent fall in pretax margins pretax income dropped -26.6 percent to $449.0 million from $612.0 million. Net income fell to $255.0 million compared with $291.0 million in the previous period. In view of significantly rising sales/share, sharply decreased pretax margins and higher tax retention earnings/share declined substantially from $6.18 to $4.68.

Net sales rose in three years and dropped in two years. The maximum rise was 22 percent while the highest drop was -5 percent. Pretax margins advanced in two years and declined in three years. The greatest climb was 133 percent whereas the largest decrease was -70 percent. Earnings/share increased in three years and fell in two years. The greatest increase was 156 percent and the highest decline was -70 percent.

Between 1968 and 1973 net sales rose significantly to $11774.0 million from $7445.0 million. The advance in net sales reflected substantially increased average equity capital, somewhat rising total leverage, sharply increased average assets and higher asset turnover. Total leverage increased 4.7 percent to 2.21 from 2.11. Asset turnover advanced to 2.02 from 1.79. Average equity capital increased to $2608.0 million against $1951.0 million in the preceding interval.

Between 1968 and 1973 net return on equity dropped significantly from 14.8 to 9.7. The fall in net return on equity was caused by rising asset turnover, substantially falling pretax margins, slightly higher total leverage and increased tax retention.

Acknowledgment

The early research was supported in part by a grant from the Ford Foundation.

References

Chomsky, Noam, *Syntactic Structures,* Mouton, The Hague, 1969.

Goldman, Neil M. (1975), "Sentence Paraphrasing From a Conceptual Base," *CACM*, 18,2, pp. 97-106.

Simmons, R. F. (1970), "Natural Language Question Answering Systems 1969," CACM, 13, pp. 13-50.

Weisenbaum, J. (1966), "Eliza - A Computer Program for the

Study of Natural Language Communications Between Man and Machine," *CACM*, 9, pp. 36-45.

Winograd, Terry, "Understanding Natural Language," *Cognitive Psychology* , Volume 3, Number 1, January, 1972.

17

Financial Ratios, Discriminant Analysis and the Prediction of the Odds of Corporate Deficit

In recent years considerable research has been devoted to the use of financial ratios and discriminant analysis in the prediction of corporate bankruptcy. This work produced discriminant-ratio models which proved to be extremely accurate in predicting bankruptcy correctly. Despite the importance of the question of profit or loss of the individual industrial firm, little work has been done on the use of ratio analysis, discriminant analysis, or other procedures in predicting corporate deficits. It is quite conceivable that the techniques used in predicting corporate bankruptcy can also be applied to the prediction of operating profits or losses.

The purpose of this paper is to attempt to assess the issue of the use of ratio analysis as an analytic technique in the prediction of corporate deficits. A set of financial ratios is investigated in the context of prediction of corporate profits and losses, utilizing both multiple discriminant statistical methodology and frequency analysis. The results are converted to estimates of the relative probability of profit or loss. The data is limited to that of industrial corporations.

In Section I of the paper a review of the significance and incidence of corporate profits and losses is made. In Section II relevant studies in related areas are discussed. Section III consists of an examination and discussion of the sample used in making the study and the techniques employed. Section IV reviews the empirical results obtained from the initial sample and presents the results of actual published predictions made on the original study. Section V discusses the applicability of the model of practical decision making situations and explores the potential benefits in various areas of financing. The final section summarizes the findings and conclusions of the study and attempts to assess their role and significance.

I. The Significance of Corporate Losses

The profitability of the individual firm is of importance from

Unpublished manuscript 1972

a number of standpoints. Financial analysts, common stock and bond investment managers, and corporate officers and directors are all interested in the question of whether or not the firms with which they are concerned will be profitable or unprofitable in the future. The decision to purchase or hold a debt or equity security, the question of acquiring or not acquiring another firm, the decision to lend or not to lend, all hinge in important measure on an estimate of the future profitability of the firm in question. Profits, particularly continued profits, are essential to the maintenance of common dividends and to the repayment of the interest and principal of loans. Net losses have been determined to be one of the major explanatory variables in the prediction of corporate bankruptcy or failure.{1} The results of a study of corporate bankruptcy indicated that the mean profits of the bankrupt group were negative as measured by earnings before interest and taxes to total assets. Non-bankrupt firms, on the other hand, reported substantial positive profits. In the same study, an examination of 66 firms which reported deficits in two out of three years in the period 1958 to 1961, 14% of the firms ultimately became bankrupt. While negative net income in a single year may be a temporary phenomena, continued deficits generally result in the deterioration of the firm and in the likelihood of discontinuance. The results of this study indicate that losses in a particular year are extremely good measures or predictors of losses in future years.

In the context of this paper, losses or deficits are defined as negative net income excluding non-recurring items. Excluded from the definition of operating deficits are write-offs of good will, realized capital gains or losses from discontinued businesses, etc. The frequency of losses among large industrial corporation has varied. Among the sample of major industrial firms used in this study the percentage experiencing deficits in the period 1955 through 1970 ranged from a high of 6.4% in 1971 to a low of 1.0% in 1955.{2} The incidence of deficits, while much higher among small firms and among newly organized firms, pervades the entire scene of American industry. In the last few years the heavy incidence of operating losses among the airlines, the failure of W. T. Grant, the earlier discontinuance as a profitable private operating company of the Penn Central, are illustrative examples of major corporation which can experience continuing losses and ultimate discontinuance.

The frequency of losses is also a function of the economic cycle. When business activity is rising and sales are increasing and gross national product is expanding, the relative incidence of losses among major corporations declines. In periods of recession and declining economic activity, the percentage of firms experiencing losses tends to rise.

II. Relation to Other Studies

Although the author is not aware of any other studies which attempt to predict future profit or loss of individual corporations, a number of studies have been conducted in related areas, specifically the prediction of corporate failure or discontinuance, the prediction of loan quality and experience and the use and prediction of credit ratios. Extremely useful studies on prediction of firm failure were done in the 1930's by Merwin.{3} These studies utilized financial rations to distinguish firms which would fail from firms which would not and reported discrimination among failed and unfailed firms for as many as five years in advance of failure. The work of Merwin was expanded upon in the 1960's by Beaver, using ratios as the basis of discrimination.{4} The results of Beaver's work corroborated that of Merwin. Subsequently, Altman made extensive studies of failure among industrial and then railroad firms, using techniques of discriminant analysis.{5} Other unpublished work using discriminant analysis in the prediction of corporate bankruptcy has been done.{6} In all of these studies, financial ratios proved successful in one degree or another in forecasting future failure.

All of the studies used, for the most part, ratios. The ratios which proved to have forecasting ability consisted both of credit, liquidity and insolvency ratios and of profitability ratios. Among the most useful ratios were the relationship between cash flow and debt, between working capital and total assets, and net income to total assets. Altman was the first to attempt to use discriminant analysis in the prediction of corporate failure. In so doing, he was able to determine the relative importance of each variable to the ultimate prediction and to weight that variable according to its proportional significance. All of the studies are common with respect to their attempt to forecast a two state result, with failure or non-failure. While the results of discriminant analysis procedures used in this study also derive a prediction of deficit or non-deficit the initial work and the final test derive estimates of the relative probability of deficit. The latter prediction, while it has the disadvantage of being less concrete, may provide an easier tool in the decision making process.

The final part of this study also differs in the point of view from which it examines the evidence. In Merwin's work on failure and in the use of discriminant analysis in bankruptcy, firms are classified into one of two categories, failed or non-failed. The ratios of each group are then examined in terms of their mean and the standard deviation of the mean. In this study, the initial work was based on categorization of firms by ratio and then the relative frequency of deficit within various levels of a given ratio was examined. This approach permitted derivation of relative frequency and the development of relative probabilities of deficit. In a sense, this approach is analogous to the various categories of credit rating used by the standard credit rating services, except that those services do not attach any specific incidence of a future occurrence to rating categories.

III. The Sample

The sample is based on the Compustat 900 primary industrial tape published by a subsidiary of McGraw-Hill, Inc. It contains most of the 900 largest industrial firms in the areas of manufacturing, distribution and transport. These industries include all of the major firms in the oil, chemical, drug, retail, steel, machinery and other related industries. The tape also includes certain finance and utility companies which were excluded for the purpose of this study. The advantage of this sample is that it covers the predominant share in terms of sales, employees and investment of U.S. industry. As a result, it comprises the bulk of the publicly held equity capital, a majority of publicly issued debt instruments, and perhaps the major share of bank credit. Because large firms are less subject to failure and bankruptcy, the sample contains a smaller share of potential instances of failure.

The sample was used in its entirety and not broken down by industry. This procedure is contrary to that used in most other studies and has the disadvantage that it excludes whatever influence the industry may have on the nature of particular variables. Individual profitability and credit ratios differ significantly from one industry to another and the frequency of profit or loss differs substantially among industries. Consequently the study may have dropped from use as a result of non-discriminating ability, certain ratios which on an individual industry basis might possess predictive power. The ratios that were ultimately selected based on their ability to distinguish between deficit and non-deficit firms, on the other hand, have broader applicability in potential decision making activities.

In order to derive relative probability of profit or loss, it is beneficial to have a large sample. This consideration led to use of all of the data that was available and roughly comparable on the Compustat tape. The results do not apply, as indicated by subsequent investigation, to firms in entirely different areas of activity, such as utility and finance. They do apply to some capital intensive industries such as air transport. Certain of the ratios developed from and applicable to the broad cross-section of industries are somewhat less applicable to individual industries. For example, pre-tax margins, which prove to be a useful variable, tend to indicate higher odds of deficit for retail companies and other distribution companies where margins are low, than is in fact the case.

The study restricts the date used in the calculation of a ratio to the single year preceding the profit or loss. Careful consideration was given to use of the most recent data. From the standpoint of ultimate usage, a single year's data is more efficient in that less data is required. In many instances recent data is most reliable from the standpoint of accuracy, as in the case of new security offerings where the latest fiscal results may be the only audited data. Use of a single year's data also made it possible to use a larger sample without overlapping figures, which again facilitated the derivation of frequencies or probabilities. Average figures over a longer period could be more reflective of the future, though several studies suggest that the best estimate of next year's data is the current evidence.{7}

Furthermore, the results of this study indicate that the predictive power of ratios decline as the period of forecast lengthens. From this fact one may infer that the most recent data provides greater predictive power than past data. Though trends in individual series such as earnings on equity may be valuable, an examination of the usefulness of changes in ratios suggested that they are not useful in predicting future profit or loss. The variability of any given figure might add significant additional information, though this question was not examined in this paper.

A total of 16 separate periods were used in making the investigation which resulted in the derivation of ratios for use in predicting future deficits. these periods span the years 1956 through 1971, inclusive. Over these years a variety of economic changes occurred, including war, recession and expansion. The frequency of deficits varied during this period, although in every year at least some major corporation experienced deficits.

Careful consideration was given to the various kinds of information which might be used in forecasting future deficits. The variables considered included ratios, size variables, industry variables, change variables and trends, current variables, past average ratios, and the variability of ratios and trends. The results of work on bankruptcy suggested that ratio variables might be the most useful predictors that could be used in arriving at forecasts of future of profit or loss. The initial variables tested consisted of 45 different ratios, which included measures of liquidity, solvency, capital adequacy, profitability and coverage. The use of ratios had the advantage of reducing the effects of scale, which were particularly prevalent in the sample used which contained firms ranging in size with revenues in excess

232

of $20 million to several hundred million. The ratios included in the original examination contained most of those used in the preceding studies on failure.

The ratios can be divided into three categories: those consisting solely of balance sheet items, those combining income statement data with balance sheet data and those restricted entirely to income statement data. The balance sheet ratios examined included those which measured liquidity, debt to equity, working capital, etc. Balance sheet ratios are commonly used in loan and credit analysis, and have proved to be extremely useful in the prediction of corporate failure. It was quite surprising, therefore, that none of the ratios composed solely of balance sheet information proved to have any univariate discriminatory ability in predicting future profit and loss. The question of failure, however, is quite different from that of profit or loss, particularly since the existence of assets which are available to pay interest or principal or maintain survival of the firm do have an effect on failure rates but may not bear any necessary relation to profitability. The only ratios which did possess significant discriminatory abilities were those which included income statement items, particularly those which contained elements directly related to net profits, the quantity to forecast. Of the 45 variables studied, only 10 proved to have significant univariate discriminatory capacity. These variables were the following:

1. Capital Expenditure Coverage. This is defined as depreciation plus earnings available for common stock less common dividends paid divided by capital expenditures. In a sense, this is a measure of coverage, the capacity to pay for future needed capital. The ratio's significance may have been a direct result of the fact that it includes earnings.

2. Cash Flow/Total Assets. This variable, which is defined as earnings available for common stock plus depreciation divided by total assets, was found to have predictability in studies of corporate failure. In a sense, it measures the total amount of cash generated and scales that value to total assets. On a univariate basis, this measure has significant discriminating ability.

3. Interest Coverage. Interest coverage is defined as fixed charges plus income taxes plus preferred dividends plus earnings available for common divided by fixed charges. It is a traditional credit ratio and proved to be significant in this particular study.

4. Operating Margin. Operating margin is defined as operating income before depreciation divided by net sales.

5. Pre-tax Margin. Pre-tax margin is defined as income taxes plus preferred dividends plus earnings available for common stock divided by net sales.

6. Net Margin. This variable is defined as preferred dividends plus earnings available for common stock divided by net sales.

Operating margins, pre-tax margins, and net margins all reflect the same general characteristics. They measure the profitability of the firm's volume, e.g. the productivity of sales. To an extent, they discriminate against those industries where margins are predominantly low, such as the distribution industry, particularly retail and wholesale trade.

7. Return on Equity. Return on equity is defined as earnings available for common stock divided by common stock and surplus, including intangibles. This basic measure records the profitability of the corporation to its common stock shareholders. It is the ultimate measure of profit or loss scaled by the equity capital. From the standpoint of predicting future net income profit or loss, however, it may underestimate the safety margin of current profits among those firms where the equity capital is very small in relation to total assets. As a univariate measure, it proved to have less significance in predicting future profit or loss than either net income to total assets or cash flow to total assets.

8. Return on Total Capital. This variable is defined as earnings available for common plus preferred dividends plus fixed charges divided by common stock and surplus plus preferred dividends and long term debt. This stands as the ultimate measure of the overall profitability of the firm. It is a common measure in the industry and proved to be useful in predicting future profit or loss.

9. Cash Flow to Total Debt. The ratio defined as net income

plus depreciation divided by long term plus short term debt. On a univariate basis, it proved to be one of the most discriminating variables, although less discriminating than the following variable.

10. Net Income to Total Assets. Defined as net income before payment of preferred dividends divided by total assets, this ratio proved to be the most predictive on a univariate basis. The numerator represents the ultimate variable to be predicted, or net profit or loss. The denominator takes into account not only the capital position but also the effect of long and short term debt, reducing the effect of differing capital structures. The final discriminant function was based solely on this ratio. This ratio and cash flow to total debt were found by Beaver and Merwin to be useful predictors of failure.

IV. Empirical Results

The Initial Discriminant Function

The initial discriminant analysis was performed on a sample of 965 firms, of which 218 reported deficits and 747 reported profits. The deficit firms were drawn from the Compustat tape for the period 1962 through 1971, inclusive. The profitable firms were those contained on the tape in 1971. To test the individual discriminating ability of the variable, an F test was performed as part of the discriminant analysis. This test related the difference between the average values of the ratios in each group to the variability of values of the ratios within each group. The variables were computed one financial statement prior to the experience of a deficit or profit. The F statistics, together with the means for each variable for each group are presented in Table 1. The means for the two coverage figures, capital expenditure coverage and interest coverage, are shown as normally used in financial reporting, although for the discriminant analysis the inverse of the traditional ratios were used. The inverse was used for the coverage ratios to avoid the very high values which sometime occur.

As can be seen in Table 1, nine of the ten ratios were significant at the .001 level and the tenth ratio was significant at the .05 level. Therefore, all variables indicated significant differences between groups on a univariate basis. Individually, each of the ten variables showed a significantly higher ratio for non-deficit firms than for the deficit firms. It is noteworthy that only one variable in this sample record a negative figure for the deficit group. As can be seen from the F ratios, the variable which possessed the greatest discriminatory ability alone without other variables was net income to total assets. Only slightly lower F ratios were exhibited by the ratio of cash flow to total assets and the return on total capital. Interest coverage showed the least discriminatory ability by itself with an F ratio of only 5.7.

The final discriminant function utilized nine of the ten variables. The variable excluded was pretax margin, despite the fact that it had an F ratio 140.6, the fourth highest F ratio of all ten variables. Generally speaking, when there is a high correlation between two variables, as there is between pretax and after-tax margins, little additional information is provided by one of those two variables. Negative correlations are generally more helpful than positive correlations in adding new information to the function.

A test to evaluate the overall discriminating power of the model is the F-value which is the ratio of a sum-of-squares between-groups to the within-groups sums-of-square. This test is appropriate because one of the purposes of multiple discriminant analysis is to utilize those variables which provide the best discrimination between groups and which are most similar within groups. The approximate F value of the nine variable functions was 27.48, which was significant at the .001 level. This significance test rejects the null hypothesis that the observations come from that same population. One must conclude that the a priori groups are significant.

Having made the estimation of the discriminant coefficients, discriminant scores were calculated for each observation to assign the observations to one on the two groups. In this procedure the profile of an individual firm was compared to that of the alternative groupings and then the firm was assigned to the group it most resembled. Comparisons were measured by use of a chi-square value and the firm was assigned to one of the two groups based on the closeness of the firm's score to the various group centroids. The results are presented according to the classification chart shown in Table 2.

The model attempted to classify firms according to a priori groupings based on the original discriminant function. Although the model was basically explanatory at this point, when new companies were classified, the nature of the model became predictive. The c's stand for correct classification and the e's stand for incorrect classifications. Symbol e_1, represents a Type 1 error and e_2 a Type 2 error. The sum of the diagonal elements equal the total number of correct classifications, which when divided by the total number of firms classified gives the percentage of firms which were correctly classified.

Based on the initial model which resulted from the above discriminatory function, the sample was examined, using the data one financial statement prior to profit or loss. A high degree of successful classification was expected since the group distributions and the discriminant coefficients were derived from the sample itself. The classification matrix of the initial sample is shown in Table 3.

Since the incidence of loss is relatively small among industrial corporations of the size considered here, a high proportion of correct predictions will be achieved if one simply predicts that all firms will be profitable. This prediction applied to the sample shown on Table 3 would have been 77% correct since 77% of the firms in that sample were profitable in 1971. This percentage compares with the model's accuracy classification of 77%, the same accuracy on an overall basis.{8} The overall statistics, however, do not provide a reliable indication of the discriminatory ability of the model. While the model on an overall basis was only 77% accurate, it correctly identified 73% of the firms which actually went bankrupt, a type 1 error of 27%. And it correctly identified 78% of the firms which proved to be profitable, a Type 2 error of 22%.

In the investment or lending decision, one normally selects the investment or loan, a sub-set of the total population. Therefore, if one can segregate the total population into separate risk categories in terms of future profit or loss, one has a useful device for decision making. The results of the discriminant function can be looked at from the following point of view. The actual loss among firms predicted to be profitable was 9.0%. This compares with an actual loss among all firms in the population of 22.6%. The critical question then becomes, was the instance of loss among firms predicted to have future losses significantly greater than the instance of losses among firms predicted to be profitable. One may compare these percentages, 49.4% for those predicted to have losses against 9.0% for those predicted to be profitable and may test the statistical significance of the difference between the two ratios. An appropriate test to use is the t test which may be applied when frequencies are low or the proportion in one category is extremely small. The appropriate t test is show in Table 3 and results in a value of 14.2 which is significant at the .001 level.{9} Application of the chi-square test to the data show in Table 2 also produces a statistic which is significant at the .001 level. One might conclude as a result of these tests that the model has significant discriminatory ability.

Derivation of a One Variable Discriminant Function

In view of the high F ratio, 201.3, for the ratio of net income to total assets, it was decided to derive a discriminant function for this variable alone. The sample chosen for this test was the single period 1970-1971. The importance of having functions which are generally independent of time or the time period chosen cannot be overemphasized, since descriptive equations or predictive equations which are time dependent will inevitably have questionable predictability. The sample chosen consisted of 839 companies. The ratios computed for 1970 data and the profits or deficits of the sample were computed for the subsequent year 1971. Of the total sample, 774 experienced profits in 1970 and 65 incurred deficits. The function resulted in an F ratio of 99.57, which is significant at the .001 level and which reveals significant discriminatory capacity of the function. The mean value of the ratio for the deficit groups was minus 0.6%, while the mean value of the non-deficit group was 5.5%. The standard deviation of the former group was 6.5% and that of the latter group was 4.6%. The equation for the discriminant score is as follows:

$p = e^x / (e^x + e^y)$
where e = 2.718
x= -.009 -2.844r
y= -.663   + 23939r
r is the ratio of net income to total assets, and
p is the discriminant score.

Having derived the discriminant function, it was then possible to test the function in its ability to classify firms as between those which were likely to experience deficits in the following year and those which were not. The results of this classification are shown in Table 4. Of the 65 firms which experienced deficits the following year, the function correctly classified 48, or 74% of the deficit firms. Of the 774 firms which were profitable the following year, the function correctly identified 639, or 82%. A chi-square test of the results indicates that the function provided significant discriminatory ability. The type 1 error was 26% and type 2 error was 18%.

The frequency of loss among the firms predicted to have loss was 25.6%, while the frequency of loss among firms predicted to be profitable was 2.6%. Application of the t test to these two ratios results in a statistic of 10.4, which is significant at the .001 level. The results of this function proved superior to those of the nine variable functions revealed in the preceding table.

Test of the one variable discriminant function on independent time periods.

In order to examine the discriminatory power of the function it was decided to test its usefulness on sixteen separate time periods. In the test of each time period the ratios in one year were used to forecast deficit or profit in the following year. The number of firms in the test in any year depended on the number available on the Compustat tape in that period. This number ranged from 781 in 1968 to as few as 405 in 1954. The results of these tests are given in Table 5 which records the accuracy of classifying firms in independent time samples.

In the table is given the percent of firms forecast to experience deficits which reported deficits, the percent of firms forecast to experience profits which experienced deficits, and the percent of the total number of firms which reported losses. As may be seen in the table, ratios in 1969 were used to forecast profit or loss in 1970. In that test of 793 firms, 51 experienced deficits the following year. Of the 51, 60.8% were correctly classified as prone to deficits. Of the firms forecast to have deficits, 30% experienced deficits. Of the firms predicted to be profitable, only 2.9% experienced losses. The t test was used to evaluate the difference between the actual frequency of deficits among firms forecast to be profitable and firms forecast to report deficits. At the right of Table 5 is given the results t test. As can be seen, all the tests were significant at the .001 level. The results of these tests indicate that discriminant analysis may be applied to ratios of one accounting period in order to forecast profit or loss in a subsequent accounting period. The analysis significantly separates the sample into two groups on the basis of relative likelihood of experiencing future deficits.

Test of one variable discriminant function on an independent sample and independent time periods.

The discriminant function was derived from data on industrial companies contained in the Compustat primary tape which pertains to large industrial corporations. The function was derived in 1973 on the basis of data reported through calendar 1971. The test of the data described here was based on an independent sample of companies drawn from the Compustat tertiary tape. These companies are primarily smaller industrial companies. The period of the test covers the years 1965 through 1974, or a span of years which both precedes and is subsequent to the original year from which the discriminant function was derived. This test sample consists of a smaller number of companies, approximately 186 industrial firms. The results on a year by year basis are shown in Table 6. Again, the firms were classified into two groups: firms which were likely to report a profit and firms which were likely to report a deficit. For each group a percent of firms which actually incurred deficits is given. In each test year the number of firms in the sample is

186. Based on the ratio of net income to total assets in 1973, 30 firms reported deficits in 1974, or 16.1% of the total. Of this sample, 137 firms were forecast to be profitable. Of these, 8 firms or 5.8% reported deficits. Of the 49 firms which were classified as being likely to experience deficits the following year, 22 firms or 44.9% actually reported deficits. To test the significance of the difference between the incidence of actual deficits among the two groups, or difference between 5.8% and 44.9%, the t test is used. In this year the t value was 6.4, which is significant at the .001 level. In other words, the odds of obtaining by chance the above results is less than one in a thousand. Table 6 shows the same statistics for each of the forecast periods, 1966 through 1974, together with the percentages of deficits in each groups. As may be seen, the results were significant in every year at the .001 level. In the aggregate for all periods, 3.5% of the firms predicted to record losses, 23% reported losses and 76.5% of actual deficits were predicted to by the discriminant function. This analysis of independent time periods affords evidence of the ability of the function to correctly classify firms on the basis of profit or loss in one period as predicted from data derived from the preceding accounting year.

Prediction of deficits in subsequent years

The next test was more stringent in that from the data in one accounting period an attempt was made to predict deficits two, three, four, five and six years later. To derive a two year forecast, for example, data was derived in one accounting period and then a forecast was made of the profit or loss of the firm in question two years subsequent to the year of the forecast. One would expect that as the length of the forecast increases, the accuracy of the forecast would diminish. The sample used in making these tests with the same sample as was used in the preceding test, or the 186 firms in the tertiary tape which were in the general industrial category. the data was based on the years 1965 through 1974. All possible forecasts within that span were calculated. The results of this test are shown in Table 7. The results for the one year forecast are precisely the same as those shown in Table 6. For the two year forecast, there were 1,488 firms in the sample. Of these, 10.43% reported a deficit two years subsequent to the year in which the ratio was derived. Of those which were predicted to be profitable, 6.9% reported deficits and of those which were forecast to be unprofitable, 17% were profitable. The t test measure of the significance of the difference between the two ratios was significant at the .001 level. Furthermore, 55.6% of those firms which actually reported deficits two years later were identified as being prone to deficit on the basis of the discriminant function. As might be expected, the percentage of firms which were forecast to be profitable that actually experienced deficits increased from 3.5% for one year forecast to 8.3% for the six year forecast. The percentage of firms that were forecast to be unprofitable that actually experienced losses declined from 23.1% to 14.8% as the forecast period lengthened from one to six years. Yet in every forecast period, the difference between these two ratios was significant at the .01 level, and significant at the .001 level for one and two year forecasts. The percentage of firms which actually experienced deficits that fell into the group for which deficits were forecast, declined from 76.5% to 42.1%. On the basis of these tests, one may conclude that the discriminant function revealed significant forecasting ability for as much as six years out. Furthermore, the accuracy of the forecast declined as the period of forecast lengthened.

The results of longer forecasts for the sample of firms from which the function was derived but for independent time periods was also calculated. Tests of these results were similar to those obtained in the independent firm sample. Forecasts of up to six years subsequent to the year of derivation of the ratio were significant at the .01 level.

Increasing the degree of discrimination

The results so far have been based on a two by two table which categorizes companies into two classes. The discriminant function scales firms from 0 to 1 on the basis of their likelihood of being profitable or unprofitable in the subsequent year. It is quite possible to use this scale in more detail so as to provide greater classification of firms than the simple two-way classification of deficit and non-deficit. One approach is to examine the actual frequency of deficits among various orders of magnitude for the discriminant function produced for all of the firms in the sample. To accomplish this, the frequency of deficits was examined for various ranges of the scale so as to derive classes based on those frequencies. Six final classifications were derived. The classifications were based on frequencies of 0 to 1% deficit, 1 to 2% deficit, 3 to 4% deficit, 5 to 10% deficit, 11 to 20% deficit, and over 20% deficit. This classification reflects the actual experience of deficits of the firms in the Compustat primary tape over the period 1964 through 1971, inclusive. Letters were assigned to each group ranging from A through F, based on the relative frequency of deficit. The discriminant function used to derive the frequencies was the one variable discriminant function based on net income to total assets in the preceding year and derived on the basis of 1970-71 data. Based on the statistic derived by applying equation 1 to the net income to total asset ratio of a particular firm in a particular year, each firm was assigned a classification of A through F. The entire procedure was equivalent to the procedure discussed previously, except that a greater degree of classification was made.

In the preceding procedure the firm was assigned to the deficit or non-deficit group, depending on whether or not the statistic derived from the equation was 0.5 or less, or 0.5 or greater. Here tests were made of the accuracy of one year forecasts based on six classifications. The results of this test are shown in Table 8. These tests were based on the independent sample of firms derived from the Compustat tape. The table aggregates the results of all possible periods in the interval 1965 through 1974. As may be seen from the table, 2.8% of the firms classified A experienced deficits the following year, 3.4% of the firms classified B experienced deficits the following year, 7.5% of the firms classified C, 11.7% of the firms classified D, 21.1% of the firms classified E and 46.9% of the firms classified F.

The table also shows the results of two and five year forecasts. As may be seen, the accuracy of the forecast declined as the period of forecast increased. For all forecast periods, the firms ranked A recorded the lowest incidence of deficits, and the firms ranked F recorded the highest incidence of deficits. The right side of Table 8 portrays the results for firms in the primary Compustat tape where the sample is much larger; however, the firms in the sample represent the same firms as those from which the original function was derived and the same periods in part from which the relative frequencies of deficits for various classes were derived.

As may be seen, the results for this test were comparable to the results for the preceding test. On a one year basis, firms ranked A experienced less than 1% deficit the following year, and firms ranked F recorded a frequency of 37% deficits the following year. The two year forecast resulted in 1.7% of firms ranked A recording deficits, and 22.6% of firms ranked F experiencing deficits. In the five year forecast, 3.7% of the A firms experienced deficits and 15.7% of the F firms experienced deficits. In each forecast period there is a direct correlation between the discriminant category and the actual frequency of deficits in that category. A chi-square test may be used to evaluate the significance of the frequency of deficits among each of the six categories. In this instance, the chi-square test measures the relationship between the actual frequencies deficits in each category and the expected frequency of deficits in that category. For five of the six tests in Table 8, chi-square was significant at the .001 level, and in the remaining test it was significant at the .02 level.{11}

V. Applications

The one variable multiple discriminant model has revealed significant advantages for the projection of future profit or loss. It displayed a predictive capacity which was equal to, if not superior to, that displayed by the nine variable discriminant model. From the point of view of application, the use of a single variable has significant advantages over a multi-variable model in that its use may be reduced to a simple table. Use of a table which has more than two classifications has the additional advantage of permitting the user to evaluate the relative odds of profit or loss. Such a table would be of use to bankers, credit managers, executives, and investors. The final table, which displays the six categories used in the final tests, together with the estimated frequencies of deficits for each category, could be used to assess the risk of profit or loss of the individual industrial firm.

Business Loan Evaluation

Several studies have examined the effectiveness of discriminant analysis in evaluating loans. The assessment of business loans is a major activity of commercial banks and other lending institutions. Certainly, analysis of the loan applicant's financial statements is only one part of the entire evaluation process, but it is an important part. An efficient and simple device for identifying unfavorable credit risks might permit the lending officer to avoid potentially costly decisions. It might also facilitate the efficient and rapid audit of loans currently carried on the books. Comparison of the classification of loans made by the above discriminant function and the evaluation of those loans by the credit department of a large bank holding company revealed a very close correlation between the two assessments. The questionable loans identified by the credit department tended to be the firms with high probabilities of deficit, of those rated D, E and F in the classification scheme described above. Use of a discriminant function to identify questionable loans also permits the loan officer to investigate more thoroughly questionable loans and to spend less time on those which the discriminant function shows to be satisfactory.

Investment Criteria and Internal Management

An important task of corporate management is to periodically assess the present condition of the firm and of its subsidiaries. In this task significant strengths and weaknesses may be identified and corrected. If the odds of loss or negative profits are higher than normal, this consideration might significantly affect policies in regard to payment of dividends, capital expenditures, etc. The decision to acquire another firm or to continue or discontinue operations of internal subsidiaries will also be affected by management's assessment of future profit or loss of those entities. The discriminant function might appropriately and efficiently be applied to identify potential problems.

A related use lies in the application of an accurate deficit predictor in the investment area. An efficient predictor of future profit or loss could be used as a screening technique to ferret out undesirable investments, either in the equity area or the fixed income area. Since the model is predictive, the analyst can utilize those predictions to recommend an appropriate policy on individual securities. One use, which is currently in effect at a major trust department, is to use the discriminant function to identify those fixed income issues which are questionable. Securities which fall into the lower categories, particularly those labeled D, E or F, are singled out for further investigation and potential removal from portfolios. A list is prepared automatically on a monthly basis of all securities which fall into the latter category and of all portfolios which hold any securities in those categories. Simulation of the use of the discriminant function for identification of such issues as the Penn Central, which ultimately went bankrupt, revealed that the function would have provided an early warning of future problems.

VI. Conclusion

The purpose of this paper was to assess the quality of ratio analysis in the prediction of corporate deficits. In order to evaluate its potential, a large set of financial ratios was screened for their univariate ability to identify future profit or loss. From this set a group of nine ratios was combined in a discriminant analysis approach to the problem of predicting corporate deficits. From within this set, a single ratio, net income to total assets, proved to possess a discriminatory predictive capacity equal to or superior to that possessed be the larger set of variables.

The discriminant ratio model proved to be significantly accurate in predicting corporate profit or loss on the initial sample. Moreover, the discriminant function was accurate in time periods other than the time period from which the model was derived. Investigation of the accuracy of the model applied to an independent sample of companies revealed that the model possessed considerable accuracy. While the initial tests were limited to a one year forecast, subsequent tests of forecasts over the next 2, 3, 4, 5 and 6 year periods revealed that the model was useful in longer periods. The final parts of the analysis convert the discriminant score to an estimate of the relative probability of deficit based on the actual frequencies of deficit for various scores. The results of this classification are tested and found to be significantly accurate.

Several applications of the model are suggested, including investment screening, loan credit evaluation, and internal control procedures. Current examples of some of these applications currently in use are referred to.

Footnotes

1. E. L. Altman, "Financial Ratios, Discriminant Analysis and the Prediction of Corporate Bankruptcy." *Journal of Finance,* Vol. XXIII (September 1968), pp. 601-602.

2. The sample understates the proportion of firms experiencing deficits in past years since firms which fail or merge after continued losses are deleted from the Compustat tape.

3. C. Merwin, *Financing Small Corporations,* (New York: Bureau of Economic Research, 1942).

4. W. H. Beaver, "Financial Ratios as Predictors of Corporate Failure." *Empirical Research in Accounting: Selected Studies,* 1966 (Institute of Professional Accounting, January 1967), pp. 77-111.

5. E. L. Altman, *Corporate Bankruptcy in America,* (D.C. Heath and Company, 1971).

6. M. P. Blum, "The Failure of Company Doctrine." Unpublished Ph.D. dissertation, Columbia University, 1969. L. G. Gru, "Financial Ratios, Multiple Discriminant Analysis and the Prediction of Small Corporate Failure." Unpublished Ph.D. dissertation, University of Minnesota, 1973.

7. See various studies of the behavior of financial variables, e.g. A. C. Rayner and I. M. Little, *Higgledy, Piggledy Growth Again.* (Oxford, Basil Blackwell, 1966). J. E. Murphy and J. R. Nelson, "Random and Nonrandom Relationships Among

Financial Variables: A Financial Model." *Journal of Financial and Quantitative Analysis*, Vol. VI, No. 2 (March 1971), pp. 875-885.

8. The accuracy on an overall basis is obtained by dividing the number of correct classifications by the total number of observations.

9. The t test used is appropriate for examining the difference between proportions where the frequencies are small.

10. Single variable models were as effective as multivariate models in predicting company failure, according to Blum, who states: "It was expected that a multivariate models would be more accurate than a univariate approach." Yet comparison indicates that the "models seems to be about equally effective overall," a conclusion that is "especially surprising" since the multivariate model includes cash flow to total debt, the ratio used in the univariate approach. Blum, op. cit., pp. 130, 178-9.

11. A comparison of ratings published in August 1973 with operating results available a year later reveals that the rating provided highly accurate forecasts of the probability of deficit. Of the 30 firms rated F, 13 reported deficits. Results for all rating categories are shown in the table below.

August 1973		August 1974	
		Deficit	Percent
Rating	Firms	Firms	Deficit
A	377	1	0.3%
B	228	2	0.9
C	107	4	3.7
D	73	4	5.5
E	26	4	15.4
F	30	13	43.3

Ratings were published in *Corporate Deficits*, Volume 1, Number 1 (Northwestern National Bank, 1973).

References

1. Altman, Edward I., *Corporate Bankruptcy in America*, (D.C. Heath and Company, 1971).

2. Altman, Edward I., "Financial Ratios, Discriminant Analysis and the Prediction of Corporate Bankruptcy." *Journal of Finance*, (September 1968), pp. 589-609.

3. Altman, Edward I., "Predicting Railroad Bankruptcies in American", *Bell Journal of Economics and Management Studies*, Spring, 1973, pp. 184-211.

4. Beaver, William H., "Financial Ratios as Predictors of Failure", *Empirical Research in Accounting: Selected Studies*, 1966, pp. 71-118.

5. Blum, M. P., "The Failing Company Doctrine", Unpublished Ph.D. dissertation, Columbia University, 1969.

6. Chesser, Dalton L., "Predicting Loan Noncompliance", The Journal of Commercial Bank Lending, August 1974, pp. 28-38.

7. Gru, L. G., "Financial Ratios, Multiple Discriminant Analysis and the Prediction of Small Corporate Failure", Unpublished Ph.D. dissertation, University of Minnesota, 1973.

8. Horrigan, James O., "Small Empirical Bases of Financial Ratio Analysis", *The Accounting Review,* July 1965, pp. 558-568.

9. Johnson Craig G., "Ratio Analysis and the Prediction of Firm Failure", *Journal of Finance*, December 1970, pp. 1166-1168.

10. Lomax, K. S., "Business Failures: Another Example of the Analysis of Failure Data", *Journal of the American Statistical Association*, December 1954, pp. 847-852.

11. Merwin, C., *Financing Small Corporations* (New York: Bureau of Economic Research, 1942).

12. Meyer, Paul A. and Fifer, Howard W., "Prediction of Bank Failures", *Journal of Finance*, September 1970, pp. 853-858.

13. Northwestern National Bank of Minneapolis, Corporate Deficits, Vol. 1, No. 1, August, 1973.

14. Sinkey, Joseph F., "A Multivariate Statistical Analysis of the Characteristics of Problem Banks", *Journal of Finance*, March 1975, pp. 21-35.

15. Winaker, Arthur and Smith, Raymond F., *Changes in Financial Structure of Unsuccessful Industrial Companies,* (Urbana: University of Illinois Press, 1935).

Table I
Variable Means and Tests of Significance

Variable	Deficit Group Mean (1962-1971)	Non Deficit Group Mean (1971)	F Ratio
n	218	747	
Cap. Expend. Coverage	0.9x	1.2x	17.8*
Cash Flow/Assets	4.1%	9.0%	176.3*
Int. Coverage	2.9x	4.7x	5.7**
Oper Inc./Sales	5.4%	12.2%	110.4*
Pretax Net/Sales	0.6%	7.8%	140.6*
Net Inc./Sales	0.1%	4.3%	93.6*
Net Return Equity	-1.4%	10.5%	85.8*
Return/Total Cap.	2.7%	9.9%	160.5*
Cash Flow/Debt	10.8%	26.4%	79.7*
Net Inc./Total Assets	0.4%	5.2%	201.3*

```
 * Significant at .001 level
** Significant at .05 level
```

Note: In actual computation the inverse of the coverage ratio was used

Table II

Actual Group Membership	Predicted Group Membership	
	Deficit	Non-Deficit
Deficit	c1	e1
Non-Deficit	e2	c2

Table III
Nine Variable Predictions of Profit or Loss Following Year

Loss Data   1954-55 to 1970-71
Function and Test Based on Same Data

	Predicted Loss	Predicted Profit	
Actual Loss	160	58	218
Actual Profit	164	583	747
	324	641	965

Actual loss among firms predicted loss	49.4%
Actual loss among firms predicted profit	9.0
Actual loss among all firms	22.6
Predicted loss as precent of firms reporting loss	73.4

$$t = \frac{P_1 - P_2}{(p(1-p)(1/n_1 + 1/n_2))^{\frac{1}{2}}}$$

where $n_1 = c_1 + e_2$ $n_2 = e_1 + c_2$

$P_1 = c_1/n_1$ $P_2 = e_1/n_2$

$p = (c_1 + e_1)/(n_1 + n_2)$

$$= \frac{160/324 - 58/641}{((218/965)(747/965)(1/324 + 1/641))^{\frac{1}{2}}}$$

$= 14.2$

Table IV
One Variable Function Predicting Profit or Loss
Following Year

1970 Net Income/Total Assets and 1971 Profit or Loss
Function and Test Based on Same Data

	Predicted Loss	Predicted Profit	
Actual Loss	48	17	65
Actual Profit	139	635	774
	187	652	839

Actual loss among firms predicted loss	25.6%
Actual loss among firms predicted profit	2.6
Actual loss among all firms	7.7
Predicted loss among firms reporting loss	73.8

t = 10.4   significant at .001 level

Table V
Net Income/Total Assets as Predictor of Deficits

- Firms From Which Function Derived - Independent Time Periods

YEAR RATIO DERIVED	YEAR DEFICIT PREDICTED	INCIDENCE OF DEFICITS			PERCENT OF DEFICITS PREDICTED	SIGNIFICANCE TEST t
		TOTAL	PROFIT PREDICTED	DEFICIT PREDICTED		
1969	1970	6.4%	2.9%	30.1%	60.8%	10.5*
1968	1969	2.8	1.8	13.8	40.9	4.3*
1967	1968	2.0	1.0	13.1	53.3	6.4*
1966	1967	1.8	0.7	22.2	61.5	9.5*
1965	1966	1.2	0.5	17.1	66.7	8.7*
1964	1965	1.5	0.5	14.0	70.0	7.5*
1963	1964	1.5	0.4	11.9	77.8	6.9*
1962	1963	1.2	0.2	9.5	85.7	8.4*
1961	1962	2.4	0.6	15.9	76.9	7.5*
1960	1961	2.5	0.9	15.3	69.2	6.7*
1959	1960	3.1	1.7	21.9	50.0	6.4*
1958	1959	1.4	0.5	7.4	66.7	4.3*
1957	1958	2.6	1.2	25.0	58.3	7.7*
1956	1957	1.4	0.5	10.8	60.7	5.1*
1955	1956	1.7	1.0	9.7	42.9	3.6*
1954	1955	1.0	0.3	6.2	75.0	3.9*

* Significant at .001 level

Table VI
Net Income/Total Assets as Predictor of Deficits

Independent Firms and Time Periods, 186 Firms

YEAR RATIO DERIVED	YEAR DEFICIT PREDICTED	INCIDENCE OF DEFICITS			PERCENT OF DEFICITS PREDICTED	SIGNIFICANCE TEST t
		TOTAL	PROFIT PREDICTED	DEFICIT PREDICTED		
1973	1974	16.1%	5.8%	44.9%	73.3%	6.4*
1972	1973	7.0	0.8	20.0	92.3	4.8*
1971	1972	7.0	1.7	15.7	84.6	3.6*
1970	1971	10.8	3.7	20.8	80.0	3.7*
1969	1970	15.1	7.4	25.6	71.4	3.4*
1968	1969	10.2	5.4	21.1	63.1	3.2**
1967	1968	7.0	1.6	18.6	84.6	4.2*
1966	1967	9.1	3.7	24.0	70.6	4.3*
1965	1966	7.0	1.5	22.0	84.6	4.9*
All Periods		9.9	3.5	23.1	76.5	12.6*

* Significant at .001 level
All chi-squares are significant at .001 level except 1954-5 and 1955-6 test which
are significant at .05 level

Table VII
Net Income/Total Assets as Predictor of Deficits over Next One to Six Years

Independent Firms and Time Periods#

FORCAST PERIOD YEARS	n	INCIDENCE OF DEFICITS			PERCENT OF DEFICITS PREDICTED	SIGNIFIANCE TEST t
		TOTAL	PROFIT PREDICTED	DEFICITS PREDICTED		
1	1,674	9.9%	3.5%	23.1%	76.5%	12.6*
2	1,488	10.3	6.9	17.0	55.6	6.0*
3	1,302	10.5	8.5	14.3	46.3	3.2**
4	1,116	11.0	9.0	15.1	45.5	3.1**
5	930	11.2	9.0	16.0	45.2	3.2**
6	744	10.2	8.3	14.8	42.1	2.7**

*Significant at .001 level   ** Significant at .01 level
#One of the time periods overlaps

Table VIII

Classification of Firms by One Variable Discriminant Function Into Six Categories and Actual Frequency of Deficits One, Two and Five Years Later

1965 - 1974 Data

CATEGORY	INDEPENDENT SAMPLE YEARS FORCAST			ORIGINAL SAMPLE YEARS FORCAST		
	1	2	5	1	2	5
A	2.8%	5.8%	8.3%	0.6%	1.7%	3.7%
B	3.4	8.7	11.6	1.2	4.1	5.8
C	7.5	11.7	13.4	4.7	5.1	8.2
D	11.7	12.1	12.1	10.9	11.5	10.5
E	21.1	14.9	16.0	21.1	13.1	11.3
F	46.9	28.5	22.5	37.8	22.6	15.9
x^2 sig. at	.001	.001	.02	.001	.001	.001
Number of Firms	186	186	186	790	790	790
Observations	1,674	1,488	930	7,110	6,320	3,950

x^2 20.5 significant at .001   11.1 significant at .05

Table IX
Probability of Deficit - Industrial Firms

Classification	Net Income/ Total Assets %	Probability of Deficit %
A	4.7 or more	Under 1
B	3.9 - 4.6	2 - 3
C	3.1 - 3.8	4 - 5
D	1.6 - 3.0	6 - 10
E	-0.1 - 1.5	11 - 20
F	Less than -0.1	Over 20

18

A NOTE ON ALTERNATIVE FORMULAS FOR THE COEFFICIENT OF AUTOCORRELATION.

This article describes the differences in coefficients of auto-correlation and correlograms produced by three standard but alternative formulas. The principal differences arise with linear series and with series exhibiting a strong linear trend.

KEY WORDS: Autocorrelation; Correlogram; Serial Correlation

The Equations

The equation for computing the ordinary correlation coefficient with N pairs of observations and two variables x and y, is

$$r = \frac{\Sigma(x_i - \bar{x})(y_i - \bar{y})}{\sqrt{[\Sigma(x_i - \bar{x})^2 \Sigma(y_i - \bar{y})^2]}}$$

the following

The same concept can be applied to time series to determine whether successive observations are correlated.

Equation 1.

Given n observations $x_1,...,x_n$ we can form (N-1) observations $(x_1,x_2), (x_2, x_3),...,(x_{n-1},x_n)$. We can regard the first observation in each pair as one variable and the second observation as a sec

$$r_1 = \frac{\sum_{t=1}^{N-1} (x_t - \bar{x}_{(1)})(x_{t+1} - \bar{x}_{(2)})}{\sqrt{[\sum_{t=1}^{N-1} (x_t - \bar{x}_{(1)})^2 \sum_{t=1}^{N-1} (x_{t+1} - \bar{x}_{(2)})^2]}} \tag{1}$$

where

$$\bar{x}_{(1)} = \sum_{t=1}^{N-1} x_t/(N-1)$$

is the mean of the first (N-1) observations and

$$\bar{x}_{(2)} = \sum_{t=2}^{N} x_t/(N-1)$$

Unpublished manuscript 1996

is the mean of the last (N-1) observations.

The coefficient formed between successive observations is the autocorrelation coefficient or serial correlation coefficient.

Equation 2.

In Equation (2) it is assumed that the means of the lead and lag variables are approximately the same. Equation (1) is then simplified to:

$$r_1 = \frac{\sum\limits_{t=1}^{N-1} (x_t - \bar{x})(x_{t+1} - \bar{x})}{(N-1) \sum\limits_{t=1}^{N} (x_t - \bar{x})^2 / N} \tag{2}$$

where $\bar{x} = \sum\limits_{t=1}^{N} x_t / N$

= overall mean

Equation 3.

In Equation (3) the factor N/(N-1) is dropped giving:

$$r_1 = \frac{\sum\limits_{t=1}^{N-1} (x_t - \bar{x})(x_{t+1} - \bar{x})}{\sum\limits_{t=1}^{N} (x_t - \bar{x})^2} \tag{3}$$

Equations (2) and (3) produce similar coefficients.

In a similar way we can compute the correlation between observations k distance apart

$$r_k = \frac{\sum\limits_{t=1}^{N-k} (x_t - \bar{x})(x_{t+k} - \bar{x})}{\sum\limits_{t=1}^{N} (x_t - \bar{x})^2}$$

An alternative form of equations (2) and (3) is the following.
Autocovariance function at lag 1 (first version)

$$c_k = (1/n-1) \sum_{t=1}^{n-k} (x_t - \bar{x})(x_{t+k} - \bar{x}) \qquad (4a)$$

Autocovariance function at lag 1 (second version)

$$c_k = (1/n) \sum_{t=1}^{n-k} (x_t - \bar{x})(x_{t+k} - \bar{x}) \qquad (4b)$$

Variance

$$c_0 = (1/n) \sum_{t=1}^{n} x_t - \bar{x})^2 \qquad (5)$$

where the mean is

$$\bar{x} = \sum_{t=1}^{n} x_t/n$$

Coefficient of Autocorrelation at lag 1

$$r_k = c_k/c_0 \qquad (6)$$

Substituting the covariance of (4a) and the variance of (5) in (6), gives equation (2). Substituting the covariance of (4b) and the variance of (5) in (6) gives (3).

The Comparative Results of the Equations

For a perfectly linear series, equation (1) gives r values of 1 .00 (the correct value). Equations (2) and (3) give r values which decline monotonically with increases in the lag. The same holds for a random walk with a strong trend.

The following figures illustrate the differences for linear, periodic and random walk series.

For the linear series (Fig. 1, upper left panel), the correct value of r is 1.00. Only Equation (1) gives a values of 1.00 for all lags. Equations (2) and (3) give monotonically declining values of the coefficient. Equation (3) gives the lowest values of r. Neither (2) nor (3) would correctly identify a linear series.

For the sine series (Fig. 1, upper right panel), the correct value of r is periodic, with a range of +1 to -1. The coefficients of (1) fall within this range. The coefficients of (2) are very close, those of (3) less so. Overall, all three equations provide generally satisfactory results, although (3) fails to identify a perfect sine curve.

For a random walk, the expected coefficient of autocorrelation is 0. For this random series (Fig. 1, lower left panel) all three formulas provide values of r which are very similar. Each equation performs satisfactorily.

For a cumulative random series, a random walk, with a marked trend (Fig. 1, lower right panel), only (1) reveals the trend and demonstrate that it is not purely linear. Equations (2) and (3) show continuously declining values of r. On the basis of the correlograms of Equations (2) and (3), it might be difficult to distinguish the cumulative random series (in the lower left panel) from the purely linear series (in the upper right panel). For a cumulative random walk with a strong trend, only Equation (1) provides a clear identification of the nature of the series.

The panels in Figure 2 present correlograms for Equations (2) and (3) for four financial series. They demonstrate the sharp differences given by the two equations.

Conclusion

The three equations produce correlograms which differ in varying degree, depending on the series under examination. The coefficient of autocorrelation given by (1) is quite close to the coefficients given by (2) and (3) for purely random data and to a lesser degree for periodic data, but not for linear data, nor for cumulative random data with a strong trend.

For an unknown time series, Equation (1) is least likely to lead to misinterpretation of the data. Unfortunately, that is not the equation used in most statistical software packages.

References

Chatfield, C., (1984) *The Analysis of Time Series*, Chapman and Hall, London, 66, 24-5.

Cryer, Jonathan D., (1986) *Time Series Analysis*, Duxbury Press, Boston, 45.

Fuller, Wayne A., (1976) *Introduction to Statistical Time Series*, John Wiley & Sons, New York, 236.

Harvey, (1986) *Time Series Models,* Philip Allan, London, 23-25.

Kendall, M.G. and Yule, G. Udny, (1944) *An Introduction to the Theory of Statistics*, Griffin & Company, London, 13th ed., 639.

Kendall, M.G., (1976) Time-Series, 2nd edition, Hafner Press, N.Y., 39-40.

Kendall, M.G., and Stewart, A., (1976) *The Advanced Theory of Statistics*, 3rd edition, Hafner, New York, 3, 375-376.

Statgraphics Formula Guide, (1987) Statistical Graphics Corporation, Princeton, N.J., 32.

Tietjen, Gary L., (1986) *A Topical Dictionary of Statistics*, Chapman and Hall, New York, 106.

Figure 1

Correlogram - Linear Series

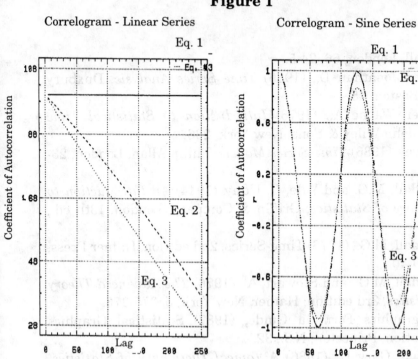

Correlogram - Sine Series

Correlogram- Random Series

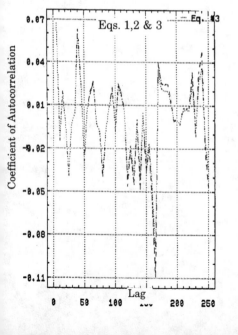

Correlogram-Cumulative Random

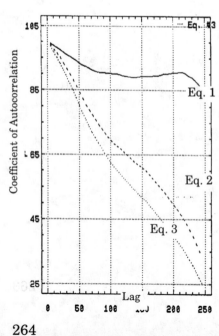

Figure 2

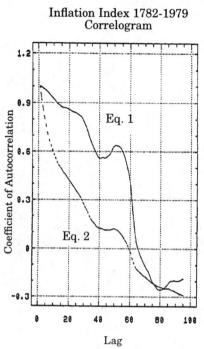

Inflation Index 1782-1979
Correlogram

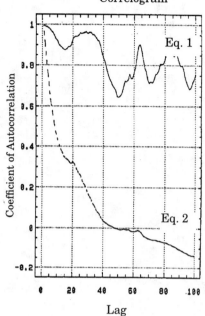

New York Stock Exchange Index 1790-1992
Correlogram

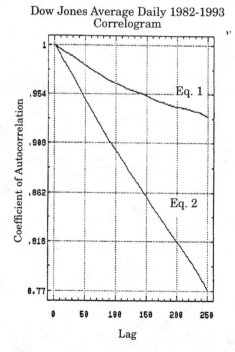

Dow Jones Average Daily 1982-1993
Correlogram

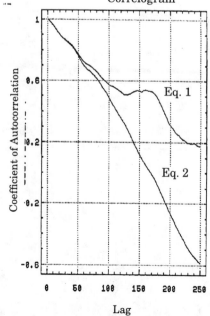

U.S. 20 Year Bond Yield Index 1950-1993
Correlogram

19

EVIDENCE OF NON RANDOMNESS IN DAILY CHANGES IN NEW YORK STOCK EXCHANGE PRICES

Joseph E. Murphy & M.F.M.Osborne

Although extensive research had been done on the sequential distribution of price changes of New York Stock Exchange stocks, comparatively little has been done on the cross-sectional distribution of price changes, despite the importance of the subject. Prior studies are largely silent, for example, on whether the cross-sectional distribution is skewed or symmetrical, whether these attributes are related to price level, or to the direction of price change, or whether they vary over time. An exception is the work of M.F.M Osborne who plotted on probability paper the cumulative cross sectional distributions of $\Delta\log_e$ price of New York Stock Exchange prices [3].

Apart from the strictly scientific interest in these questions, there is economic interest, for the answers have bearing on the behavior of stock portfolios and the behavior of the market. A good example is the expected return from a portfolio consisting of a sample of possibly several hundred stocks. The value of such a portfolio is the sum of the values of its components; changes in the value of the portfolio will reflect the cross sectional distribution of changes in prices. If the distribution of price changes is log normal, and we assume continuous changes in prices, the expected change in value in $ of the portfolio price can be calculated from the mean $\Delta\log_e$ price and the standard deviation of $\Delta\log_e$ price; if the distribution is not log normal, however, the estimated expected change of value of the portfolio must be adjusted. Consequently, the presence and the nature of any departures from normality in the cross-sectional distribution of price changes is important to know. This paper investigates the degree and nature of these departures.

This paper takes a close look at the consequences and the limitations or imperfections of applicable conditions for the Central Limit Theorem. We can spell this out. There is more

Unpublished manuscript 1994

than one form of the Central Limit Theorem. The word limit means a limit of a finite number of observations as the number approaches infinity, or for an infinitely long time if the observations occur at finite time intervals. Real data is finite in amount and finite in range over a finite time interval, so the data are an imperfect and approximate picture of that which the Central Limit Theorem describes.

If the limit is a "normal" distribution, it means each one of the +1 and -1 values of coin flips are small compared to the sum of all of them. If this condition is not met, but the other conditions are (i.e. steady state in time, no time dependence in the process of summations), you get the Pareto-Levy or Cauchy distribution; fat tails and infinite variance, or for Cauchy an infinite or ambiguous mean also.

In practice, as will be seen by the data below, there is some time dependence, some era or calendar effects. In addition, there is discreteness, both in price ($1/8th) and discreteness in time. Prices exist only at the ends of finite time intervals, a few minutes or seconds, at least. These non-continuities really matter for market making and for the profit you can or cannot achieve. Market making is much simplified and safer with discrete price changes.

The paper reveals the small but statistically significant departure from "pure" steady state in time randomness, as described by the Central Limit Theorem. The effects which we describe below can be seen qualitatively on cumulative plotted distributions on normal probability graph paper. These are given in Osborne [3]. With 100 data points, you cannot plot anything less than .01 probability or greater than .99. Finite amounts of data gives a finite range, although the limit of a normal distribution is from minus infinity to plus infinity. A normal distribution will be a straight line with a slope of 1/standard deviation. If the plot resembles an S-curve, you have excess in the tails.

I
Cross Sectional Versus Sequential Dispersion

It is useful to define carefully the difference between the cross sectional versus the sequential differences and their distributions. Imagine the data in a rectangular table, the rows labeled by individual stocks, the columns labeled by dates, with the starting date at the left. The cross sectional distribution of differences is the distribution of differences between successive columns 1, 2, 3,..., 8 days apart. The sequential distribution is that of differences for a single row. The entire table is not that of prices, but of the natural logarithms of prices. We could, of course, do the same thing with the prices, but in this paper we deal with the logarithms of prices.

As a physical example, we can think of a column of smoke from a chimney. The spreading or distribution of the plume of smoke as it drifts down wind would be the cross sectional distribution. The sequential distribution would be obtained from the trajectory of a single smoke particle. The same could be imagined for a dye, or chemical, in a river, or in the ocean.

For small time intervals, small meaning less than 2 years, any distribution which is normal will still be normal approximately if you go from price to log price, or in fact to any continuous variable transformation, simply by Taylor's theorem, which is for small intervals approximately a linear transformation.

Equation (1) gives the probability distribution density of $P(t)=P$ where $P_0(t)$ is the price of a randomly selected stock at random time t, and $P=P(t+t)$, the price of the same stock t later.

The probability distribution density of P itself is

$$F(P)dP=\exp\{-\log_e(P/P_0)^2/2\sigma^2\tau\}dP/P(2\pi\sigma^2\tau)^{1/2} \qquad (1)$$

The median value of P is P_0

The expected value E of P itself is

$$E(P)= \int_{p=0}^{p=\infty} P\,F(P)dP= P_0\,\exp\{\sigma^2\tau/2\}\approx P_0(1+\sigma^2\tau/2) \qquad (2)$$

The variance of P is

$$\sigma^2(P) = P_0^2\{\exp 2\sigma^2\tau - \exp\sigma^2\tau\} \tag{3}$$

$$\approx P_0^2\sigma^2\tau$$

The range of P is 0 to $+\infty$

For the normal distribution, putting

$$x = \log_e P, \qquad x_0 = \log_e P_0$$

$$F(x)dx = [\exp\{(x-x_0)^2/2\sigma^2\tau\}/(2\pi\sigma^2\tau)^{1/2}]dx \tag{4}$$

$$\text{Mean} = \text{median} = x_0 = \log_e P_0 \tag{5}$$

The range of x is $-\infty$ to $+\infty$

For τ small the dispersion is $\sigma(P) = P_0\sigma\sqrt{\tau}$. Thus we see that the expectation value of log P does not change with τ, but the expectation value of P itself does.

The purpose of the paper is to examine closely the departures of real data from either or both of these formulae for cross sectional distributions, as distinct from sequential distributions. The paradoxical behavior of the log normal distribution, is that the expectation value of $ per share P, and shares per $, 1/P, both increase in an identical manner with time interval t. We have examined this for $ per share P, but not for shares per $, 1/P. The identical behavior of $ per share P, and shares per $, is worth examining both in manufactured random and real price series. Any such examination should take into account the birth and death of firms. See [4] page 275, also [5], discussion pp. 324-5.

This paradoxical behavior expresses a symmetry of the operation of numerical measurement - which is always a relation or ratio between two objects or circumstances being compared. Thus, a pencil may be half a foot long - equivalently the foot ruler is two pencils' length. One second is a small fraction of the period of time of the rotation of the earth. The earth rotates in a time (seconds) equal to the reciprocal of a small fraction of a year on a given date. A German mark may be worth 1/2 a dollar, a dollar worth 2 marks. The measured value is different on different dates. In a stochastic (and nonstationary) setting, where real fluctuations in time, errors, or uncertainties matter, (much as in a market where dollars and shares are constantly and symmetrically exchanged) the above paradoxical behavior of expectations expresses this symmetry of their operation of measurement, or in finance, their "evaluation." Note that this paradoxical behavior is a property of any even probability distribution density function of the logarithm, not just the normal distribution.

II

Data and Method of Investigation

The underlying data for this investigation is the change in the logarithms of prices of 871 individual NYSE securities for one to eight day intervals for the 252 trading days in 1987.

The method of analyzing the data was the following. We divided the trading days into 28 separate time intervals, or time samples. Time interval one covered days 1-9; time interval two covered days 10-18; time interval three covered days 19-27; and so on up to time interval 28 which covered days 244-252. In each time interval, we computed the price change for 1 day, 2 days, 3 days,..., up to 8 days. We computed the one day price change as the logarithm of the price on day two less the logarithm of the price on day one. We computed the two day price change as the logarithm of the price on day three less the logarithm of the price on day one. And so on for the other intervals.

From these computations, we obtained eight changes of $\log_e$ price for each stock, one for each time difference interval of 1, 2, 3, ..., 8 days. For the first part of the investigation, we used only 1-day and 8-day difference intervals; that gave us 871 x 28 one day changes of $\log_e$ price and 872 x 28 eight day changes of $\log_e$ price. The reason for restricting our analysis in the first part of the study to 1-day and 8-day differences was to keep the samples as independent as possible. In these two samples, only one-eighth of the data overlap. In calculating the change of log, we used natural logarithms for all computations. We used logarithms because the distribution of stock price changes is more nearly log normal than normal, keeping in mind that our purpose was to describe the distribution, and to investigate departures from normality, or log normality.

Once we had the one day changes of $\log_e$ price for the first interval, day 1-9, we sorted that set of changes of $\log_e$ price by the magnitude of the stock price on day one. We then divided the price changes into four price classes, or quartiles, basing each quartile on the beginning price so that the first quartile contained the one-fourth lowest priced stocks on day one of the time interval, the second quartile the next lowest one-fourth prices, the third quartile, the third one-fourth lowest prices, and the fourth quartile the highest prices. Since log price is an increasing function of price, quartiles of price, or log price contain exactly the same stocks. Next, within each quartile, we sorted the price changes by amount of change so that we could examine the distribution of changes of $\log_e$ price of that quartile. The word "changes" refers strictly to changes of natural logarithms of price.

We repeated this entire process for the eight day price changes. We also repeated it for one and eight day price changes for each of the other twenty seven nine-day intervals in the year. The result was that we obtained a set of changes of $\log_e$ price distributions giving, for each of four price quartiles and for twenty-eight independent time intervals, or time samples. Each quartile, but the last, contained 218 stocks; the last contained 217 stocks.

Since the price data was adjusted for all stock splits and stock dividends through December 31, 1987, before determining the quartiles, some of the prices used to construct the quartiles were lower than their historical values. Thus, if a stock which was priced at $50 in January of 1987 and subsequently split 2-for-1 in July, that stock was priced at $25 in January (i.e. the post split price). Consequently, it probably was in a different quartile than if the actual January price of $50 were used.

Ideally, we would have used the actual price on the date of the split.

Our reason for dividing the data into price quartiles was to enable us to examine the relationship between price level, of trading prices, and such properties as median change of $\log_e P$, skewness, or the degree of symmetry in the distribution, and kurtosis, or the behavior of the tails. We examined kurtosis by looking at the degree to which the tails were too long for a normal, or Gaussian, distribution.

We wanted to examine symmetry and kurtosis, both for the full distribution, and for the four price quartiles, to see what they looked like for two difference intervals, one day and eight days, and for different time intervals. We also wanted to examine the presence, or lack, of symmetry, both for the central part of the distribution, the middle two thirds, or "symmetry in the core," as we call it, and "symmetry in the tail" of the distribution.

The reason for using different time samples was that we wanted to see whether the results were invariant over time, or were dependent on the particular historical or calendar era, and also whether they bore any relationship to the direction of change in the market as a whole, to the mean or median change in the market.

In our investigation, we used four formulas and applied each to the price changes in the quartile. These formulas designate percentiles of $\log_e$ prices by the letter "p" and a number, so that the 83rd percentile is designated p.83, the 50th percentile, or median, is designated p.50, and so forth. The formulas are given below:

Note that in formulas 1 to 4 "$\log_e$ p" refers to changes in the natural log of price.

1. Skewness in the core.

$$((((\Delta\log_e p).83 - (\Delta\log_e p).50) - ((\Delta\log_e p).50 - (\Delta\log_e p).17))/((\Delta\log_e p).83 - (\Delta\log_e p).17)$$

2. Skewness in the tails.

$$((\Delta\log_e p).95 - (\Delta\log_e p).83)/(\Delta\log_e p).17 - (\Delta\log_e p).05)$$

3. Flatness of the tails.

$((\Delta \log_e p).95 - (\Delta \log_e p).05)/((\Delta \log_e p).83 - (\Delta \log_e p).17)$

4. Skewness

$(3 \times (\text{mean} \Delta \log_e p - \text{median} \Delta \log_e p))/(\text{standard deviation} \Delta \log_e p)$

Formula #1 shows whether the distance covered by the third of the distribution of $\Delta \log_e$ price just above the median is longer, or shorter, than the third just below the median. If it is longer, the distribution is skewed upward in the core toward higher price changes; if shorter, the distribution is skewed downward in the core toward lower or negative price changes.

Formula #2 shows whether the distance in $\Delta \log_e$ price from the 83rd percentile to the 95th percentile of the distribution was longer, or shorter, than the distance from the 5th percentile to the 17th percentile. If it was longer, the tails of the distribution are skewed upward, to the right, toward larger price changes; if shorter, the tails of the distribution were skewed downward, to the left, toward smaller or negative price changes.

Formula #3 shows by how much the distance covered from the 5th to the 95th percentile of the distribution exceeded the distance covered by the 17th percentile to the 83rd percentile. For a normal distribution the former should be 1.74 times the latter. If the ratio was greater than 1.74, the distribution had wider tails than a normal distribution.

Formula #4 is another measure of skewness which shows whether the mean is greater, or less than, the median. When the mean is greater than the median, the distribution is skewed in a positive direction toward larger price changes; when the mean is less than the median, the distribution tends to be skewed in a negative direction toward smaller price changes.

III

Skewness in the Core. (Formula #1)

$((p.83-p.50)-(p.50-p.17))/(p.83-p.17)$

In the above shortened formula, p.83 refers to the 83rd percentile, with "p" representing "percentile" of the distribution of $\log_e$ price.

To determine whether the core of the distribution is skewed, we counted the number of positive and negative values of Formula #1 for all quartiles for the first and second halves of the year and then for the full year. If, in the first half of the year, the positives and negatives were equal, indicating no skewness on balance, there would be 28 of each (4 quartiles, 14 values each half year). If we divide the difference between the number of positives and negatives by the standard error, we obtain the z statistic. The standard error would be the square root of n, or the square root of 56, or 7.5 Thus, in the first half there were 40 times of positive skewness and 16 times of negative skewness, the difference is 24, and 24 divided by 7.5 gives a z score of 3.2 for the first half.

The results of the count of positive and negative skewness, together with the z statistics for the difference, are shown in Table I. The z statistic will be greater than 2.05 (see legend of Table I) when there is a clear excess in one side of the core versus the other, an excess that cannot be ascribed to random chance at the 5% level of significance.

As we can see, the distribution of changes of $\log_e$ price price is skewed upward toward greater changes in log price, in the core, in both the first half of 1987 and overall, for both the one day interval and the eight day interval. In the second half of the year, which included the Big Crash of October 19, the skewness is still present, but now it is slightly negative for the one day interval (z=-1.2). If we use two standard deviations as the criterion of significance, the difference between the number of positive and negative asymmetries is significant for the first half of the year (z=3/2 for one day, z=2.4 for 8 days) and for the full year the eight day interval only (for which z=2.2).

The evidence of the test shows that skewness is present in the central part of the distribution of changes in the logarithms of stock prices. This is not the distribution you would expect from a purely random process in changes of the log of prices; it

Table I

Skewness in the Core (Formula #1)

Evidence of Skewing in the Central Portion of the Distribution of Price Changes Toward Higher Price Changes (Excess of +'s), Toward Lower Price Changes (Excess of -'s), or Absence of Skewing (Equal Number of +'s and -'s) for Each of Four Price Quartiles (Q1 Lowest Prices, Q4 Highest Prices) for Intervals of 1-Day and 8-Days. (z > 2.05 Significant at 5% Level of Significance)

$$((((\Delta\log_e p).83-(\Delta\log_e p).50)-((\Delta\log_e p).50-(\Delta\log_e p).17))/((\Delta\log_e p).83-(\Delta\log_e p).17)$$

Interval		First Half +	-	Second Half +	-	Full Year +	-
1 Day	Q1	10	4	5	9	15	13
	Q2	8	6	6	8	14	14
	Q3	12	2	4	10	16	12
	Q4	10	4	8.5	5.5	18.5	9.5
Total		40	16	23.5	32.5	63.5	48.5
z =		3.2		-1.2		1.4	
8 Days	Q1	11	3	7	7	18	10
	Q2	9	5	10	4	19	9
	Q3	9	5	8	6	17	11
	Q4	8	6	6	8	14	14
Total		37	19	31	25	68	44
z =		2.4		0.8		2.2	

represents a departure. Moreover, the degree of asymmetry is similar for both the one and eight day time intervals; it declines with increases in the difference interval in the first six months only, as would be expected from the Central Limit Theorem; and it changes from the first to the second half of the year, revealing that the distribution is not invariant over time. Finally, as shown in the quartile data, the skewness to the larger values (+sign) is present in the first half of the year and, for the one day interval, mostly to the smaller values (-sign) in the second half of the year.

IV

Skewness in the Tails. (Formula #2)

(p.95-p.83)/(p.17-p.05)

In the next part of the study, we wished to determine whether there was skewness in the tails of the distribution, i.e. whether the tails were symmetric, or asymmetric. To determine this, we divided the distance covered by the 95th to 83rd percentiles by the distance covered by the 17th to 5th percentiles. For any distribution (including the normal) with symmetry about the median, these would be equal, giving a ratio of 1.0. If the tails are skewed toward higher or positive price changes, the ratio will be greater than 1.0. If the skewness is toward the lower or negative price changes, the ratio will be less than 1.0.

Table II gives the summary results for this measure of skewness in the tails for the first and last half of 1987 and for the full year.

As you can see, the majority of the tails of the distributions were skewed positively, toward higher price changes, not only overall, but in all four price quartiles. None of the differences were likely to arise by chance, as can be seen by the level of the z-statistics. All z-statistics are significant at the 5% level of significance.

V

Flatness of the Tails (Kurtosis) (Formula #3)

(p.95-p.05)/(p.83-p.17)

Formula #3 does not measure skewness, but the extent to

Table II

Skewness in the Tails (Formula #2)

Evidence of Skewing in the Tails of the Distribution of Price Changes Toward Higher Price Changes (Excess of >1's), Toward Lower Price Changes (Excess of <1's), or Absence of Skewing (Equal Number of >1's and <1's) for Each of Four Price Quartiles (Q1 Lowest Prices, Q4 Highest Prices) for Intervals of 1-Day and 8-Days. (z > 2.05 Significant at 5% Level of Significance)

$$((\Delta\log_e p).95 - (\Delta\log_e p).83)/((\Delta\log_e p).17 - (\Delta\log_e p).05)$$

Interval		First Half >1	<1	Second Half >1	<1	Full Year >1	<1
1 Day	Q1	10	4	9	5	19	9
	Q2	11	3	8	6	19	9
	Q3	10	4	9	5	19	9
	Q4	10	4	11	3	21	7
Total		41	15	37	19	78	34
z =		3.5		2.5		4.2	
8 Days	Q1	13	1	8	6	20	7
	Q2	11	3	9	5	20	8
	Q3	11	3	8	6	19	9
	Q4	9	5	13	1	22	6
Total		44	12	38	18	82	30
z =		4.3		2.7		4.9	

which the distribution is piled up in the tails. We examined the flatness of the tails by dividing the 95th to the 5th percentile range by the 83rd to 17th percentile range, formula #3 above. For a normal distribution, this ratio is given by (p.95-p.05)/(p.83-p.17) = 1.645/0.967 = 1.74. When the ratio exceeds 1.74, it means the tails contain more probability, relative to the core, than they would in a normal distribution. In other words, the tails are more spread out than they would be in a normal distribution. Table III shows the results for both halves of 1987 and for the full year.

As you can see the tails are significantly more spread out than they would be in a normal distribution for both the one day interval and the eight day interval. There is somewhat less spreading (smaller z-values) as the difference interval increases from one to eight days, suggesting a move toward the normal distribution as the difference interval is lengthened.

Comments on skewness formulas #1, #2, and #3 and what they do and don't measure are relevant here. Formula #1 only covers the distribution between p.17 and p.83, i.e. the inner two-thirds of the frequency distribution. Whether the tails are long and thin, or closely bunched up, makes no difference. This skewness measure only covers the shape of the "core" (p.17 to p.83) of the distribution.

Skewness Formula #2, by contrast, only covers the asymmetry of the tails, from p.95 to p.83 and from p.05 to p.17. Formula #1, on the other hand, the shape of the distribution in the "core" (p.17 to p.83), has absolutely no effect on the skewness measure given by Formula #2.

Also, the shape of the extremes of tails, p.00 to p.05 and p.95 to p.100, has no effect on skewness measure #2. But, it is precisely these extremes of tails, p.00 to p.05 and p.95 to p.100, which have the biggest effect on the skewness measure given in most textbooks. This measure is the third moment about the mean, μ_3. The ratio μ_3/σ, σ being the standard deviation, is also

Table III

Flatness in the Tails (Formula #3)

Evidence in the Distribution of Price Changes of Flatness in the Tails (Excess of >1.74's) or Absence of Flatness in the Tails (Excess of <1.74's) for Each of Four Price Quartiles (Q1 Lowest Prices, Q4 Highest Prices) for Intervals of 1-Day and 8-Days. (z > 2.05 Significant at 5% Level of Significance)

$$((\Delta\log_e p).95 - (\Delta\log_e p).05)/((\Delta\log_e p).83 - (\Delta\log_e p).17)$$

Interval		First Half >1.74	<1.74	Second Half >1.74	<1.74	Full Year >1.74	<1.74
1 Day	Q1	14	0	14	0	28	0
	Q2	14	0	13	1	27	1
	Q3	11	3	13	1	24	4
	Q3	13	1	11	3	24	4
Total		52	4	51	5	103	9
z =		6.4		6.1		9.1	
8 Day	Q1	13	1	13	1	26	2
	Q2	12	2	11	3	23	5
	Q3	10	4	9	5	19	9
	Q4	13	1	10	4	23	5
Total		48	8	43	13	91	21
z =		5.3		4.0		6.8	

commonly used as a skewness measure.

VI

Skewness. (Formula #4)

(3x(mean-median))/(standard deviation)

The final formula #4 reveals skewness toward greater price changes, positive skewness, when the mean is greater than the median, when the ratio is positive; it shows skewness toward the lowest or negative price changes, or negative skewness, when the mean is less then the median, or when the ratio is negative. During the first half of 1987 there was definite and significant positive skewness for both the one and eight day intervals, but this diminished somewhat in the second half, particularly for the one day interval where skewness became slightly negative (26+, 30-). There was not a great deal of difference between the one and eight day data. The overall result was that skewness was clearly observable, as can be seen in Table IV.

VII

The Effect of the Direction of Price Change on Skewness of the Core (Skewness Formula #1)

One may ask whether the direction of skewness is related to the direction of the price movement. We can test this question by examining how the direction of skewness given in formula #1 (skewness of the core) relates to the median change in price for the one day interval. The results are given in Table V.

In the 47 times the median price rose, 36 times the skewness was positive and 10 times the skewness was negative, revealing skewness in the direction of price change. The direction of skewness was the same as the direction of price change three and a half times as often as it was in the opposite direction. When the median price was unchanged, skewness was positive as often as it was negative. When the median price was negative, skewness was negative twice as often as it was positive (14 to 7). The Chi-square for Table V is 15.6 and barely significant at the 1% level of significance. Thus, the direction of skewness is generally related to the direction of price change, based on

281

Table IV

Skewness (Formula #4)

Evidence of Skewing in the Distribution of Price Changes Toward Higher Price Changes (Excess of +'s), Toward Lower Price Changes (Excess of -'s), or Absence of Skewing (Equal Number of +'s and -'s) for Each of Four Price Quartiles (Q1 Lowest Prices, Q4 Highest Prices) for Intervals of 1-Day and 8-Days. (z > 2.05 Significant at 5% Level of Significance)

$$(3x(\text{mean}\Delta\log_e p-\text{medium}\Delta\log_e p))/(\text{standard deviation}\Delta\log_e p)$$

Interval		First Half +	First Half -	Second Half +	Second Half -	Full Year +	Full Year -
			Mean - Median				
1 Day	Q1	10	4	5	9	15	13
	Q2	10	4	6	8	16	12
	Q3	11	3	7	7	18	10
	Q4	12	2	8	6	20	8
Total		43	13	26	30	69	43
z =		4.0		0.5		2.5	
8 Days							
	Q1	11	3	7	7	18	10
	Q2	10	4	12	2	22	6
	Q3	8	6	9	5	17	11
	Q4	8	6	7	7	15	13
Total		37	19	35	21	72	40
z =		2.4		1.9		3.0	

Table V

Skewness (Formula #1)

Evidence of Skewing in the Central Portion of the Distribution of Price Changes Toward Higher Price Changes (Positive), Toward Lower Price Changes (Negative), or Absence of Skewing (Zero) for 1-Day Interval When the Median Price Was Up, Down, or Unchanged. (Chi-Square is barely Significant at 1% Level of Significance).

$$(((\Delta\log_e p).83-(\Delta\log_e p).50)-((\Delta\log_e p).50-(\Delta\log_e p).17))/((\Delta\log_e p).83-(\Delta\log_e p).17)$$

Median Price Change	One Day Change in Price Skewness		
	Positive	Zero	Negative
Up	36	1	10
Unchanged	22	0	22
Down	7	0	14
Chi-Square		15.6	

the above data. This should be of interest to people who use formulae to estimate the value of options. Note that the above conclusion is for simultaneous changes of median and skewness. It does not say whether skewness leads or lags median changes. Note that the 8-day data shows coupling of skewness to the median more strongly than the one-day data. In other words, it takes more than one day for the effect of the market to be felt.

Table V.a

Skewness (Formula #1)

Evidence of Skewing in the Central Portion of the Distribution of Price Changes Toward Higher Price Changes (Positive), Toward Lower Price Changes (Negative), or Absence of Skewing (Zero) for 8-Day Interval When the Median Price Was Up, Down, or Unchanged. (Chi-Square Significant at much less than 1% Level of Significance).

$$(((\Delta\log_e p).83-(\Delta\log_e p).50)-((\Delta\log_e p).50-(\Delta\log_e p).17))/((\Delta\log_e p).83-(\Delta\log_e p).17)$$

Median Price Change	Eight Day Change in Price Skewness		
	Positive	Zero	Negative
Up	43	0	7
Unchanged	10	0	5
Down	15	0	32
Chi-Square	30.0 highly significant		

Over the eight day interval, there were 50 increases in price. Of these instances, skewness was positive in 43 and negative in 7, revealing skewness in the direction of price change. When the price dropped, skewness was negative in 32 instances and positive in 15, again revealing skewness in the direction of price change. The Chi Square for Table V.a is 30.0 with four degrees of freedom - a significant statistic.

VIII

Increase in Dispersion with the Square Root of the Difference Interval

Now let us look at a quite different question. We will look at how dispersion rises with increases in the length of the time difference interval, or the length of the time interval over which the price change is measured. For a random process, dispersion measured by the standard deviation, rises with the square root of the time difference interval.

In Figure 1, we give the semi-intersextile range (SISR) of changes in the natural logarithms of price for four different quartiles for difference intervals of from one to eight days for four different 8-day pricing periods. The slope of the line is approximately 0.5 which reveals that the semi-intersextile range rises roughly with the square root of the difference interval. This square-root of time difference interval relationship is typical of random series and corroborates other work on the relationship.

A better test of the square root rule is to examine the instances in which the 8-day semi-intersextile range is more, or less, than $8^{.5}$ times the 1-day semi-intersextile range. This is a more accurate test than the graphs in Figure 1 since the samples are seven-eights independent. In the graphs, on the other hand, there is a high degree of overlap between the 1, 2, 3,..,8 day difference intervals. The variability of the data will not give us perfect relationships.

There were 61 cases when the ratio 8-day SISR's/1-day SISR's was greater and 48 instances where it was less. The standard deviation is $109^{.5}$, or 10.4. The observed difference is 61 minus 48, or 13. The z-value is 13/10.4 = 1.25. The probability of the value of z being greater than 1.25 (two tailed test) is 0.21. In other words, the $t^{.5}$ law cannot be rejected at the 20% level. The square root law looks to be a fairly good fit, based on the frequency in which the semi-intersextile range rose by more and less than $8^{.5}$ in the 8-day interval from its value in the 1-day interval. Note that these figures refer to cross-sectional, not sequential SISR's.

In Figure 2, we give the same data, but for the standard deviation of changes in the natural logarithms of prices for difference intervals of from one to eight days.

When we compare the ratio SD 8-day/SD 1-day to $8^{.5}$, the ratio is less than $8^{.5}$ in 76 instances and greater than 8.5 in 36 cases. The sum is 112 and the difference is 40. The standard deviation of 112 is 10.5 giving a z-score of 40/10.5 = 3.8. The difference is significant revealing that the standard deviation rises more slowly than $t^{.5}$.

IX

How the Standard Deviation Moves Toward the Semi-Intersextile Range as the Difference Interval Rises from One to Eight Days

The semi-intersextile ranges measures half the middle two-thirds of the distribution. That is by definition. The standard deviation of a normal distribution also measures half the middle two-thirds of the distribution. If the distribution is not quite normal, or has wide tails, the standard deviation will generally be higher than the semi-intersextile range. Thus, the relationship between these two measures is a test of normality. For a random series, as the difference interval of changes in the series is increased, the distribution should become more normal, under the Central Limit Theorem.

The ratio of SD/SISR is higher for 1-day data than for 8-day data, tending to move more toward the semi-intersextile range as the difference interval is increased to 8 days. We can test the significance of this by counting the number of instances in which the ratio of SD/SISR for the 1-day difference interval was higher than the same ratio for the 8-day difference interval. If it was, the standard deviation declined toward the semi-intersextile range. The results of this test, with separate tests for each quartile, are the following. In 81 instances, the ratio SD/SISR moved down toward 1.0; in 29 instances it did not, for a total of 110 cases. In 2 instances there was no change. The standard deviation of the total of 110 is 10.5. The difference between 81 and 29 is 52, well beyond two standard deviations. The z-score (52/10.5) is 5.0 indicating significant movement of the standard deviation toward the semi-intersextile range, as would be expected under the Central Limit Theorem.

X

Effect of Price Level on the Standard Deviation of Cross Sectional Changes in the Natural Logarithms of Price

Also in Figure 2, you can see that the standard deviation of changes in the natural logarithms of prices is related to the absolute value of the price. Quartile 1 contains the lowest prices, Quartile 4 the highest prices. The standard deviation of $\Delta\log_e$ price for the low price stocks is higher than the standard deviation for high price stocks. Why this is so is an interesting question. This point is of interest for its implications on expected returns from low price stock portfolios versus high price stock portfolios, as described below. It also means that the cross-sectional distribution cannot be precisely log normal, i.e., normal in $\Delta\log_e$ price.

The standard deviation is systematically larger than the semi-intersextile range (SISR). The standard deviation converges to the SISR as we go from a 1-day difference interval to an 8-day difference interval. We have observed this above. It means that the Central Limit Theorem is operating, and that for the 1 to 8 day interval, the (cross sectional) standard deviation increases somewhat less rapidly than the square root of 8.

XI

Conclusions

The following conclusions are based on cross-sectional price changes in the natural logarithms of prices of from 1 to eight days, tabulated by quartiles. The 4th quartile has the highest prices; the 1st quartile has the lowest prices. Most of the conclusions below are based on one-day price changes and 8-day price changes.

1. For cross-sectional changes of $\log_e$ price, the distribution of changes in the natural logarithms of prices reveals significant departures from normality. (Table III)

2. The distributions often tend to be skewed both in the central part of the distribution and in the tails. (Tables I and II)

3. The skewness is in the same direction for all four quartiles far more often than would occur by chance, suggesting that the direction of skewness is not dependent on price level. (Tables I & II)

4. The tails of the distributions tend to be more flat than normal and the central portion of the distributions tend to be more skinny than normal, as shown by other studies (e.g., Osborne, 1959). (Table III)

5. Departures from the normal curve are not invariant over time, but depend on the particular part of the year.

6. The direction of skewness is more often than not in the same direction as the median price change. Thus, if price changes are positive, the skewness tends to be in the positive direction. If price changes are negative, the skewness tends to be in the negative direction. This correspondence of direction of price change and direction of skewness occurs both in the central part of the distribution and in the tails. (Table V)

7. The semi-intersextile ranges of changes in the natural logarithms of prices (measured by the semi-intersextile range) rises approximately with the square root of the difference interval for 1 to 8 day differences. The standard deviation rises at a slightly lower rate over the same intervals.

8. The standard deviation, which is systematically larger than the semi-intersextile range, converges toward the semi-intersextile range as the difference interval is increased from 1 to 8 days. This movement toward normality may be expected for a random process under the Central Limit Theorem.

9. The standard deviation of changes in the natural logarithms of prices is higher for lower price stocks and lower for higher priced stocks. (Figure 2)

10. Many of the above characteristics are found in the sequential dispersion of individual stock prices. Why these characteristics should also be true of cross-sectional dispersion is an interesting but unanswered question.

References

[1] Fisher, Lawrence and Lorie, James H., 1970, "Some Studies of Variability of Returns on Investments in Common Stocks," *Journal of Business*, 43, 99-134.

[2] McEnally, R. W. and Todd, R. B., 1992, "Cross-Sectional Variation in Common Stock Returns,", *Financial Analysts Journal*, May-June, 59-63.

[3] Osborne, M.F.M., 1959, "Brownian Motion in the Stock Market," *Operations Research*, 7, 145-73, also in Cootner, P.H., Ed., 1964, *The Random Character of Stock Prices* (M.I.T. Press, Cambridge, MA).

[4] Osborne, M.F.M., 1995, *The Stock Market and Finance from a Physicist's Viewpoint* , Crossgar Press. Originally published in 1977.

Figure 1

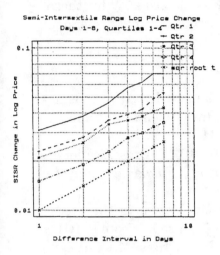

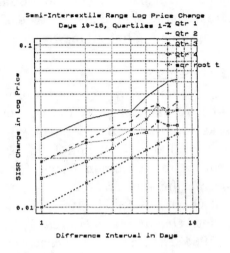

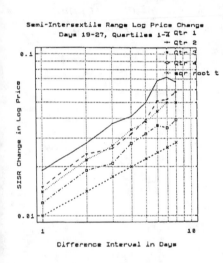

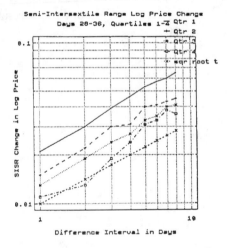

Figure 2

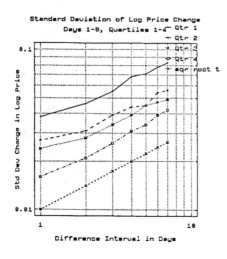

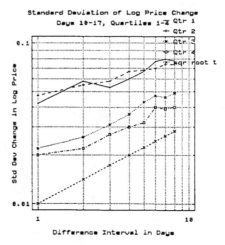

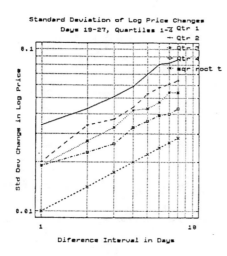

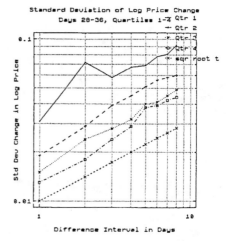

20

STATISTICAL ANALYSIS OF CHANGES IN EARNINGS PER SHARE

Introduction

Knowledge of the characteristics of changes in earnings is of practical importance to managers of corporations and investors and of theoretical importance to economists. Yet relatively little is known of the underlying statistical characteristics of earnings changes.

The kind of investigation which has recently and substantially enlarged our knowledge of (stock and commodity) prices[1] has not generally been applied to earnings.[2] This lack of application exists despite the appropriateness of available earnings data to statistical analysis in terms of the large number of series available, the care with which the data has been compiled and verified, and the length of most series (many cover a generation or more).

Using the variables defined in equation (1) below, we treat the following topics:

1. Frequency distribution of earnings changes.

2. Correlation of rates of earnings changes in successive periods.

3. Analysis of variance: the effect of the company.

4. Analysis of variance: the effect of the year.

5. Dispersion of earnings changes and the length of the period.

6. Dispersion of earnings changes and the industry.

7. Stability of earnings changes of the company by industry.

8. Correlation of stability of rates of earnings changes in successive periods.

9. Serial correlation, by company.

The Data

All of the data is drawn from the Value Line Investment Survey[3] which presents per share earnings data for some 1100 U.S. corporations, including virtually all major publicly owned

Unpublished manuscript 1966

corporations. Of importance to those interested in prediction, this earnings data is as originally reported, adjusted only for stock splits and stock dividends. To insure uniformity of the data over an extended period, to avoid the frequently arbitrary nature of interim data and to permit use of logarithms (which cannot be applied to negative numbers), we used annual earnings, included only companies reporting on a calendar year, rejected companies which reported any deficits or which failed to have published records for the full period 1950-1964.

Most of the results are presented on an industry basis. In these tests we usually restricted the sample to some 400 companies and eleven industries as defined and grouped by Value Line. In other tests the sample becomes larger. Sometimes the sample was cut to meet the requirements of programming or keypunching. The principal effect of exclusions was to reduce the number of companies with high fluctuations in earnings.

The variable used in the study is the series of first differences in the natural logarithms of earnings per share as defined in equation (1).[4]

$$x_t = \log_e v_t - \log_e v_{t-1} \tag{1}$$

where v_t equals earnings per share in the year t.

We use first differences in the logarithms of earnings per share (rather than earnings per share) for several reasons. First, the absolute value of earnings per share is an arbitrary quantity determined by the number of shares outstanding. Second, variability in earnings per share may be, and probably is, an increasing function of the value of earnings. This effect will be neutralized by use of natural logarithms. Third, for changes of ± 15 percent, the log change is practically the same as the percentage change.

I

Frequency Distributions

The frequency distribution[5], which is simply a breakdown of the data into groups, can reveal important information. Upon plotting and testing, we found the frequency distribution of earnings per share (1964), first differences in earnings per share (1963-1964), and the natural logarithms of earnings per share (1964) to be significantly skewed to the left and slender (leptokurtic), though skewness declined successively as we shifted from the original values to first differences and then to logarithms.[6]

The frequency distribution of first differences in the natural logarithms of earnings per share (entire sample, 1963-1964) was not skewed, thought it was more slender than the normal curve. These characteristics were indicated by applying the Chi-square test to a fitted curve and by using other tests.

II

Correlation of Rates of Earnings Change in Successive Periods

Correlation simply means relation. Positive correlation means that the same companies report high rates of change in both periods (and visa versa); negative correlation denotes that companies with high rates in one period have low rates in the other period. Correlation is nil when rates of change in one period bear no systematic relation to rates in the next period.

A presumption of much investment theory and practice is that relative per share earnings changes in successive periods are positively correlated. The intuitive basis for this presumption rests in quantitative and qualitative differences, such as the return on investment, management, etc. These differences are believed to cause differences in rates of change in earnings that will persist over extended periods of time.

The two alternate hypotheses are: non correlation and negative correlation. The principal intuitive arguments which may be raised for non correlation rest in the random effect probably produced by the multitude of uncontrollable and unpredictable factors constantly affecting changes in per share earnings. Negative correlation could result from negative serial correlation or other causes.

To eliminate the effect of industry on the results, the correlations are made by industry, using eleven industries.[7] For each industry, four correlations were made: 1950-1954 versus 1954-1959; 1954-1959 versus 1959-1964; 1953-1957 versus 1957-1960; 1957-1960 versus 1960-1964.

The first correlations are made with nearly equal or equal time spans. The second two correlations are made using peak to peak periods of the "business cycle" to eliminate the effect of the cycle. The definition used was that of the Department of Commerce and the National Bureau of Economic Research. The coefficients are given in Table 1.

Table 1
Correlation of Earnings Changes in Successive Periods

Industry	1950-54 versus 1954-59 r^2	1954-59 versus 1959-64 r^2	1953-57 versus 1957-60 r^2	1957-60 versus 1960-64 r^2
Auto Parts (18)	+.00	-.30*	-.00	-.45*
Building Materials (35)	-.21*	+.04	+.00	-.00
Chemical (34)	-.01	+.08	-.10	-.40*
Drug (24)	+.18*	+.03	+.04	-.01
Machinery (29)	-.06	-.01	-.04	-.03
Electric Machinery & Electronics (29)	+.01	+.09	-.34*	+.00
Steel (31)	-.03	-.06	+.03	-.19*
Petroleum (29)	-.00	-.01	-.04	-.04
Natural Gas (31)	+.00	— .18 '	-.04	-.00
Electric Utility (93)	+.01	-.00	+.02	-.00
Bank (33)	-.03	-.04	-.12*	+.01
Railroad (24)	-.00	-.00	-.03	-.06

* Significant at .05 level of significance. Approximate number of companies in sample given in parentheses.

The results indicate that generally (over 80% of the tests) earnings changes in successive periods are not correlated. When significant correlation is present, it is predominantly (over 85%) negative. These results apply to comparisons within individual industries.

III
Analysis of Variance: Effect of the Company

Next we turn to the question of whether rates of change in earnings of various companies in a single period (1950-1964) differed by more than might be accounted for by chance.[8] The correlations of the last section suggest that we will find no significant differences.

To remove the influence of industry, separate analyses were made for each industry. In addition, we chose a method of analysis which would eliminate the effect common to all companies in each industry of shifts in the annual change in earnings. This method also negated the effect of the business cycle.[9]

The low values of our statistic (the F-ratio) show that in each of the 21 industries there is no significant difference in rates of change of earnings of various companies; the company means are homogeneous. In retrospect, of course, one might pick two companies whose growth rates differed significantly. Our analysis indicates that one could not pick them in advance.

IV
Analysis of Variance: Effect of the Year

As a by-product of the preceding analysis, we obtained measures of the significance of differences in the yearly changes in earnings for each industry. Our results (the high values of the F-ratios) indicate that the yearly changes were significantly different in over 85% of the industries. At a slightly lower level of significance (0.10 instead of 0.05) the yearly means were heterogeneous in all but one industry. The effect of the year is substantial and significant in nearly all industries.

The contribution of the yearly change to total variance was much higher in some industries than in others, however. It was especially important in the cyclical industries such as the steel, auto parts, metals & mining and building materials industries. It was of comparatively small importance in certain utility industries, such as telephone and natural gas and in the bank and finance industries.

Table 2
Analysis of Variance

Industry	Annual Average	Variance of Yearly Means	Variance of Company Means	Residual Variance
Auto Parts (16)	.032	.929	.014	.067
Bank (33)	.058	.077	.005	.013
Building Materials (31)	.025	.653	.019	.048
Chemical (28)	.038	.566	.027	.029
Container (12)	.022	.195	.013	.041
Drug (24)	.089	.269	.071	.040
Electric Utility (93)	.052	.187	.005	.010
Elec. Equip. & Electronics (24)	.047	.494	.086	.077
Finance (11)	.045	.016	.007	.013
Machinery (24)	.042	.308	.027	.052
Machine Tool (5)	.007	.344	.008	.087
Metals & Mining (23)	.028	.737	.024	.097
Natural Gas (33)	.055	.091	.020	.032
Paper (4)	.016	.424	.016	.041
Petroleum (29)	.034	.285	.013	.017
Railraod (21)	.000	.397	.019	.036
Steel (24)	.033	1.448	.025	.073
Telephone (7)	.050	.055	.015	.014
Textile (6)	.021	.175	.020	.070
Tobacco (12)	.047	.109	.017	.030
Truck & Bus (6)	.071	.159	.051	.059

The F-ratio, not given here, is obtained by dividing the value in the second, or third, column by the corresponding value in the fourth column. None of the F-ratios for the company means were large enough to be significant at the 0.05 level. In all cases but three it was significant at the 0.05 level for yearly means. The three exceptions were the textile, truck & bus and finance industries.

V

Dispersion of Earnings Changes and the Length of the Period

In this section, we measure dispersion from the mean change for the industry.[10] Our unit of measurement is the standard deviation (s). We wish to know how dispersion changes as the time period is lengthened. Separate tests are made for each industry.

Values for s for various time periods are given for eleven industries below. In all industries, dispersion tends to increase as the period of time is lengthened. For every industry the mean value of the standard deviation for one-year periods is less than the mean value for five-year periods. The latter value is always less than the value for the fourteen-year period.

VI

Dispersion of Earnings Changes and the Industry

Here, as in the preceding section, dispersion (s) measures the degree of spread of earnings changes from the mean change for the industry.[11] We wish to know how dispersion varies from one industry to another. The results are shown in the table. As may be seen in the table, dispersion is very low in the electric utility and bank industries, fairly low in the oil industry, higher (on a one-year basis, much higher on a long-term basis) in the natural gas and chemical industries, and very high in the electrical equipment & electronics industry.

In most industries, if dispersion is low on a one-year basis, it is also low on a long-term basis; and visa versa. In the chemical industry, however, dispersion is relatively low in the one-year period and high in the longer period; in the auto parts industry the reverse is true.

In three industries, bank, electric utility and natural gas, dispersion has tended to decline since 1950.

Table 3

Standard Deviation of First Differences in Natural Logarithms of Earnings Per Share

	Bank	Elec. Utility	Oil	Auto Parts	Rail-Road	Bldg. Materials	Natural Gas	Steel	Machinery	Chemical	Drug	Elec. Equip.& Electronics
No. of Companies	33	93	29	18	21	31	33	24	24	28	24	24
1950-1	.149	.159	.143	.306	.234	.214	.320	.288	.284	.212	.150	.337
1951-2	.213	.151	.098	.219	.202	.246	.209	.262	.168	.202	.233	.294
1952-3	.130	.114	.124	.168	.188	.181	.187	.183	.125	.112	.187	.222
1953-4	.152	.104	.120	.269	.172	.234	.225	.327	.233	.253	.356	.219
1954-5	.108	.073	.096	.238	.148	.257	.186	.281	.291	.169	.340	.303
1955-6	.107	.070	.160	.317	.142	.165	.105	.281	.227	.141	.166	.291
1956-7	.071	.067	.120	.223	.218	.185	.197	.202	.168	.190	.142	.272
1957-8	.084	.086	.181	.384	.185	.297	.111	.350	.259	.174	.158	.298
1958-9	.084	.086	.125	.297	.128	.229	.143	.352	.264	.153	.145	.307
1959-60	.058	.076	.124	.218	.201	.177	.155	.304	.229	.135	.213	.312
1960-1	.070	.056	.118	.238	.309	.180	.105	.214	.222	.133	.164	.205
1961-2	.054	.094	.104	.156	.163	.194	.142	.202	.268	.215	.234	.219
1962-3	.086	.090	.116	.247	.117	.236	.124	.169	.145	.118	.130	.314
1963-4	.060	.044	.154	.122	.126	.135	.104	.189	.160	.109	.078	.263
Average	.102	.071	.127	.243	.181	.209	.165	.257	.217	.165	.193	.275
1950-54	.212	.174	.255	.454	.345	.460	.417	.423	.402	.358	.480	.519
1954-59	.175	.138	.260	.299	.349	.368	.228	.462	.352	.435	.457	.490
1959-64	.139	.128	.273	.318	.319	.337	.231	.379	.366	.250	.380	.652
Average	.175	.147	.263	.357	.338	.388	.291	.421	.373	.348	.439	.554
1950-64	.254	.273	.429	.449	.516	.519	.526	.587	.609	.615	1.001	1.100

VII

Stability of Earnings Changes of the Company, by Industry

In the previous section we were concerned with how rapidly earnings of companies diverged and how this divergence varied by industry.

In this section, we are concerned with the degree of stability of earnings changes of individual companies and with how this stability varies by industry[12]. We wish to know whether companies in some industries have highly stable changes in earnings and companies in other industries have unstable changes in earnings. Our measure of stability is the standard deviation; in this section, however it is computed for each company and measured from the mean change for the particular company. Low values of s indicate high stability of earnings change.

Two industries have very high stability, the bank and electric industries. For more than half the companies in these industries the standard deviation is less than 0.12. For 80% of the companies it is below 0.18. Earnings changes are fairly stable in the petroleum industry.

VIII

Correlation of Stability of Rates of Earnings Change in Successive Periods

Our measure of stability is the same as in the last section, the standard deviation (s); it is computed for each company and measured from the mean change for that company.

We wish to know whether stable changes in one period are correlated with stable changes in the next period[13]. To determine this we correlated standard deviations in the period 1950-1955 with standard deviations in the period 1955-1960. A separate analysis was made for each of the nine industries.

The analysis showed significant positive correlation in one third of the industries: electric equipment and electronics ($r^2 = 0.44$), machinery and electric utilities. (The coefficients of determination were 0.10 or higher in three other industries - auto parts, steel and bank - but not high enough to be significant at the 0.05 level.)

There was no significant evidence of negative correlation.

IX

Serial Correlation

Serial correlation, as used here, refers to the relation between neighboring terms in a series, such as annual rates of change in earnings per share.[14] If the rates of change in all periods are similar, serial correlation will be positive; if high and low rates occur in alternate years, serial correlation will be negative. If there is no systematic relationship, serial correlation will be nil.

The purpose of this section is to determine whether annual changes (in the natural logarithms) of earnings are serially correlated. To determine whether they are, correlation analysis was performed on each of 248 companies in eleven industries over the period 1950-1964.

The analysis showed almost no significant evidence of positive serial correlation in earnings changes. The coefficient was positive and significant at the 0.05 level for only one company.

Negative serial correlation was more frequent, but significant in only 8% of the companies. The highest incidence of negative serial correlation occurred in the auto parts industry and in the two regulated industries: natural gas (over one-fifth of the companies) and electric utility. Negative signs to the coefficient of serial correlation were more common than positive signs in a ratio of over two to one.

The major conclusion of the analysis is that serial correlation is not present in most companies (92%).

Table 4
Serial Correlation

Industry	TOTAL Percent Negative	SIGNIFICANT (AT 0.05) Percent Negative	SIGNIFICANT (AT 0.05) Percent Positive
		Coefficients of Correlation	
Auto Parts (11)	91%	18%	none
Building Material (22)	59	5	none
Chemical (22)	59	none	none
Drug (14)	29	none	7
machinery (19)	53	none	none
Electric equipment & Electronics (14)	71	none	none
Steel (19)	89	11	none
Petroleum (18)	61	6	none
Natural Gas (23)	83	22	none
Electric Utility (61)	80	18	none
Bank (22)	73	none	none
Railroad (3)	67	none	none
Total (248)	69%	8%	< 1%

Number of companies in each industry given in parentheses.

X

Summary of Conclusions

The major conclusions are listed below:[15]

1. Our tests indicate that the frequency distribution of first differences in the natural logarithms of earnings per share in a given year tends to approach a normal distribution.[16]

2. In each of the 12 major industries studied, there was little correlation between rates of growth of per share earnings in two consecutive periods; when significant correlation was present, it was predominately negative.

3. In the period 1950-1964 there was no significant difference between the rates of change in per share earnings of various

companies.[17] This was true in 18 of 21 industries studied. In retrospect, one might pick two companies whose growth rates differed significantly. Our analysis indicates that one could not pick them in advance.

4. Rates of change in earnings per share in any industry varied significantly from one year to another.[18] This effect, which was significant in all but three industries, was especially pronounced in the cyclical industries, such as steel and auto parts, but of relatively minor importance in the bank, telephone, and natural gas industries.[19]

5. From any point in time, rates of change of earnings per share of companies in an industry tended to diverge from one another, or disperse. The amount of dispersion was directly related to the length of the period.[20]

6. The degree of dispersion of earnings per share of companies in an industry is low in a few industries, particularly the electric utility and bank industries. It is very high in others, especially the electronic and electric equipment industry.

7. Volatility of annual rates of change in earnings per share of individual companies is very low in the electric utility ad bank industries, below average in the petroleum industry, and very high in the steel industry.

8. Within some industries, companies with stable rates of change of earnings per share in one period also record stable rates of change in the next period. We found significant positive correlation in one third of the industries tested. Our tests of serial correlation between annual rates of change in earnings per share of individual companies over the period 1950-1964 indicated that significant positive serial correlation was rare, significant negative serial correlation was infrequent, and lack of significant serial correlation was characteristic of over 90 per cent of the companies tested.

Implications of Conclusions

The conclusion that rates of change of per share earnings in successive periods are uncorrelated[21] has important implications in at least four related areas: theory of valuation of the firm; practical valuation of the firm; relation of changes in earnings to other characteristics of the firm; and fluctuations in stock market prices.

Assumptions about earnings growth form an important element in most theoretical work on valuation of the firm, ranging fro the early work of J. B. Williams[22] to more recent studies. This theoretical work generally, or frequently, makes two assumptions: that growth rates are fixed (increasing, decreasing, unchanging or a combination) and that different firms have different rates of growth. If earnings changes in successive periods are uncorrelated, the appropriateness of these assumptions and of applying different growth rates to different companies is questionable.

Most financial analysts, investment managers, appraisers and others concerned with day to day appraisal of securities make analogous assumptions about growth rates. The most common example is the application of different price-earnings multiples to companies which have had different past rates of growth of earnings. If earnings in successive periods are uncorrelated,[23] the utility of using higher price earnings multiples for some companies than for others is very questionable. It presumes positive correlation of past and future earnings changes. Since this assumption is basic to much practical valuation of companies, the presence of random correlation would call into question a wide-spread practice.

A less concrete implication concerns differences in management, location, market domination, access to raw materials, profit margins, return on capital, etc. These characteristics are generally felt to affect growth of earnings. If there is no significance in rates of change in earnings, is that assumption correct?[24] Rating management on the basis of changes of per share earnings would seem to be a questionable practice. The rate of return on investment may not be a reliable indicator of future growth earnings

Changes in stock prices have been shown to be a random process, and changes in earnings bear an important relation to changes in stock prices. If changes in earnings are uncorrelated or random, as the evidence suggests, randomness in earnings changes would serve as partial explanation of randomness in stock prices.

Finally, our measures of stability of changes in earnings of individual companies could serve as one tool for measuring security of dividend payment, as a complementary measure in estimating adequacy of coverage of fixed charges or for other purposes.

Footnotes

1. The widely scattered studies on the statistical analysis of speculative prices were assembled by P. H. Cootner in *The random Character of Stock Market Prices*, The M.I.T. Press, Cambridge, 1964.

2. References to the statistical analysis of profits (similar to the statistical analysis of prices) are rare, or incidental to other studies. A reference of the latter type occurs in M. FG. Scott, "Relative Share Prices and Yields", *Oxford Economic Papers*, October 1962, p. 242 & 249. Scott correlated changes in earnings in consecutive time intervals and found, as we did, "virtually no correlation" though he attributed the lack of correlation to the "existence of overlap between periods." A similar reference occurs in H. Benishay, "Variability in Earnings Price Ratios of Corporate Equities," *America Economic Review*, March 1961, p. 88, where the author finds the suggestion of low "correlation between growth in earnings in two consecutive time intervals." R. F. Wippern analyzed variability in earnings, though he did not use reported after tax per share earnings as a variable. See R. F. Wippern, "Earnings Variabilitv, Financial Structure, and the Value of the Firm," doctoral dissertation, Stanford University, 1964.

3. The *Value Line Investment Survey*, Arnold Bernhard & Co., Inc., New York, Volume XX.

4. Formula (1) may be stated in more general form as:

$$x_{ij} = \log_e v_{ij} \log_e v_{i,j-1} \qquad (1a)$$

where v_{ij} equals earnings per share of the i_{th} company in the

j_{th} year. The x_{ij} equals the difference between the natural logarithm of earnings per share in the year j and the natural logarithm of earnings per share in the year j-1. Sometimes we shall be concerned with the change in the natural logarithm of earnings per share over a period longer than one year in which case formula (la) becomes:

$$x_{ia} = \log_e v_{ij} - \log_e v_{i,j-1} \qquad \text{(lb)}$$

where k may exceed one year. In this case x_{ia} is the difference between the natural logarithm of earnings per share in the year j and the natural logarithm of earnings per share in the ear j-k

5. We computed four types of frequency distributions:

(a) the frequency of distribution of v_{ij}

(b) the frequency distribution of v_{ij}-$v_{i,j-1}$

(c) the frequency distribution of $\log_e v_{ij}$, and

(d) the frequency distribution, of x_{ij} each for j = 1964 and i = 1,2,....,n, with the variables v_{ij} and x_{ij} as defined in equation (la).

6. Frequency Distribution

	Earn. Per Share 1964	1st Dif. Earn. Per Sh. 1963-4	1st Dif. Earn. Per Sh. 1963-4	Nat. Log. Earn. Per Sh. 1964	1st Dif Nat. Log. Earn. Per Sh. 1963-4
# excluding electric utility					
No of Companies	527	413	320	413	448
π_1	1.979	0.155	0.186	0.267	0.029
π_2	3.168	0.071	0.066	-0.044	-0.000
π_3	1.976	0.180	0.214	0.303	0.005
β_1	1.295*	1.367*	0.688*	0.102*	0.030
β_2	5.04**	7.50**	6.37**	5.90**	6.16**
Sample	Gp I&II	Gp I	Gp I#	Gp I	Gp I&II

Excluding electric utility industry.

Skewness: π_3 is a measure of absolute skewness; π_3 equals 0 when no skewness is present; when a curve is perfectly symmetrical, $\beta_1 = 0$. The * indicates that significant skewness is present.

Kurtosis: π_4 is an absolute measure of kurtosis. β_2 is a relative measure of kurtosis. For a normal curve $\beta_2 = 3.0$. β_2 is less than 3.0 for a platokurtic(flat) curve and greater than 3.0 for a leptokurtic (slender) curve. The ** indicates that the curve is significantly leptokurtic.

7. In correlating rates of earnings changes in successive periods we used first differences in the natural logarithms as the measure of rates of change.

8. We used the standard formula for analysis of variance. See C. U. Yule & M. G. Kendall, *An Introduction to the Theory of Statistics*, C. Griffin & Co., London, 1958, pp. 54, 513. E. Croxton & D. J. Cowden, *Applied General Statistics*, Prentice-Hall, 1959, p. 713. Also *Unstat Computer Programs Manual*, Numerical Analysis Center, University of Minnesota, 1964, Umstat 51, p. 11.

9. Our procedure was to use the analysis of variance and to divide the variance of company means by the residual variance in obtaining the F-ratio. This procedure permits us to determine whether the company means are homogeneous even though the annual means are not.

10. Dispersion is defined as the root-mean-square deviation: The standard deviation was computed for fourteen one-year periods, two five-year periods (1954-9 and 1959-64) one-four year period (1950-4), and one fourteen-year period (1950-64).

13. The standard formula was used in computing the coefficient of correlation.

14. See *Umstat Computer Programs Manual*, Umstat 51, p. 21, Kendall uses a slightly different formula: Yule & Kendall, o. cit., p. 639.

15 Rates of growth, or rates of change, of earnings per share refer to differences in the natural logarithm of earnings per share.

16. As defined in equation (1).

17. Specifically, the company means were homogeneous. See Section III.

18. The yearly means were not homogeneous. See Section IV.

19. The effect of the year, as measured by analysis of variance, is probably related to the effect of the economy on rates of change of earnings.

20. This is similar to the relationship observed by Osborne, "Brownian Motion in Stock Market Prices", Cootner, op. cit.

21. Section X, Conclusion 2.

22. Section X, Conclusion 2. Also Conclusion 9. Lack of serial correlation would call into question Williams' assumptions.

23. Section X, Conclusion 2.

24. Section X, Conclusion 3.

Note: A few editorial changes were made in the article and several standard statistical formulas given in the original have been omitted.

PRINCIPLES OF FINANCIAL RELATIONSHIPS

Joseph E. Murphy

Talk Before the Institute for Quantitative Research in
Finance, Phoenix, Arizona, April 22-24, 1970

The material which I will present today is a generalized form
of the principles which I presented at the Computer
Applications Seminar of the New York Society of Security
Analysts a month ago in New York City. Any of you here today
who heard that earlier talk will find, I believe, that the increase
in generality is very great, indeed. Whereas the earlier principles covered a restricted set of relationships, the restated principles cover most relationships.

For the past five years at the University of Minnesota and
the Northwestern National Bank we have been examining decision rules for selecting stocks. This work has been done by
Harold Stevenson, now at Arizona State University, Russell
Nelson, myself and others. Dr. Nelson and I collaborated on the
present paper. In examining decision rules for selecting stocks,
we found a high correlation between relative changes in earnings per share and prices per share in the same time period. The
results of this work appeared in the January-February 1968
issue of the *Financial Analysts Journal* and will be reprinted in
the forthcoming *C.F.A. Readings in Financial Analysis* to be
published by Irwin and Company. The high correlation between
concurrent relative changes in prices and changes in earnings
established the importance of earnings changes as a determinant of price changes.

Having established the importance of earnings changes as a
determinant of price changes, we became interested in finding
decision rules for predicting earnings changes. We wished to be
able to distinguish those stocks which would record superior
growth of earnings from those stocks which would record infe-

rior growth of earnings. In attacking this problem, we asked the following kinds of questions: Does past percentage change in earnings per share give reliable information as to which stocks will record the best future growth of earnings per share? Does the price/earnings ratio give a means of determining which companies will exhibit the best future growth of earnings? Is the dividend yield useful in attempting to predict superior earnings growth? How helpful are payout ratios and rates of return on equity capital in selecting companies which will show the greatest growth of earnings?

As you can see these questions are basic; they treat stock selection rules which are in general used and they concern some of the essential parts of general theories of finance. Our interest in the questions of course, was not restricted to selecting stocks. We were concerned with improving our understanding of financial and price changes. Moreover, as you know, other persons were investigating these same questions, both in this country and abroad.

We were surprised at the answers we obtained to our questions. In nearly all cases, the answers tended to be negative. Past percentage changes in earnings per share gave little indication of future changes. Price/earnings ratios were not very indicative of which companies would record the highest future rates of earnings growth. Payout and rate of return on equity capital were not good predictors of future earnings growth.

The negative results to the question created doubt about the usefulness of the usual or traditional approaches to forecasting earnings. They also suggested that we run tests on other variables. Initially we planned to compute all possible correlations among all pairs of major financial variables. The existence of the high speed computer and the availability of the Compustat data base made it possible to find all possible correlations of pairs of major variables. We completed a general program which would compute, print and test the significance of correlation for any pair of variables for any sample of companies for varying sample sizes.

But even with the availability of enormous computing power, a general program and all the required data, this approach had potential problems. One possible problem was: Given the results of correlations of all possible pairs of variables, how could one make any sense out of the resulting data? We were likely to be inundated by so much data that we could not bring any order to it.

Another approach occurred to us. That was to postulate the kinds of general relationships which might exist between any two variables, and then to test the postulates. If we could find some general rules or principles which covered a number of pairs of variables, then we could test these rules. If the rules seemed to work, then we would not need to run correlations on all pairs of variables. If the rules or principles held in most or all cases, we would have a framework in which to place the results.

So we turned to the problem of attempting to formulate some general principles which might govern the relationships among various financial variables. In so doing, we first considered the possibility of distinguishing among two or more general kinds of financial variables. Perhaps some classes of financial variables behaved differently than others. Some variables, for example, might be quite stable and predictable. Other financial variables might be very unstable, erratic, unpredictable.

We divided financial variables into two classes or categories. The first class is composed of dollar variables and ratio variables. A dollar variable is simply a financial variable which is expressed in dollars. Sales of Minnesota Mining in 1969 is a dollar variable. Earnings per share is a dollar variable. Market price per share is a dollar variable. Examples of dollar variables are shown in Exhibit I. A ratio variable is formed by dividing one dollar variable by another dollar variable. Price divided by earnings is a ratio variable. Profit margins, rate of return on equity, payout and dividend yield are all ratio variables. Examples of ratio variables are also shown in Exhibit I. Both dollar variables and ratio variables are relatively stable, relatively predictable.

The second class of variables which we distinguished consists of percentage change variables. Percentage change variables tend to be highly volatile, erratic, unpredictable. The values of percentage change variables change rapidly from period to period. Percentage change in earnings per share is a percentage change variable. Rate of appreciation of market price is a percentage change variable. All growth variables are percentage change variables. Examples of percentage change variables are shown in Exhibit II.

We thus made a distinction between dollar and ratio variables, on the one hand, and percentage change variables, on the other hand. Having made the distinction, we turned to the problem of formulating rules which governed the relationships among values of the two kinds of variables.

Initially we developed a group of five principles which covered a limited set of relationships among pairs of variables. We tested those principles through over 20,000 correlations and found that they were very accurate.

The original principles were limited in several respects, however; they covered only pairs of variables; they did not extend to relationships involving more than two variables; the pairs of relationships were incomplete in that only coincident or adjacent time periods were considered, not more distant time periods; and many classes of relationships were not considered. As a result of these shortcomings, we reexamined the principles, restructured them and rewrote them.

We have not had time to test completely the revised principles. However, the validity of the broadened principles can be deduced in large part, I believe, from the tests that have been done on the original principles. Limited testing to date suggests that the revised principles will be corroborated.The final validity of the revised principles, of course, will await final testing which we are in the process of conducting. For these reasons, some of the principles which will be presented today will be in the form of hypotheses or postulates.

I will present the principles in five sections. The first section will concern relationships between two percentage change variables. The second section will concern the relationship between two dollar or ratio variables. The third section will concern relationships between a percentage change variable and a ratio variable. The fourth section will concern many variable relationships when the dependent variable is a percentage change variable. And the fifth section will concern many variable relationships when the dependent variable is a ratio or dollar variable.

In presenting each section I will list the principles or postulates in that section and examine one or more of the principles in detail giving illustrations, evidence and some of the implications. The important point to keep in mind is that the principles or rules will permit you to predict the relationships between one variable and other variables. My associate, Dr. Nelson, tells me that now when he receives a research paper by one of his students involving relationships between financial variables he can for the first time generally predict what the results will be before he has read the paper. For my part, I now generally know what to expect in any given correlation and I would be quite willing to bet on the results. Last year I never knew quite what to expect. Let me now turn to a description of the principles.

The first section concerns relationships involving up to two percentage variables. There are four principles. They are:

1.1 The values of a percentage change variable in one period typically will not be related to the values of the same, or any other, percentage variable in a different period.

1.2 The values of one percentage change variable can, but need not, be related to the values of another percentage change variable in the same period.

1.3 If one percentage change variable is a component of another, the values of the first variable typically will be related to the values of the other variable in the same period. The degree of relationship will depend on the extent to which the one variable includes the other variable.

1.4 The above relationships will apply to a group of firms in one or two time periods, or to a single firm in many time periods.

The principle labeled 1.1 stated: The values of a percentage change variable in one period typically will not be related to the values of the same, or any other, percentage change variable in a different period. This principle applies to a group of firms in two periods, or to a single firm in many periods. You will find in Exhibit III an illustration of the principle applied to a group of companies in two periods. That exhibit shows the percentage change in earnings per share of nine companies in the chemical industry in two periods, 1966-1967 and 1967-1968. The companies are listed in order of percentage change in earnings per share in the first period, 1966-1967. If you will examine the percentage changes in earnings per share in the second period, 1967-1968, you will see that they bore no relation to percentage changes in earnings per share in the first period. Relative growth in one period was not related to relative growth in the next period. The company with the best percentage change in earnings in the first period, Dow Chemical, recorded the next to worst percentage change in earnings in the second period. The company with the highest percentage increase in earnings in the second period, Du Pont, recorded the third to worst percentage change in the first period. The coefficient of correlation between the values of percentage changes in one period and percentage changes in the next period was not significantly different from zero.

The example refers to a single variable for a group of firms in successive periods. The example could have dealt with a single variable in widely separated periods, or with two variables for a group of firms in different periods. The example could also have dealt with lagged variables of a single firm in many periods. The only specification of the principle is that percentage changes in one period will not be related to percentage changes in a different period.

What is the evidence in support of the principle? Extensive published evidence exists in support of the principle when applied to percentage changes in stock prices in successive periods and to percentage changes in earnings per share in successive periods. The articles contained in Paul Cootner's The Random Character of Stock Prices (M.I.T. Press, 1964) give substantial evidence revealing that percentage changes in 0stock prices in one period are not related to percentage changes in stock prices in a different period. Evidence for the principle with respect to percentage changes in earnings per share has been published by Rayner and Little, in England, and by Richard Brealey and by myself in this country.

To test one part of the principle we performed 4,800 separate tests similar to the one shown in Exhibit III. Tests were conducted on eight separate industries: Business and Electrical Equipment, Chemical, Drug, Finance, Machinery, Petroleum, Retail Trade and Steel. The data used was the Compustat annual data, based on calendar year companies in all industries except Retail Trade.

The number of companies in the sample for the test on a particular variable of a particular industry ranged from ten to thirty, depending on the availability of the appropriate data. For each variable in each industry tests were conducted for successive one year periods, successive two year periods, successive three year periods, successive four year periods and successive five year periods. For each length period, ten tests were made similar to the test shown in Exhibit III. The results for successive one year periods are shown in Exhibit IV. If you will look at the results for percentage changes in sales for the Chemical Industry, you will see that there was no significant correlation in ten out of ten tests in successive one year periods.

The totals for all tests are given in the right hand columns of Exhibit IV. Altogether 748 tests resulted in no significant correlation. This represented 78% of all tests and 87% of the predicted number of tests. The predicted number of tests is simply 90% of the total number of tests. Results for longer periods were similar to the results for the successive one year periods shown in Exhibit IV.

Our tests provide substantial evidence in support of the principle when applied to values of a single variable for a group of firms in successive periods. We do not have evidence for the relationship between values for a group of firms of one variable in one period and another variable in a different period. Nor do we have explicit evidence for the principle when applied to a single firm. Consequently the application of the principle to those cases remains hypothetical until the evidence is in hand. We are presently conducting tests on those aspects of the principle. Limited testing to date suggests that the principle will be borne out.

What are some of the implications of principle 1.1? The principle states that relative past growth of a variable will be unrelated to relative future growth of that variable. The company with the highest growth of price or earnings will have only an even chance of recording above average future growth of price or earnings. The company with the highest percentage increase in sales will have only an even chance of recording above average increases in sales. This inconsistency between relative growth in one period and relative growth in the next period casts doubt on the superiority of one management over another management in respect to their supposed ability to consistently achieve superior growth of sales, earnings, market prices or any other variable you care to name. The principle also casts doubt on the supposed advantages which are allegedly conferred by strategic location of plants or markets, patent protection, degree of integration, specialization, or relative size.

Principle 1.2 stated: The values of one percentage change variable can be, but need not be, related to the values of another percentage change variable in the same period. This principle is stated for clarification of the other principles and for completeness. It concerns two percentage change variables which are not components of one another in the same period, an area not covered by the other principles. The primary instance is that of percentage changes in prices and percentage changes in earnings in the same time period. As stated earlier we found a high correlation between relative changes in earnings per share and prices per share in the same time periods.

Principle 1.3 stated: If one percentage change variable is a component of another percentage change variable, the values of the first variable typically will be related to the values of the other variable in the same time period. The degree of relationship will depend on the extent to which the one variable includes the other variable. If one variable includes all of the other, the values of the two variables will, of course, be perfectly correlated.

Now let us turn to relationships between two dollar or ratio variables. As you will recall, those are the variables listed in Exhibit I. Dollar and ratio variables tend to be relatively stable, comparatively predictable. There are two principles. They are:

2.1 For a group of firms, the values of a dollar or ratio variable will typically be related to the values of that same dollar or ratio variable in another period. The degree of relationship will be inversely proportional to the time interval between the periods.

2.2 For a group of firms, if one dollar or ratio variable is a component of another dollar ratio variable, the values of the two variables typically will be related. The degree of relationship will depend on the extent to which the one variable includes the other variable.

You will find an illustration of principle 2.1 in Exhibit V. In that exhibit you will see listed the sales of nine companies in the Chemical Industry in two years, 1967 and 1968. You will see on examining Exhibit V that the values of sales in one year were directly related to the values of sales in the next year. This direct relationship is shown by the rankings of sales of the companies in 1967 and 1968. You will note that the ranks are the same in both years revealing a direct relationship. Du Pont, for example, ranked first in both years and Rohm and Haas ranked last in both. The coefficient of correlation between the values of sales in 1967 and the values of sales in 1968 was extremely high and positive, revealing a direct relationship.

There is very little published evidence regarding the principle. Russell Nelson and I did a short article last year in the Financial Analysts Journal which substantiates the principle when applied to the ratio variable price/earnings ratio. But we needed evidence on the application of the principle to other variables. To test the principle we performed 6,100 separate tests similar to the one shown in Exhibit V. The results for successive one year periods are shown in Exhibit VI. If you will look at the results for sales for the Chemical Industry, you will see that in ten out of ten tests, the coefficient of correlation was significantly positive. This means that in ten tests similar to the one in Exhibit V, a direct relationship existed between the values of sales in one year and the values of sales in the next year. If you will look at the results for pretax income per share for the Chemical Industry, you will see that in ten out of ten tests the correlation was again significantly positive, again corroborating the principle.

On the far right of Exhibit VI are listed the totals for all tests. In 1,194 tests, or ninety-eight percent of all tests, the coefficients of correlation were significantly positive. This provides substantial evidence in support of the principle. Tests on longer periods, up to five years, produced similar results.

What are the implications of the principle? The principle implies that a company will tend to maintain its same rank among other companies in its industry with respect to any particular dollar or ratio variable. A company with a low price/earnings ratio, for example, will tend to continue to have a low price/earnings ratio. A company with a low profit margin will tend to continue to have a low profit margin. A company with a low rate of return on capital will typically continue to earn a low rate of return on capital. There will be no tendency, on average, for companies at either end of the spectrum of any particular ratio variable to move toward the industry average.

If the principle is true, as I believe the evidence indicates that it is, it is unrealistic to expect that a company's price/earnings ratio will move toward the industry average, or that its profit margins will tend to shift up or down to the industry median. This implies that the statement, "this company is statistically cheap", or the statement "this company's margins are too low and will move up" are open to serious question.

These statements are open to question because companies which are statistically cheap are likely to continue to be statistically cheap and companies which have low profit margins are likely to continue to have low profit margins. Relative price/earnings ratios and relative profit margins do change, of course, but relatively low price/earnings ratios and relatively low profit margins are about as likely to go down as they are to go up.

Principle 2.2 stated: For a group of firms, if one dollar or ratio variable is a component of another dollar or ratio variable, the values of the two variables typically will be related. The degree of relationship will depend on the extent to which the one variable includes the other variable. If one variable includes all of the other the values of the two variables will, of course, be perfectly correlated. An illustration of Principle 2.2 is given in Exhibit VII and evidence is given in Exhibit VIII.

Now let us turn to the section of principle concerning the relationship between a percentage change variable and a dollar or ratio variable. These principles state:

3.1 The values of a percentage change variable typically will not be related to the values of a dollar or ratio variable in the same period or in any other period.

3.2 This will be true of a group of firms in one or two periods, and of a single firm in many periods.

You will see an illustration of this principle in Exhibit IX. In that exhibit, values of a ratio variable, rate of return on common equity in 1967, are compared with values of a percentage change variable, percent change in earnings per share between 1967 and 1968, for nine companies in the Chemical Industry. As you can see in the exhibit, there is no relation between the values of the ratio variable and the values of the percentage change variable. The company which ranked first in rate of return on common equity ranked next to last in percentage change in earnings. The company which stood second in rate of return, on the other hand, ranked first in percentage change in earnings. The ranks of the values of the ratio variable bear no systematic relation to the ranks of the values of the percentage change variable. The coefficient of correlation is not significant.

Several past studies provide evidence for the principle. These studies have demonstrated that no relationship exists between the ratio variable price/earnings, for example, and the percentage change variable growth of earnings per share. Other studies have revealed that little or no relationship exists between values of the percentage change variables growth of earnings and values of any of the ratio variables rate of return on equity, payout or leverage.

To provide evidence on more variables we conducted 6,750 tests similar to the one shown in Exhibit IX on twenty-five pairs of ratio variables and percentage change variables. The results for successive one year periods are shown in Exhibit X. If you look at the results for the Chemical Industry you will see that there was no significant correlation in ten of ten tests between the debt/capital ratio and percent change in sales per share. If you examine the results of the relationship between the debt/capital ratio and percentage change in pretax income per share, you will see that no significant relationship was found in eight out of ten tests.

On the far right of Exhibit X you will see the totals. In 1047 of 1350 tests there was no significant relationship between values of the ratio variables and values of the percentage change

322

variable. This number represented 78 percent of all tests and 86 percent of the predicted number of tests. Results for periods longer than one year were comparable. This evidence gives substantial support to the principle. What are the implications of the principle? There are several. First, it implies that none of the stock selection decision rules which use the price/earnings ratio to predict price changes will be usually unsuccessful. Second, it implies that here is little evidence in the real world for some of the rules of thumb that are derived from traditional theories of finance. There is little relation between percentage change in earnings, for example, and debt/equity, payout, rate of return on capital and other ratios for a group of firms.

The next group of postulates concern the relationships between a percentage change dependent variable and two or more independent variables. The postulates state:

4.1 In relationships among more than two variables, if the independent variables include a percentage change variable in the same time period, a relationship with the dependent variable can, but need not, exist between the values of the dependent variable and the values of the independent variables.

4.2 In relationships among more than two variables, if the independent variables do not include a percentage change variable in the same time period, no relationship typically will exist between the values of the dependent variable and the values of the independent variables.

The above postulates were deduced from the principles stated earlier and from the mathematical relationships between two variable and many variable linear correlations. Principles 1.1, 1.2, 3.1 and 3.2 state that no relationship can exist between a percentage change variable and another variable unless the other variable is another percentage change variable in the same time period. The multivariable postulates simply extend that idea to many variable relationships.

The formula which converts two variable coefficients of determination to three variable coefficients of determination is the following:

$$R^2_{1.23} = (r^2_{12} + r^2_{13} - 2r^2_{12}r^2_{13}r^2_{23})/(1-r^2_{23}) \qquad (1)$$

The formula states the relationship between the dependent variable (variable 1) and the two independent variables (variables 2 and 3).

In the formula the capital R refers to the relationship between variable 1 and variables 2 and 3. The small r's refer to the relationships between the two variables indicated by the subscripts. Thus, r_{12} refers to the relationship between variables 1 and 2. For sake of initial discussion let us assume that r^2_{23} is zero or tends to zero. In other words, the two independent variables are not related to one another. If that is so, the far right hand expression of the numerator will also tend to zero. Then our formula reduces to:

$$R^2_{11.23} = r^2_{12} + r^2_{13} \qquad (2)$$

where

$$r^2_{23} = 0 \qquad ((3)$$

In other words, the relationship between the dependent variable and two independent variable is equal to the sum of the relationships between the dependent variable and each of the independent variables. From principles 1.1, 1.2, 3.1 and 3.2 we know that the only instances in which the expressions on the right of the equation are significantly different from zero is when the independent variable is also a percentage change variable in the same time period. In all other cases the relationship will not be significant. Under these circumstances principles 4.1 and 4.2 will both be true.

So far we have assumed that no relationship exists between the values of the two independent variables, variables 1 and 2. We have assumed that r^2_{23} tends to zero. What about the cases when this is not true, when r^2_{23} is significant. This will occur under two circumstances: when variables 2 and 3 are both dollar or ratio variables or when variables 2 and 3 are both percentage variables in the same time period. Under the former instances the two expressions on the right of equation (1) will tend to zero; in the latter instance the two expressions on the right of equation (1) will also tend to zero if the dependent and independent variables are not in the same time period. Under both of these circumstances the numerator of the equation will tend to zero, and the relationship will tend to zero. This corroborates principle 4.2. If the dependent and independent variables are in the same time period the numerator of equation (1) will be positive and principle 4.1 will be corroborated.

I have only talked about three variable relationships. The same kind of analysis could be extended to more than three variables. The argument for the postulates has been deductive, not empirical. We are now examining empirical evidence.

The final group of postulates concerns multi-variable relationships when the dependent variable is a dollar or ratio variable. The principles are:

> 5.1 When a dollar or ratio variable is the dependent variable, a relationship will exist typically between the values of the dependent variable and the values of the independent variable if, and only if, one of the independent variables is the same variable as the dependent variable in a different time period, or if one of the independent variables is a component of the dependent variable, or vice versa.

The same kind of deductive analysis that was used in the previous section can be applied to this principle.

What are some of the implications of the principles stated in this paper? First, the principles question many of the prevalent practices used by professional investors in selecting and evaluating securities. Second, they question approaches used by academic persons in describing financial relationships. They question, for example, use of a percentage change variable on one side of an equation and a dollar or ratio variable on the other side. I would guess that this question would affect over half of the equations which appear in academic publications.

If the principles, or postulates, are correct, as I believe they are, a considerable body of academic research and publication is suspect. Third, the principles provide a device or model for predicting general relationships among financial variables. This use has not been provided in such a general form by previous theories. Fourth, the principles provide a gauge for deciding what avenues of research in quantitative techniques are likely not to be useful and what roads might be useful. Fifth, the principles provide a general framework for understanding the relationships among various financial variables.

EXHIBIT I
ILLUSTRATIVE EXAMPLES OF DOLLAR AND RATIO VARIABLES

TOTAL DOLLAR VARIABLES	PER SHARE DOLLAR VARIABLES	RATIO VARIABLES
Sales	Sales/Share	Sales/Total Capital
Operating Income	Operating Income/Share	Sales/Equity Capital
Pretax Income	Pretax Income/Share	Pretax Income/Sale
Income Taxes	Income Taxes/Share	Net Income/Sales
Net Income	Net Income/Share	Net Income/Capital
Dividends Paid	Dividends Paid/Share	Dividends/Net Income
Inventory	Inventory/Share	Curr. Assets/Current Liabilities
Receivables	Receivables/Share	Plant/Equity Capital
Current Assets	Current Assets/Share	Net Current Assets/ Debt
Total Assets	Total Assets/Share	Equity Capital/Total Assets
Current Liabilities	Current Liabilities/Share	
Long Term Debt	Long Term Debt/Share	
Common Equity	Common Equity/Share	
Market Value	Market Price/Share	Price/Earnings

EXHIBIT II
ILLUSTRATIVE EXAMPLES OF PERCENTAGE CHANGE VARIABLES

PERCENT CHANGE IN:	PERCENT CHANGE IN:	PERCENT CHANGE IN:
Sales	Sales/Share	Sales/Total Capital
Operating Income	Operating Income/Share	Sales/Equity Capital
Pretax Income	Pretax Income/Share	Pretax Income/Sales
Income Taxes	Income Taxes/Share	Net Income/Sales
Net Income	Net Income/Share	Net Income/Capital
Dividends Paid	Dividends Paid/Share	Dividends/Net Income
Inventory	Inventory/Share	Curr. Assets/Current Liabilities
Receivables	Receivables/Share	Plant/Equity Capital
Current Assets	Current Assets/Share	Net Curr. Assets/Debt
Total Assets	Total Assets/Share	Equity Capital/Total Assets
Current Liabilities	Current Liabilities/Share	
Long Term Debt	Long Term Debt/Share	
Common Equity	Common Equity/Share	
Market Value	Market Price/Share	Price/Earnings

EXHIBIT III
ILLUSTRATION OF PRINCIPLE 1.1

	Per Cent Change in Earn/Share 1966-1967	Rank	Per Cent Change in Earn/Share 1967-1968	Rank
Dow Chemical	7%	1	-2%	8
GAF Corp.	-4	2	5	6
Stauffer Chemical	-7	3	-2	7
Hercules, Inc.	-12	4	14	3
Monsanto	-13	5	11	5
Rohm & Haas	-17	6	18	2
DuPont	-20	7	19	1
Grace, W. R.	-22	8	13	4
Union Carbide	-26	9	-8	9

Correlation not significant $r^2 = .08$

Exhibit IV

Tests of Principle 1.1

Per Share Percentage Change Variables in Successive One-Year Periods

Number of Zero Correlations Out of Every Ten Tests

Industry	Dollar Variables														Ratio Variables					Total			Percent of	
	Sales	Pretax Income	Cash Flow	Depr.	Fixed Chgs.	Income Tax	Earn	Div	Inv Cap	Cap Exp	Price High	Price Low	Price close	Debt/ Cap	Price/ Earn	Earn/ Eqty	Pretax Margin	Div/ Earn	Div/ Price	Actual	Predicted	Possible	Predicted	Possible
Business & Elec. Equip.	6	5	7	3	9	7	NA	9	3	4	8	8	8	NA	NA	6	6	6	10	101	144	160	70	63
Chemical	10	10	9	10	NA	10	NA	9	8	8	10	9	10	NA	NA	9	9	10	10	149	135	150	104	93
Drug	5	7	NA	NA	NA	10	10	NA	NA	NA	NA	NA	NA	NA	NA	NA	NA	NA	NA	32	36	40	88	80
Finance	9	10	NA	NA	9	8	NA	7	8	6	8	9	8	9	NA	9	8	8	9	126	135	150	93	84
Machinery	7	7	7	8	NA	8	NA	NA	8	NA	10	9	10	NA	NA	8	6	NA	NA	88	99	110	89	80
Petroleum	9	10	10	10	5	4	10	10	7	7	9	10	9	8	7	9	9	9	8	160	171	190	94	84
Retail Trade	6	3	7	8	NA	5	NA	NA	8	NA	9	9	10	NA	NA	2	2	NA	NA	69	99	110	70	63
Steel	NA	4	7	8	NA	NA	NA	NA	10	NA	NA	NA	NA	NA	NA	3	NA	NA	NA	32	45	50	73	64
Total																				748	864	960	85	76

NA designates those tests which the sample size was less than 10 or the required data was not available.
In all other tests the sample size ranged between 10 and 30 companies. If, for example, between 65% and 75% of the tests were zero correlations, then a 7 was recorded representing approximately 7 out of 10.

EXHIBIT V

ILLUSTRATION OF PRINCIPLE 2.1

	Sales 1967 (Millions $)	Rank	Sales 1968 (Millions $)	Rank
DuPont	$3,100	1	$3,480	1
Union Carbide	2,540	2	2,680	2
Monsanto	1,630	3	1,790	3
Grace, W. R.	1,580	4	1,740	4
Dow Chemical	1,380	5	1,650	5
Hercules, Inc.	640	6	720	6
GAF Corp.	520	7	570	7
Stauffer Chemical	420	8	480	8
Rohm & Haas	370	9	420	9

Correlation Positive r^2 = .99

Exhibit VI

Tests of Principle 2.1

Per Share Variables in Successive One Year Periods

Number of Significantly Positive Correlations Out of Every Ten Tests

Industry	Dollar Variables														Ratio Variables					Total			Percent of	
	Sales	Pretax Income	Cash Flow	Deprec. Chgs.	Fixed Chgs.	Income Tax	Earn	Div	Inv Cap	Cap Exp	Price High	Price Low	Price close	Debt/ Cap	Price/ Earn	Earn Eqty	Pretax Margin	Div/ Earn	Div/ Price	Actual	Pre-dicted	Pos-sible	Pre-dicted	Pos-sible
Business & Elec. Equip.	10	10	10	10	10	NA	10	10	10	10	10	10	10	10	NA	10	10	5	10	165	153	170	108	97
Chemical	10	10	10	10	10	NA	10	10	10	10	10	10	10	10	NA	10	10	9	10	164	153	170	107	96
Drug	10	10	10	10	10	10	10	10	10	NA	NA	NA	NA	10	NA	10	10	10	NA	130	117	130	111	100
Finance	10	10	NA	NA	10	NA	10	10	10	NA	10	9	10	9	NA	8	8	10	10	135	126	140	107	96
Machinery	10	10	10	10	NA	10	10	10	10	NA	10	10	10	10	NA	10	10	10	10	150	135	150	111	100
Petroleum	10	10	10	10	10	10	10	10	10	10	10	10	10	10	9	10	10	8	10	187	171	190	109	98
Retail Trade	10	10	10	10	10	10	10	10	10	NA	10	10	10	10	7	10	10	7	10	174	162	180	107	97
Steel	NA	10	10	10	NA	NA	10	10	10	NA	NA	NA	NA	10	NA	10	NA	9	NA	89	81	90	110	99
Total																				1184	1098	1220	109	98

NA designates those tests which the sample size was less than 10 or the required data was not available.

In all other tests the sample size ranged between 10 and 30 companies. If, for example, between 65% and 75% of the tests were positive correlations, then a 7 was recorded representing approximately 7 out of 10.

EXHIBIT VII

ILLUSTRATION OF PRINCIPLE 2.2

	Cash Flow Per Share 1968	Rank	Earnings Per Share 1968	Rank
DuPont	$14.31	1	$7.82	1
Rohm & Haas	10.41	2	5.68	2
Dow Chemical	9.70	3	4.27	3
Monsanto	8.53	4	3.30	4
Union Carbide	6.41	5	2.60	8
Grace, W. R.	6.17	6	2.86	6
Stauffer Chemical	6.12	7	3.11	5
Hercules, Inc.	5.03	8	2.69	7
GAF Corp.	2.64	9	1.22	9

Correlation Positive $r^2 = .99$

EXHIBIT VIII

TESTS OF PRINCIPLE 2.2

Dollar Variables (Per Share) in One-Year Periods

Number of Significantly Positive Correlations Out of Every Ten Tests

Industry	Sales & Pretax Income	Sales & Cash Flow	Sales & Deprec.	Sales & Income Tax	Sales & Earn	Sales & Div	Pretax Income & Income Tax	Pretax Income & Earn	Pretax Income & Div	Cash Flow & Deprec	Cash Flow & Earn	Cash Flow & Div	Earn & Div	Total
Elec. Equip.	2	2	0	3	NA	8	10	NA	9	10	NA	5	NA	
Chemical	10	10	10	10	NA	8	10	NA	10	10	NA	10	NA	
Drug	9	10	10	0	0	0	10	10	10	10	10	8	10	
Finance	3	NA	NA	1	5	3	10	8	1	NA	NA	NA	10	
Machinery	4	8	10	5	NA	4	10	NA	10	9	NA	10	NA	
Petroleum	6	10	10	0	4	5	10	10	10	10	10	8	10	
Retail Trade	0	5	10	0	0	3	10	9	8	9	9	9	10	
Steel	NA	NA	NA	NA	NA	NA	10	NA	10	10	NA	10	NA	
Total	34	45	50	19	9	29	80	37	68	68	29	60	40	568
Possible	70	60	60	70	40	70	80	40	80	70	30	70	40	780
Percent of All Tests	48	75	83	27	23	41	100	92	85	97	97	86	100	73

A designates those tests which the sample size was less than 10 or the required data was not available. In all other tests the sample size ranged between 10 and 30 companies. If, for example, between 65% and 75% of the tests were zero correlations, then a 7 was recorded representing approximately 7 out of 10.

EXHIBIT IX

ILLUSTRATION OF PRINCIPLE 3.1

	Rate of Return on Common Equity in 1967	Rank	Per Cent Change in Earn/Sh. 1967-1968	Rank
Dow Chemical	14.1%	1	-2%	8
DuPont	13.3	2	19	1
Hercules, Inc.	13.1	3	14	3
Stauffer Chemical	11.7	4	-2	7
Union Carbide	10.3	5	-8	9
Rohm & Haas	10.1	6	18	2
Monsanto	9.1	7	11	5
Grace, W. R.	8.6	8	13	4
GAF Corp.	5.8	9	5	6

Correlation not significant $r^2 = .00$

EXHIBIT X

TESTS OF PRINCIPLE 3.1

Ratio and Percentage Change Variable in Coincident One-Year Periods

Number of Zero Correlations Out of Every Ten Tests

Industry	Debt/Cap Sales	Debt/Cap Pretax Cash Income Flow	Debt/Cap Earn	Debt/Cap Price Close	Price/Earn Sales	Price/Earn Pretax Cash Income Flow	Price/Earn Earn	Price/Earn Price Close	Earn/Eqty Sales	Earn/Eqty Pretax Cash Income Flow	Earn/Eqty Earn	Earn/Eqty Price Close (And Percentage Change to)	Pretax Margin Sales	Pretax Margin Pretax Cash Income Flow	Pretax Margin Earn	Pretax Margin Price Close	Div/Earn Sales	Div/Earn Pretax Income Flow	Div/Earn Cash Flow	Div/Earn Earn	Div/Earn Price Close	Total Actual	Total Predicted	Total Possible	Percent Predicted	Percent Possible
Business & Elec. Equip.	6	10	7	NA	9	NA	NA	NA	NA	8	7	3	NA	3	7	6	NA	7	3	1	9	93	144	160	65	58
Chemical	10	8	9	9	NA	7	9	5	7	5	8	9	NA	9	8	7	8	6	6	NA	8	120	144	160	83	75
Drug	10	10	10	NA	NA	NA	NA	NA	8	10	10	8	NA	8	10	9	10	7	8	10	NA	146	144	160	101	91
Finance	9	8	NA	9	NA	7	NA	5	9	NA	9	10	NA	7	9	9	10	9	9	NA	9	128	133	150	95	85
Machinery	6	8	9	9	NA	NA	NA	NA	6	4	7	7	NA	7	9	8	9	8	8	NA	8	120	144	160	83	75
Petroleum	10	8	10	8	10	9	8	8	8	6	8	8	7	3	7	9	9	7	8	10	8	213	225	250	95	85
Retail Trade	10	10	10	7	NA	10	9	10	8	5	7	7	10	NA	3	9	7	3	8	7	NA	189	225	250	84	76
Steel	NA	10	10	NA	NA	NA	NA	NA	NA	5	NA	NA	NA	NA	NA	NA	NA	NA	5	NA	NA	38	54	60	70	63
Total																						1047	1215	1350	85	76

NA designates those tests which the sample size was less than 10 or the required data was not available. In all other tests the sample size ranged between 10 and 30 companies. If, for example, between 65% and 75% of the tests were zero correlations, then a 7 was recorded representing approximately 7 out of 10.

22

APPENDIX

Supplementary Tables

I

List of companies and Tables III - VI for "Relative Growth of Earnings. Per Share - Past and Future". *Financial Analysts Journal*. November- December 1966. 73-76.

II

Supplementary Tables for "Five Principles of Financial Relationships." *Financial Analysts Journal*. March-April 1971. Vol. 27, No. 2. 38-52 and "Random and Nonrandom Relationships Among Financial Variables: a Financial Model." *Journal of Financial and Quantitative Analysis*. March 1971. Vol VI, No. 2. 875-885.

III

Tables for Prediction of Corporate Profit and Loss, including results of published predictions of *P/L Forecasts*

II

Relative Growth of Earnings Per Share - Past and Future

The following tables give the companies in the study and the coefficients of correlation for growth of earnings per share in successive periods of from one to five years.

Auto Parts Industry

Arvin Indust	Borg Warner	Champ Sp Plug	Clevite
Federal Mogul	Fram Corp	Houdaille Ind	Libby Owens Ford
Maremont Corp	McQuay Norris	Raybestos Man	Fockwell Standard
Stewart Warner	Timken Roller	Globe Union	

Building Materials Industry

Alpha Portland	Amer Seating	Armstrong Cork	Carey Mnf
Certain Teed	Corning Glass	Crane Company	Eagle Picher
Ferro Corp	Flinkote	Gen Portland	Georgia Pacific
Giant Portland	Ideal Cement	Johns Manville	Kaiser Cement
Lone Star Cement	Marquette Cement	Med Ptlnd Cement	National Lead
Owens Corning	Penn Dixie Cement	Pitt Pl Glass	Ruberoid
Trane Company	U S Gypsum	Wrren Bros	Weyerhaeuser

Chemical Industry

Air Reduction	Allied Chemical	Amer Cyanamid	Diamond Alkali
Dow Chemical	Du Pont	Freeport Sulpher	General Aniline
Grace W R	Hercules Powder	Interchem Corp	Koppers Company
Remingtn Arms	Rohm & Hass	Stauffer Chem	Sun Chemical
Texas Gulf Sul	Udylite Corp	Union Carbide	Wallace & Tiernan

Drug Industry

Abbot Labs	Amer Home Pro	Amer Hosp Sup[	Baxter Labs
Dentists Sup	Johnson & Johnson	Kendall Company	Lilly Eli
Merck	Miles Labs	Norwich Pharm	Parke Davis
Pfizer Chas	Plough	Rexall Drug	Rorer W H
Upjohn	Warner Lambert		

Machinery Industry

Amer Chain	Ametek Inc	Babcosk & Wilcx	Blaw Knoxx
Caterpillar	Chicago Pneum	Clark Equip	Combustion Eng
Draper Corp	Fafnir Bearing	FMC Corp	Gerdner Denver
Halliburton	Ingersoll Rand	Mesta Machine	Rockwell Mfg
Symngtn Wayne	United Eng	White Dental	Worthington

Electrical Machinery & Electronics Industry

Amphenol Corp	Amp Inc	Dynamics Corp	General Electric
High Volt Eng	Honeywell	Indiana General	International Res
Internatl Tel	Magnavox	Mallory	Maytag
McGraw Edison	Radio Corp	robertshaw Cont	Slumberger
Singer	Sprague Electric	Square D	Sunbeam
Tung Sol Elec	Wagner Elec	Westinghouse	Zenith

Steel Industry

Allelgh Ludlum	Armco Steel	Bliss & Laughlin	Continental Steel
Copperweld Steel	Crucible Steel	Detroit Steel	Eastern Stainless
General Refract	Harrison Walker	Interlake Steel	Lukens Steel
McClouth Steel	National Steel	Sharon Steel	Steel Co Canada
U S Pipe & Fdry	U S Steel	Woodward Iron	Youngstown Sheet

Petroleum Industry

Brit Amer Oil91	Cities Service	Continental Oil	Creole Petrol
Imperial Oil	Kern County Land	Marathon Oil	Pennzoil Co
Quaker State Oil	Shell Oil	Signal Oil & Gas	Skelly Oil
Socony Mobil	Standard Oil Cal	Standard Oil Ind	Standard Oil N J
Standard Oil Ohio	Sunray DX	Texaco	Union Oil

NATURAL GAS INDUSTRY

Alabama Gas	Amer Nat Gas	Atlanta Gas	Brooklyn Union Gas
Colorado Interst	Columbia Gas	Cons Nat Gas	El Paso Nat Gas
Equitable Gas	Gas Service	Houston Nat Gas	Laclede Gas
Lone Star Gas	Miss Riv Fuel	Mtn Fuel Sup	Nat Fuel Gas
Northn Nat Gas	Okla Nat Gas	Pacific Liight	Panhandle East P
Peoples Gas Light	So Jersey Gas	Southn Nat Gas	Southn Union Gas
Stone & Webster	Suburb Pro Gas	Tenneco	Texas Gas Tran
Texas East Tran	Transc Gas Pipe	United Gas	United Gas Improv

ELECTRIC UTILITY INDUSTRY

Allegh Pwr	Amer Elec Pwr	Ariz Pub Ser	Atlan City El
Baltim G & E	Boston Edition	Caroline P & L	Cent Hud G & E
Cent Ill Light	Cent Ill PS	Cent Main Pwr	Cent & So We
Cinn G & E	Cleveland Elec	Columb & So Ohio	Commwlth Edison
Comm Pub Serv9ice	Conn L & P	Consol Edison	Consumers Pwr
Dayton P & L	Delaware P & L	Detroit Edition	Duke Power
Duquene Light	East Util Ass	Empire Dis El	Florida Power
Hawaiian Elec	Houston L & P	Idaho Power Illinois	Illinois Power
Indian P & L	Interstate Pwr	Iowa Elec L & P	Iowa Ill G & E
Kansas P & L	Kentucky Util	Long Island Light	Louisville G & E
Middle South Util	Minnesota P & L	Montana Dak Util	Montana Power
New Eng Elec	New England G & E	New York Sta G & E	Niagara Mohawk
North Ind P S	Ohio States Pwr	Ohio Edison	Oklahoma G & E
Orange & Rockland	Pacific G & E	Pacific P & L	Pennsylvania P&L
Philadelphia El	Patomic El Pwr	Pub Ser Colorado	Pub Ser Indiana
Pub Ser New Hamp	Pub Ser New Mex	Pub Ser Elec & G	Puget Sound P&L
Rochester G & E	San Diego G&E	South Carolina E&G	South Calif Edison
Southern Company	Southwest P S	Tampa Elec	Texas Util
Toledo Edison	Tucson G & E	Union Elec	United Illuminating
Utah P & L	Virginia E & P	Washington Water	Wisc Elec Pwr
Wisc P & L	Wisc Pub Ser		

BANK INDUSTRY

Bank of Amer	Bankers Trust	Chase Manhatt	Chemical NY
Citizens & South	Contl Illinois	Crocker Citizens	First Nat Boston
First Nat Chicago	First Nat St Louis	First Nat City	First Penna
Franklin National	Girard Trust	Irving Trust	Manf Hanover
Marine Midland	Morgan Guaranty	Mellon National	Natl BankDetroit
Philadelphia Natl	Repub Nat Dallas	Seattle First	Security First Nat
Union Bank L A	Valley Natl		

RAILROAD INDUSTRY

Atchison	Atantic Coast	Canadian Pacific	Chicago Gr West
Deleware Hudson	Denver Rio Grand	Great Northern	Gulf Mobile
Illinois Central	Kansas City South	Louisville Nash	Norfolk West
Northern Pacific	Pitts Lake Ere	St Louis San Fran	Seaboard Air
Southern Pacific	Soo Line	Southern Rwy	Union Pacific
Western Maryland			

Table III
Rates of Change in Earnings Per Share
Coefficients of Correlation: Successive One Year Periods

Industry	56/55 and 55/54	57/56 and 56/55	58/57 and 57/56	59/58 and 58/57	60/59 and 59/58	61/60 and 60/59	62/61 and 61/60	63/62 and 62/61	64/63 and 63/62	65/64 and 64/63
Auto Parts	-.138	.165	-.038	*-.491	*-.582	-.003	-.148	.436	*-.625	.403
Building Materials	-.220	.320	-.195	*-.579	*-.456	-.356	*-.822	*-.405	.280	.202
Chemical	.163	.130	.052	-.531	-.374	-.071	-.225	-.341	.014	.014
Drug	-.013	.260	.272	.398	.239	.033	*.476	*-.405	*.417	.091
Machinery	-.277	.296	.398	*-.588	.253	-.108	-.115	*-.611	.076	.256
Elec. Mach., Electronics	*.521	*-.623	*-.544	.283	.321	-.036	*-.677	.225	-.107	.173
Steel	-.047	.294	.227	*-.643	*-.538	-.305	.245	.101	*-.678	*.708
Petroleum	-.059	-.420	-.311	.300	-.198	*.628	-.276	.159	*.608	.238
Natural Gas	-.231	.033	-.148	-.140	*-.540	-.391	-.175	-.311	*-.378	-.042
Electric Utility	-.153	-.150	*-.282	*-.295	*-.261	.069	*-.418	*-.578	-.085	.090
Bank	.089	.176	-.218	-.003	.108	.081	*.485	.213	.140	-.130
Railroad	.361	.324	-.330	-.344	-.021	.026	-.095	-.057	-.181	.216
Industrial Composite	.072	*-.314	*-.112	*-.451	*-.423	-.065	*-.306	*-.124	-.080	*.195

* Significant (at .05 level)

Table IV
Rates of Change in Earnings Per Share
Coefficients of Correlation: Successive Two Year Periods

Industry	56/54 and 54/52	57/55 and 55/63	58/56 and 56/54	59/57 and 57/55	60/58 and 58/56	61/59 and 59/57	62/60 and 60/58	63/61 and 61/59	64/62 and 62/60	65/63 and 63/61
Auto Parts	*-.614	*-.633	-.405	*-.567	-.154	-.331	*-.533	-.464	.244	-.395
Building Materials	-.321	.028	.006	*-.600	*-.667	-.137	-.046	*-.449	-.241	.310
Chemical	*-.634	-.010	.035	.180	*-.397	-.317	.178	-.115	*-.383	*-.511
Drug	.070	.240	-.092	.082	*.530	*.576	.230	*.556	-.096	-.014
Machinery	*-.808	*-.682	-.283	*-.605	*-.811	.298	.403	.090	-.297	-.298
Elec. Mach., Electronics	-.225	.060	*-.795	*-.787	-.134	.286	*.586	-.151	-.156	*-.470
Steel	*-.858	-.355	-.268	*-.620	*-.516	*-.535	*-.605	*-.651	-.170	-.399
Petroleum	-.346	-.217	-.255	*-.489	-.150	*-.443	*.492	*-.522	-.251	*.704
Natural Gas	-.332	*-.722	*-.580	-.070	-.333	-.311	.134	.259	*-.538	-.358
Electric Utility	*-.246	.006	-.090	-.036	*-.269	*-.213	-.078	-.149	*-.418	.045
Bank	*-.397	*-.473	-.122	-.219	.007	-.066	-.096	.186	-.025	-.068
Railroad	-.291	.092	*-.487	-.213	-.038	.161	-.107	*-.517	*-.561	-.177
Industrial Composite	*-.424	*-.159	-.487	*-.518	-.339	-.095	.012	*-.282	*-.225	*-.169

* Significant (at .05 level)

Table V
Rates of Change in Earnings Per Share
Coefficients of Correlation: Successive Five and One Year Periods

Industry	56/55 and 55/50	57/56 and 56/51	58/57 and 57/52	59/58 and 58/53	60/59 and 59/54	61/60 and 60/55	62/61 and 61/56	63/62 and 62/57	64/63 and 63/58	65/64 and 64/59
Auto Parts	.208	-.375	-.111	*-.529	.266	-.245	*-.814	-.329	*-.530	.275
Building Materials	.244	.256	.222	*-.631	.145	*-.554	-.269	-.132	.225	*.584
Chemical	-.261	.233	*.383	-.205	-.089	-.103	.161	.099	-.186	*-.664
Drug	.082	.079	.231	.278	.132	.200	.299	.094	*.483	-.401
Machinery	-.269	-.172	-.057	*-.663	-.016	-.338	-.045	-.281	.088	.061
Elec. Mach., Electronics	*.479	*-.522	*-.737	-.169	.104	.036	-.154	.080	-.327	*-.607
Steel	-.360	*.754	.218	*-.857	.033	*-.475	*-.707	.313	.038	.114
Petroleum	-.166	-.060	.214	-.192	-.382	.079	-.094	-.230	.249	.222
Natural Gas	-.115	*-.487	.021	-.091	*-.481	-.276	-.022	-.165	*-.397	-.021
Electric Utility	*.247	*.339	-.097	-.092	-.050	-.016	-.201	*-.243	.021	-.033
Bank	-.205	-.086	.197	-.110	.106	.001	.248	.172	.128	-.309
Railroad	.295	.340	-.359	*-.620	.261	-.045	*-.381	*-.822	.097	.632
Industrial Composite *	.123	*-.229	-.082	*-.520	-.048	-.082	*-.152	*-.111	-.101	.020

Significant (at .05 level)

Table VI
Rates of Change in Earnings Per Share
Coefficients of Correlation: Successive Five Year Periods
And Periods Coincident with the Business Cycle

Industry	60/55 and 55/50	61/56 and 56/61	62/57 and 57/52	63/58 and 58/53	64/59 and 59/54	65/60 and 60/55	60/51 and 57/53	65/60 and 60/57
Auto Parts	.050	-.069	-.215	*-.588	-.359	*-.581	-.054	*-.638
Building Materials	.254	.014	.333	-.240	.134	-.137	.092	-.043
Chemical	254	*.546	*.685	-.007	.312	.170	*.447	-.133
Drug	.336	.339	.371	*.415	.140	.405	.244	.396
Machinery	*-.452	-.187	*-.598	*-.632	.089	*-.557	*-.725	.205
Elec. Mach., Electronics	.188	*-.492	*-.507	.095	.082	-.238	*-.582	-.108
Steel	.037	*.625	-.401	*-.671	-.229	*-.799	.107	*-.869
Petroleum	.108	.077	-.069	-.375	-.234	-.110	-.122	-.007
Natural Gas	-.081	-.113	-.094	-.236	*-.508	-.117	-.189	-.070
Electric Utility	*.267	*.272	-.020	.034	-.030	-.002	.160	-.020
Bank	-.019	-.172	.183	.157	.144	.119	.155	-.138
Railroad	.245	-.385	*-.495	-.295	*-.441	-.420	-.193	-.031
Industrial Composite	-.109	-.049	-.013	*-.169	-.013	*-.224		

•Significant (at .05 level)

345

II

Supplementary Tables for "Five Principles of Financial Relationships" and "Random and Nonrandom Relationships Among Financial Variables: a Financial Model"

Financial Analysts Journal. March-April 1971. Vol. 27, No. 2. 38-52. and *Journal of Financial and Quantitative Analysis*. March 1971. Vol VI, No. 2. 875-885, respectively.

The tests in the Supplementary Tables were based on data from the Compustat tapes. Each of 19 variables was regressed against each of the other 19 variables for lags of 1 to 16 years. Regressions of each variable against the others resulted in 361 coefficients of correlation. Lags of from 1 to 16 years resulting in 120 correlations. The total number of coefficients of correlation produced was therefore 120x361, or 43,320. The underlying coefficients are contained in the single copy of *Five Principles*, Volumes I and II 1970. Tests for the initial article in the *Financial Analysts* Journal are contained in the other single copy of the identical title and date, *Five Principles*, Volumes I and II, 1970.

Dollar Variables in Successive Periods
Percent of Coefficients of Correlation Which are Significant

DOLLAR VARIABLE	Cash	Receivables	Inventories	Current Assets	Current Liabilities	Total Assets	Gross Plant	Net Plant	Long Term Debt	Common Equity	Invested Capital	Net Sales	Operating Income	Depreciation	Fixed Charges	Income Taxes	Net Income	Common Earnings	Market Value
Cash	100	100	100	100	100	100	100	100	98	100	100	100	100	100	100	100	100	100	100
Receivables	100	100	100	100	100	100	100	100	97	100	100	100	100	100	100	100	100	100	100
Inventory	100	100	100	100	100	100	100	100	100	100	100	100	100	100	100	100	100	100	100
Current Assets	100	100	100	100	100	100	100	100	100	100	100	100	100	100	100	100	100	100	100
Current Liabilities	100	100	100	100	100	100	100	100	100	100	100	100	100	100	100	100	100	100	100
Total Assets	100	100	100	100	100	100	100	100	100	100	100	100	100	100	100	100	100	100	100
Gross Plant	100	100	100	100	100	100	100	100	100	100	100	100	100	100	100	100	100	100	100
Net Plant	100	100	100	100	100	100	100	100	100	100	100	100	100	100	100	100	100	100	100
Long Term Debt	100	100	100	100	100	100	100	100	100	100	100	100	100	100	100	100	100	100	100
Common Equity	100	100	100	100	100	100	100	100	100	100	100	100	100	100	100	100	100	100	100
Invested Capital	100	100	100	100	100	100	100	100	100	100	100	100	100	100	100	100	100	100	100
Net Sales	100	100	100	100	100	100	100	100	100	100	100	100	100	100	100	100	100	100	100
Operating Income	100	100	100	100	100	100	100	100	100	100	100	100	100	100	100	100	100	100	100
Depreciation	100	100	100	100	100	100	100	100	100	100	100	100	100	100	100	100	100	100	100
Fixed Charges	100	100	100	100	100	100	100	100	100	100	100	100	100	100	100	100	100	100	100
Income Taxes	100	100	100	100	100	100	100	100	100	100	100	100	100	100	100	100	100	100	100
Net Income	100	100	100	100	100	100	100	100	98	100	100	100	100	100	100	100	100	100	100
Common Earnings	100	100	100	100	100	100	100	100	97	100	100	100	100	100	100	100	100	100	100
Market Value	100	100	100	100	100	100	100	100	95	100	100	100	100	100	100	100	100	100	100

Correlations per test 120;   Total correlations 43,370

Percent Change Variables in Successive Periods
Percent of Coefficients of Correlation Which are Significant

PERCENT CHANGE VARIABLE	Cash	Receivables	Inventories	Current Assets	Current	Liabilities	Total Assets	Gross Plant	Net Plant	Long Term Debt	Common Equity	Invested Capital	Net Sales	Operating Income	Depreciation	Fixed Charges	Income Taxes	Net Income	Common
Cash	8	9	13	9	9	13	12	12	4	12	8	13	6	11	4	5	6	6	5
Receivables	6	9	14	9	13	13	16	15	4	14	12	15	9	14	5	6	11	13	6
Inventory	4	7	9	8	9	14	11	9	5	14	9	9	5	8	4	5	10	11	3
Current Assets	4	10	9	7	10	13	14	14	4	14	9	10	8	12	3	8	9	9	3
Current Liabilities	1	7	9	5	9	13	10	10	4	15	11	11	6	11	1	8	8	8	6
Total Assets	4	8	6	2	9	9	10	9	7	12	7	11	5	8	2	8	9	9	4
Gross Plant	4	8	9	9	10	13	9	8	7	13	9	10	8	12	2	9	11	11	9
Net Plant	4	9	9	7	10	9	8	7	6	11	7	11	6	9	2	10	11	12	8
Long Term Debt	1	6	9	4	9	4	8	8	7	5	2	5	4	6	7	2	5	6	5
Common Equity	4	13	8	6	9	10	11	11	4	10	9	10	9	10	3	9	11	11	4
Invested Capital	5	9	9	6	12	8	13	10	6	11	8	12	6	8	2	8	11	12	2
Net Sales	5	9	15	9	12	16	13	10	6	16	14	13	6	12	7	9	9	9	6
Operating Income	3	8	9	5	9	9	9	12	2	14	10	8	6	9	1	8	7	8	5
Depreciation	3	4	7	4	9	6	8	8	2	10	8	7	7	8	2	4	9	8	6
Fixed Charges	4	9	6	6	7	5	8	7	12	5	4	4	3	6	4	2	5	9	4
Income Taxes	7	5	5	7	5	6	7	5	4	9	5	4	6	4	2	5	4	5	4
Net Income	4	5	5	4	6	6	6	6	4	9	7	8	7	7	2	5	5	5	2
Common Earnings	4	7	7	4	7	7	6	6	4	10	7	7	7	8	2	4	5	5	2
Market Value	4	6	7	4	9	9	9	8	2	8	9	9	9	11	3	6	8	9	4

Correlations per test 120;   Total correlations 43,370

Dollar Variable and Percent Change Variable
Percent of Coefficients of Correlation Which are Significant

DOLLAR VARIABLE

PERCENT CHANGE VARIABLE	Cash	Receivables	Inventories	Current Assets	Current	Liabilities	Total Assets	Gross Plant	Net Plant	Long Term Debt	Common Equity	Invested Capital	Net Sales	Operating Income	Depreciation	Fixed Charges	Income Taxes	Net Income	Common Earnings
Cash	0	0	0	0	0	0	0	0	0	0	0	0	0	0	0	0	0	0	0
Receivables	0	0	0	0	0	0	0	0	0	0	0	0	0	0	0	0	0	0	0
Inventory	0	0	0	0	0	0	0	0	0	0	0	0	0	0	0	0	0	0	0
Current Assets	0	0	0	0	0	0	0	0	0	0	0	0	0	0	0	0	0	0	0
Current Liabilities	0	0	0	0	0	0	0	0	0	0	0	0	0	0	0	0	0	0	0
Total Assets	0	0	0	0	0	0	0	0	0	0	0	0	0	0	0	0	0	0	0
Gross Plant	0	2	3	0	0	0	0	0	0	0	6	5	0	3	1	0	0	0	0
Net Plant	0	5	9	7	4	5	9	2	0	6	6	5	6	9	0	0	4	4	0
Long Term Debt	3	4	4	4	3	4	4	4	4	4	4	4	4	4	4	0	5	5	4
Common Equity	0	0	1	0	0	0	2	0	0	0	0	0	0	2	0	0	0	0	0
Invested Capital	0	0	0	0	0	0	0	0	0	0	0	0	0	0	0	0	0	0	0
Net Sales	0	0	0	0	0	0	0	0	0	0	0	0	0	0	0	0	0	0	0
Operating Income	4	15	22	14	7	0	0	0	0	0	0	0	4	0	0	7	0	0	0
Depreciation	0	0	0	0	0	0	0	0	0	0	0	0	0	0	0	0	0	0	0
Fixed Charges	0	9	3	2	5	0	7	0	0	3	2	6	4	8	0	5	0	0	0
Income Taxes	0	5	6	0	0	0	4	0	0	4	0	6	0	9	0	0	4	5	3
Net Income	0	0	0	0	0	0	0	0	0	0	0	0	0	0	0	0	0	0	0
Common Earnings	0	0	0	0	0	0	0	0	0	0	0	0	0	0	0	0	0	0	0
Market Value	0	0	4	0	0	0	0	0	0	0	0	0	0	0	0	0	0	0	0

Correlations per test 120; Total correlations 43,370

First Differences in Original Variable in Successive Periods
Percent of Coefficients of Correlation Which are Significant

First Difference Dollar Variable	Cash	Receivables	Inventories	Current Assets	Current Liabilities	Total Assets	Gross Plant	Net Plant	Long Term Debt	Common Equity	Invested Capital	Net Sales	Operating Income	Depreciation	Fixed Charges	Income Taxes	Net Income	Common Earnings	Market Value
Cash	2	6	8	2	7	4	4	4	3	4	4	8	9	7	5	3	6	6	4
Receivables	3	55	29	43	46	72	74	60	10	70	69	59	40	38	13	25	46	48	50
Inventory	4	32	15	27	25	40	42	35	6	40	38	30	25	21	12	16	29	29	26
Current Assets	5	36	18	25	33	43	49	35	4	40	37	34	26	22	7	15	27	30	25
Current Liabilities	4	50	30	38	47	60	62	50	11	59	54	50	33	32	19	85	37	40	41
Total Assets	8	54	26	40	44	74	75	67	7	71	70	54	36	36	13	20	47	48	47
Gross Plant	9	59	24	50	49	75	75	70	7	75	72	57	44	43	19	23	47	47	50
Net Plant	9	43	19	34	35	60	63	50	6	60	58	45	36	33	11	16	44	44	40
Long Term Debt	3	17	9	9	17	22	20	18	6	20	17	19	13	10	12	9	16	16	16
Common Equity	4	54	21	38	43	70	73	60	4	71	68	52	35	35	12	15	51	51	47
Invested Capital	6	48	23	43	44	68	72	60	6	70	65	51	35	36	11	20	44	44	43
Net Sales	3	60	31	40	51	72	75	61	9	67	65	60	42	35	21	31	49	50	52
Operating Income	9	39	19	34	36	53	50	50	6	54	49	37	27	29	15	21	36	37	40
Depreciation	4	20	14	16	21	30	39	27	4	30	27	19	16	15	17	9	22	22	25
Fixed Charges	6	29	20	24	31	39	44	33	12	39	32	32	27	23	23	19	30	61	33
Income Taxes	9	32	16	30	35	46	46	42	6	46	43	358	30	21	19	23	32	32	35
Net Income	8	41	17	33	36	51	57	48	6	50	46	39	30	26	14	19	36	37	39
Common Earnings	8	43	17	35	36	54	57	49	6	51	48	39	32	25	14	20	39	39	42
Market Value	4	31	22	26	29	40	44	36	6	42	42	33	28	21	12	22	34	34	36

Correlations per test 120; Total correlations 43,370

III

Forecasting Corporate Profit and Loss

The following exhibits portray the results of predictions of corporate loss, or corporate deficits. The first table shows the accuracy of published forecasts of corporate deficits contained in the Northwestern National Bank publication *P/L Forecasts* which appeared from 1973 through 1977. The results are based on the December issues and the results for calendar year company for the following year. The second table shows simulated forecasts. The third table shows the accuracy of using *P/L Forecasts* as a predictor of corporate bankruptcy. Seventy-seven percent of the firms rated F filed for bankruptcy, or 37 of the 48 firms which did so. The next three tables show the relative accuracy of two measures to classify firms, net income to total assets and net income to net sales. These tests were made using the Compustat Primary, Secondary and Tertiary tapes, respectively. The final chart displays the relationship between various levels of selected ratios in one year and the incidence of loss in the following year. This data was used in the initial procedures used to classify companies by probability of loss.

P/L FORECASTS
STATISTICS ON ACCURACY OF PREDICTIONS
Accuracy of Published Ratings

Rating	A	B	C	D	E		Total
1976 Firms	409	192	84	56	28	45	814
1977 Loss	0	2	3	6	5	23	39
% Loss	0.0	1.0	3.6	10.7	17.9	51.1	4.8
1975 Firms	335	201	96	99	29	65	825
1976 Loss	3	3	5	7	7	24	49
% Loss	0.9	1.5	5.2	7.1	24.1	36.9	5.9
1974 Firms	431	205	90	44	26	33	829
1975 Loss	5	12	14	13	11	18	73
% Loss	1.2	5.9	15.6	29.6	42.3	54.6	8.8
1973 Firms	416	218	91	64	15	29	833
1974 Loss	2	6	3	9	31	16	37
% Loss	0.5	2.7	3.3	14.1	20.0	55.2	4.7

Source: *Corporate Deficits* December 1973-1977

ACCURACY of P/L FORECASTS
Simulated Tests

Rating	A	B	C	D	E	F	Total
1970-7 Data	4633	686	264	377	369	387	6716
1971-8 Loss	48	47	22	48	72	165	402
% Loss	1.0	6.9	8.3	12.7	19.5	42.6	6.0
1975 Data	903	166	57	91	92	128	1437
1976 Loss	5	6	2	7	15	51	86
% Loss	0.6	3.6	3.5	7.7	16.3	39.8	6.0
1974 Data	946	124	45	85	72	93	1365
1975 Loss	18	13	8	19	20	50	128
% Loss	1.9	10.	17.8	22.4	27.8	53.7	9.4
1973 Data	966	127	45	55	53	35	1281
1974 Loss	14	22	5	10	15	15	81
% Loss	1.4	17.3	11.1	18.2	28.3	42.9	6.3
1972 Data	888	107	52	67	60	39	1213
1973 Loss	4	1	4	4	6	16	35
% Loss	0.5	0.9	7.7	5.9	10.0	41.0	2.9

Source: Compustat Primary and Tertiary tapes, 1977/78

P/L FORECASTS

P/L Ratings of Bankrupt Firms
(Rating Fiscal Year Prior to Bankruptcy)

	A	B	C	D	E	F	Total
Firms	0	0	1	1	9	37	48
% of Firms	0	0	2	2	19	77	100

Predicted vs. Realized Frequency of Loss
Comparison of Net Income/Total Assets vs. Net Income/Sales

	PREDICTED FREQUENCY (%)					
	<1	1-8	8-15	15-30	30-50	50+
	REALIZED FREQUENCY (%)					
1980-81						
Net Income/Sales (46/753)*	0.4	7.3	14.7	18.9	24.1	54.3
Net Income/T Assets (48/756)	0.6	7.1	6.3	17.0	33.3	52.6
1979-80						
Net Income/Sales (35/744)	0.6	7.3	6.5	21.4	17.5	38.1
Net Income/T Assets (38/749)	0.8	6.4	13.8	15.2	21.1	38.5
1978-79						
Net Income/Sales (22/736)	0.8	0.0	0.0	7.1	17.6	30.0
Net Income/T Assets (26/740)	0.8	0.0	3.0	5.4	19.4	34.3
1977-78						
Net Income/Sales (28/723)	0.6	0.0	6.3	15.8	14.7	42.9
Net Income/T Assets (33/729)	0.6	1.2	6.5	14.0	12.1	53.1
1976-77						
Net Income/Sales (28/714)	0.4	2.5	0.0	5.6	15.8	50.0
Net Income/T Assets (32/722)	0.2	3.1	0.0	6.8	13.9	55.6
1975-76						
Net Income/Sales (33/709)	0.4	3.8	5.7	16.7	20.5	37.9
Net Income/T Assets (37/717)	0.6	6.3	0.0	13.0	20.5	42.9
1974-75						
Net Income/Sales (32/707)	1.3	8.8	10.7	7.1	13.3	38.5
Net Income/T Assets (35/708)	0.8	11.3	15.0	8.6	25.0	34.5
1973-74						
Net Income/Sales (26/696)	1.1	10.5	3.2	12.0	12.9	28.6
Net Income/T Assets (29/697)	1.1	7.5	12.0	13.3	17.2	28.6
1972-73						
Net Income/Sales (21/674)	0.4	3.5	0.0	9.1	9.4	36.7
Net Income/T Assets (22/679)	0.6	3.0	0.0	4.8	12.5	35.5
1971-72						
Net Income/Sales (30/661)	0.8	5.7	0.0	5.7	17.4	42.9
Net Income/T Assets (31/663)	0.7	3.5	12.0	2.5	19.4	40.5
1970-71						
Net Income/Sales (36/647)	0.8	7.0	11.8	42.1	32.1	36.0
Net Income/T Assets (38/651)	0.0	8.5	11.1	25.0	41.9	36.0

* (Number of Companies Reporting Deficits/Total Number of Companies)
Source of Data: Compustat Primary Tape

Predicted vs. Realized Frequency of Loss
Comparison of Net Income/Total Assets vs. Net Income/Sales

	PREDICTED FREQUENCY (%)					
	<1	1-8	8-15	15-30	30-50	50+
	REALIZED FREQUENCY (%)					
1980-81						
Net Income/Sales (98/691)	2.1	11.3	16.3	16.7	17.1	71.6
Net Income/T Assets (98/704)	1.0	12.1	16.0	16.9	16.7	68.1
1979-80						
Net Income/Sales (66/656)	1.2	3.5	0.0	16.1	28.7	47.3
Net Income/T Assets (68/669)	1.6	1.9	6.4	16.9	27.6	45.6
1978-79						
Net Income/Sales (56/636)	1.0	6.6	7.1	7.1	22.8	45.7
Net Income/T Assets (57/647)	1.0	3.3	9.6	5.8	24.7	47.8
1977-78						
Net Income/Sales (46/611)	1.0	2.7	4.4	10.8	11.5	43.4
Net Income/T Assets (45/622)	0.7	2.4	9.1	6.0	13.9	42.3
1976-77						
Net Income/Sales (52/584)	1.1	4.4	8.3	8.5	16.4	41.9
Net Income/T Assets (52/600)	1.5	6.3	0.0	6.8	21.7	39.3
1975-76						
Net Income/Sales (59/569)	1.9	3.1	0.0	11.9	19.4	43.5
Net Income/T Assets (59/584)	1.6	4.8	5.3	4.5	24.	41.2
1974-75						
Net Income/Sales (67/539)	2.6	12.5	9.7	21.0	22.4	44.7
Net Income/T Assets (68/549)	2.3	8.8	10.8	25.4	23.9	42.6
1973-74						
Net Income/Sales (46/S13)	4.2	4.5	12.5	14.6	10.3	35.9
Net Income/T Assets (46/516)	3.2	7.4	9.3	13.0	12.3	34.9
1972-73						
Net Income/Sales (3S/489)	1.7	3.2	12.5	7.5	8.2	32.7
Net Income/T Assets (39/491)	2.2	3.0	0.0	11.8	9.6	36.8
1971-72						
Net Income/Sales (47/460)	0.0	0.0	0.0 1	6.0	24.6	43.1
Net Income/T Assets (50/462)	0.0	0.0	4.3	12.0	23.2	46.6
1970-71						
Net Income/Sales (55/430)	2.8	9.4	9.7	19.4	31.1	44.4
Net Income/T Assets (55/434)	1.5	7.7	8.3	20.4	31.9	43.5

* (Number of Companies Reporting Deficits/Total Number of Companies)
Source of Data: Compustat Supplementary Tape

Predicted vs. Realized Frequency of Loss
Comparison of Net Income/Total Assets vs. Net Income/Sales

	<1	1-8	8-15	15-30	30-50	50+
			PREDICTED FREQUENCY (%)			
			REALIZED FREQUENCY (%)			
1980-81						
Net Income/Sales (58/735)	0.4	7.5	12.8	15.6	16.4	56.6
Net Income/T Assets (61/763)	0.6	4.9	25.7	7.9	14.3	55.0
1979-80						
Net Income/Sales (52/707)	1.1	4.0	0.0	17.5	27.8	61.1
Net Income/T Assets (59/733)	0.4	5.8	5.7	17.0	27.6	62.8
1978-79						
Net Income/Sales (33/683)	0.2	3.9	3.6	17.5	16.0	40.6
Net Income/T Assets (40/706)	0.2	1.2	13.9	14.3	19.1	46.3
1977-78						
Net Income/Sales (30/623)	0.2	2.9	5.0	6.8	20.8	39.4
Net Income/T Assets (35/637)	0.5	1.5	9.7	4.7	22.0	43.9
1976-77						
Net Income/Sales (31/588)	0.5	1.5	3.6	9.1	17.8	38.1
Net Income/T Assets (34/598)	0.3	4.2	0.0	9.1	16.3	41.7
1975-76						
Net Income/Sales (38/552)	1.4	0.0	5.9	6.7	11.4	46.4
Net Income/T Assets (42/561)	1.1	3.5	0.0	6.9	12.5	46.9
1974-75						
Net Income/Sales (42/482)	1.5	11.8	12.5	29.0	19.4	65.2
Net Income/T Assets (50/493)	0.9	20.0	18.2	28.6	27.6	69.0
1973-74						
Net Income/Sales (17/430)	1.4	0.0	9.1	11.8	18.2	50.0
Net Income/T Assets (20/434)	1.5	7.7	6.7	16.7	11.1	53.8
1972/73						
Net Income/Sales (8/391)	0.0	0.0	0.0	18.2	0.0	46.2
Net Income/T Assets (9/393)	0.0	0.0	0.0	7.1	5.3	46.7
1971-72						
Net Income/Sales (10/361)	1.0	8.3	0.0	15.0	0.0	37.5
Net Income/T Assets (13/365)	1.0	5.6	16.7	0.0	20.0	50.0
1970-71						
Net Income/Sales (7/335)	0.0	6.3	16.7	25.0	22.2	33.3
Net Income/T Assets (9/338)	0.0	11.1	0.0	25.0	25.0	33.3

* (Number of Companies Reporting Deficits/Total Number of Companies)
Source of Data: Compustat Tertiary Tape

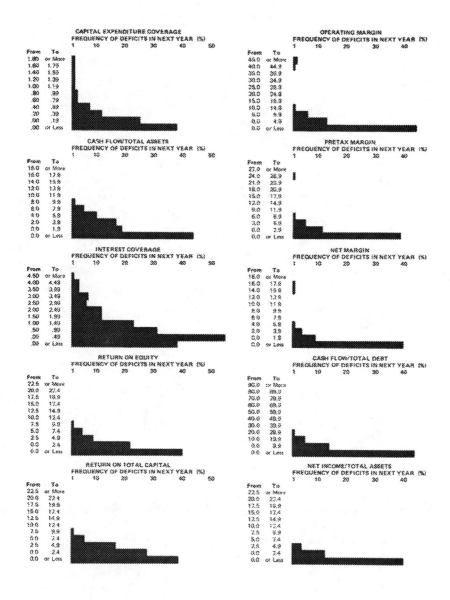

Afterward

In the process of assembling these articles and papers, I began to reflect on which approaches, in retrospect, seem most appropriate and useful and which might be improved upon.

Prediction

The approach used in "Games of Chance and the Probability of Corporate Profit or Loss" is superior to the approach used in "Financial Ratios, Discriminant Analysis and the Prediction of the Odds of Corporate Deficit" and in similar work on bankruptcy by Edward Altman (*Bankruptcy in America*) and the earlier ratio analysis of Merwin and others. It is superior because it takes advantage of the fact that logarithmic changes in profits are a random variable with an approximately normal distribution, information which can be used to give a more accurate portrait of the probable future. The realization of the connection between coin flipping, the normal distribution, and this approach to prediction came to me quite suddenly one day while vacationing on the north shore of Lake Superior. That approach is applied to a variety of other investment and corporate problems in *Stock Market Probability* (Probus 1988, rev 1994) as well as for bond analysis in *With Interest* (Dow-Jones Irwin, 1987).

The prediction of bankruptcy is a slightly different problem and I may overstate the usefulness of the "Games of Chance." solution. And since accountants now require adding "nonrecurrent" charges to the reported net income calculation, the method is likely to be less accurate, though still preferable, I believe, to other approaches. Appendix III gives the results of published estimates of future profit and loss, most of which were based on the earlier ratio and discriminant analysis.

The article "Predicting Dividend Changes" uses the dividend payout ratio that is partly related to the variable used in "Games of Chance." The denominator of the payout ratio is the earnings figure and changes (in the logs) of earnings are random. Also, the ratio itself, dividends divided by earnings, could better be expressed as 1 - dividends/earnings. Thus, a company paying out 90% of its earnings would have a ratio of 0.10 while a company paying out only 10% of its earnings would have a ratio of 0.90. The latter is much more unlikely to cut dividends. Using this, the normal distribution and a measure of the volatility of first differences in the logarithms of earnings would undoubtedly provide a more accurate way of predicting the probability of a dividend cut. When the article was written (1972) I was unaware of this possibility.

Corporate Earnings

It is perhaps redundant to include seven of the first eight articles and a talk, all of which are summarized by two of the articles. However, the articles, which are given in chronological order, illustrate how the ideas emerged leading finally to the more general statement of Five Principles. Most of the articles were controversial at the time they appeared. A lot more testing went into the rebuttal of Michael Hopewell. At the annual meeting of the Eastern Finance Association in 1971, Hopewell asserted that the principles conflicted with the "modern theory of finance." His statement was quite accurate, although he inferred from it that the principles must be wrong. The evidence, however, supported the principles. At the talk I gave in Phoenix on the principles, one of the participants said our results were in direct conflict with the results of his Ph.D. dissertation. After discussing with him later, it turned out that his results were quite different. Russell Nelson's statement that he was able to use the principles to accurately predict the results of his students' research papers before he saw their results suggests the usefulness and accuracy of the principles.

Much of current research and some investment services are probably in conflict with the principles developed in that paper. Cross-section linear regressions based on per share data, a common practice, for example, result in equation parameters that are an arbitrary function of the number of shares outstanding of the individual companies in the sample, as shown on pages 83-85. Appendix II provides reports on additional tests done in support of the first eight articles.

Two other articles (#11 and #13) and one unpublished paper (#21) deal with earnings. The unpublished paper was an attempt to look at earnings somewhat the way Osborne had looked at stock prices in his "Brownian Motion in the Stock Market." At that time I did not fully understood Osborne's reasons for plotting the standard deviation of differences in the natural logs of stocks against the length of the difference interval, on both a serial and cross-section basis and what connection that had to random variables. It took me many years to fully understand what he was about.

Interest Rates, Currencies and Stock Prices

By the mid-1980's when we did work on interest rates, earnings, and currencies, I did understand. Each of those articles and the paper concentrate on the nature of the distribution of changes in the natural logarithms of the variable. In a sense, they are a replication for a different variable of Osborne's early work on stock prices.

The paper on non-randomness in stock prices shows departures from the normal distribution, and hence departures from randomness, of first differences in the logarithms of stock prices.

Autocorrelation

"A Note on Alternative Formulas for the Coefficient of Autocorrelation," is a shortened version of a much longer paper in which I failed to elicit any interest. What bothered me was that formulas used in commercial statistical software and recommended in many books on time series (Maurice Kendall is an exception) can give the wrong answers, as may readily be seen by examining the figures on pages 282-283. A linear series like the series 1, 2, 3,...., n gives a declining coefficient of autocorrelation with a rising lag k when in fact the only correct coefficient is r=1.00 for all lags of k (provided only by Equation 1). The errant equations were originally developed as a computational shortcut in the pre-computer age.